The Quiet Zone

Critical Caribbean Studies

Series Editors: Yolanda Martínez-San Miguel, Carter Mathes, and Kathleen López

Focused particularly in the twentieth and twenty-first centuries, although attentive to the context of earlier eras, this series encourages interdisciplinary approaches and methods and is open to scholarship in a variety of areas, including anthropology, cultural studies, diaspora and transnational studies, environmental studies, gender and sexuality studies, history, and sociology. The series pays particular attention to the four main research clusters of Critical Caribbean Studies at Rutgers University, where the coeditors serve as members of the executive board: Caribbean Critical Studies Theory and the Disciplines; Archipelagic Studies and Creolization; Caribbean Aesthetics, Poetics, and Politics; and Caribbean Colonialities.

For a complete list of titles in the series, please see the last page of the book.

The Quiet Zone

Caribbean Expressive Cultures and the Feminist Aesthetics of Disturbance

PETAL KIMBERLY SAMUEL

Rutgers University Press
New Brunswick, Camden, and Newark, New Jersey
London and Oxford

Rutgers University Press is a department of Rutgers, The State University of New Jersey, one of the leading public research universities in the nation. By publishing worldwide, it furthers the University's mission of dedication to excellence in teaching, scholarship, research, and clinical care.

Library of Congress Cataloging-in-Publication Data

Names: Samuel, Petal author
Title: The quiet zone : Caribbean expressive cultures and the feminist aesthetics of disturbance / Petal Kimberly Samuel.
Description: New Brunswick : Rutgers University Press, [2025] | Series: Critical Caribbean studies | Includes bibliographical references and index.
Identifiers: LCCN 2025017750 | ISBN 9781978844704 paperback | ISBN 9781978844711 hardcover | 9781978844728 ebooks
Subjects: LCSH: Power (Social sciences)—Caribbean Area | Quietude—Social aspects—Caribbean Area | Sound—Social aspects—Caribbean Area
Classification: LCC HN49.P6 S288 2025
LC record available at https://lccn.loc.gov/2025017750

A British Cataloging-in-Publication record for this book is available from the British Library.

∞ The paper used in this publication meets the requirements of the American National Standard for Information Sciences—Permanence of Paper for Printed Library Materials, ANSI Z39.48-1992.

rutgersuniversitypress.org

For my parents, in honor of your visionary love

Contents

The Quiet Zone

Introduction

In Praise of Volume

This is a book about the uses of quiet as a transnational instrument of racial governance. By "quiet," I am referring to more than just a set of auditory phenomena—the absence or minimal presence of audible sound, but also a set of values around ways of being in public: a set of etiquettes, dispositions, behaviors, sartorial choices, and more. Quiet may be the way we describe the sound of a library; it may also be the way we describe a quality of subtlety, understatedness, or discretion. It can describe, in Kevin Quashie's lyrical and evocative words, "a metaphor for the full range of one's inner life—one's desires, ambitions, hungers, vulnerabilities, fears."[1] In and of itself, quiet is just another thread in the rich tapestry of the human experience. Yet in moments, it takes on a life as a sensory technique of racial and spatial policing, as a commodity to be bought and sold (e.g., a quiet getaway), as an entitlement of the elite. In these cases, it no longer operates as a neutral or innocent sensory preference or human quality but as an informal regime of elite privilege, spatial organization, and social control. I speak of quiet's "uses" as a technique of governance to underscore, as have others, that the senses are inextricably bound up in history, in ideology, and in struggles for power.[2] The power to shape the senses—to produce normative ways of seeing, hearing, and feeling—is the power to make worlds.

Among quiet's uses, I include a wide range of phenomena, such as the literal hushing of people, technology, cultural production, and ambient noise (whether formally by law enforcement or informally by extrajudicial agents such as neighbors and passersby); the denial of access to quiet through the systemic disruption of marginalized communities' sonic ecosystems with sounds ranging from the intrusive and terror-inducing noises of police and military technologies to the all-too-quotidian din of phobic speech hurled on the street;[3] and the racialized and gendered notions of quotidian sonic etiquette and poetic artistry that privilege the values of "restraint" and "subtlety."[4] Put simply, this is a book about what quiet means to us as a psychic resource; as a spatial feature; as an intellectual and artistic value; as an object of desire; as an entitlement, right, and commodity; and as a mechanism of exclusion. I am uniquely invested in tracing what the desire for quiet—and efforts to generate, sustain, or disrupt can reveal about the quotidian dynamics of social power. By underscoring the life of quiet as a social and political production rather than treating it merely as a matter of decibels, I aim to denaturalize it. In other words, I ask, what does quiet sound like? What are its constitutive features and why? Why and under what circumstances does it become desirable? And perhaps most pressingly, what are the formal and informal ways that the naturalization of quiet as a sonic and aesthetic ideal became entangled with colonial regimes of racial, gender, and sexual surveillance and discipline? This book asks a question about a desire so quotidian, so "obvious" that it operates as a common sense: our collective longing for quiet appears be "outside time," "persuasive precisely because we think of it as a product of Nature rather than of history."[5] This, however, is precisely why we must subject it to scrutiny.

The analyses in this study dwell on the quotidian, the "everyday."[6] The incidents I trace can appear to be so mundane, so familiar, that to even attempt an analysis of them can seem nitpicky, even punishing. By dwelling on quotidian clashes over noise, my analysis aims to "make strange" scenes (and responses to them) that otherwise may not draw our attention. As such, I am directing attention to events that are not—or not immediately—matters of life and death. Yet they are consequential and represent a form of slow violence, one small way among others that minoritized people are made to feel placeless, vulnerable, and unprotected. This is an important part of my methodology as a transnational Black feminist scholar; in particular, I build on the work of South African feminist Pumla Dineo Gqola, who writes about how systems of patriarchal policing are "normalized through repetition so that we no longer recognize it for what it is, consequently taking it for granted as 'life.'"[7] A key strategy of challenging patriarchal power, then, Gqola writes, "is interrupting it and making it strange" in order to render it "unnatural" and "to create new ways of living."[8] One goal of this work is to render strange certain formal and informal commonsense responses to noise—and expressed longing for and lavishing in quiet—to untangle the web of associations that get buried within discourse about sound.[9]

The chapters of the work are structured around the poles of limits and possibility, around a "no" and a "yes." The no is the relentless bearing down of the law, of formal and extrajudicial policing, and of public discourse in order to set limits on "acceptable" sound, to prohibit and (often literally) silence.

The yes of the chapter is the way those being policed generate imaginative, inventive ways of thinking about sound that are not limited by the constraints of acceptable or unacceptable sound. This, too, is an important feature of the work's methodology. As Gqola argues in her writing on patriarchal violence, one can never "portray patriarchy's brutality at work without gesturing toward its unmaking. . . . It is never enough to simply illustrate how patriarchy works in order to understand it. The feminist imperative is to think against it, strategise against it, and consistently work to destroy it."[10] This is not about generating facile romances of feminist victory, as Gqola stresses, but about consistently illuminating an elsewhere and an otherwise as a show of commitment to "the consistent creation of feminist hope and a patriarchy-free future."[11] The structure of the book's chapters is an effort to both render these antiblack, sexist, classist, and homophobic structures of policing strange and to highlight the principled, capacious, and hopeful work of Afro-Caribbean writers and artists to imagine otherwise.

The Peace and Quiet Capital of the World

The Caribbean—including both the loosely bounded region in the Caribbean Sea as well as its diasporas in the United States and the United Kingdom—constitutes this book's primary sites of study. There is perhaps no region that has been more aggressively marketed as the peace and quiet capital of the world, no region more freighted with the expectation to produce the stereotypical meditative soundtrack of psychic rejuvenation, leisure, and restfulness—whether palm trees swaying in the breeze, the "shhh" of steady rainfall and the chirping of birds and insects in the rainforest, waves gently washing onto white sandy shores, and the gentle trill of notes from a steel pan.[12] The production of the region as a kind of paradise to be consumed by Global North tourists—and the ways Caribbean people resist, refuse, and appropriate these productions—has been extensively cataloged by Caribbeanist scholars.[13] Krista Thompson, for example, has analyzed the ways that light specifically, and "vision and visual representation" more generally, have shaped "the imaginative geography of the islands."[14] Other scholars have elaborated on the sonic dimensions of these imaginative geographies, including the specific cultivation and maintenance of quiet as vital to the fantasy of the Caribbean as "idealized space of European idleness."[15] Susan Harewood writes, "Though much of the research on tourism has analyzed these tropical fantasies through visual culture, the fantasy is constructed as much in the auditory realm as it is in the visual realm—near silence or 'peace and quiet' is as necessary for some versions of the fantasy as the mental postcards of sunsets, pristine sands, and fruit."[16]

I build on this valuable work by querying how the expectation for quiet shapes other realms of quotidian Caribbean life outside of the tourist realms of the hotel and resort, and even outside of the region itself. In what instances—in what locations, historical periods, and in the context of which kinds of quotidian Caribbean cultural, vernacular, and political expression—did desires for quiet take on urgency, demand enforcement? Tourist representations of the Caribbean—these "imaginative geographies"—did not merely shape tourists' *ideas* about the region, they frequently shaped the actual physical environments, people, and social and artistic practices they "imagined," as the tourism industry sought to conform the region and its people to these fantasies of "tamed nature and 'disciplined' natives."[17] Though tourist images and discourses about the region are powerful, Thompson warns against presuming that "Western ideologies or notions of colonial power" overdetermine the ways we—as scholars and those with deep roots and investments in the region—understand the contours of quotidian life, creativity, imagination, and political possibility in places still marked by the legacies of colonial rule.[18] Instead, Thompson urges us to pay attention to the lived impacts of these discourses on the people and places they represent, including the ways "local constituencies interpreted and used these images toward their own social, political, or aesthetic ends."[19]

To this end, I am curious about the ways art and writing by Caribbean writers, filmmakers, and artists document a range of relationships to quiet—as an affect, a sonic etiquette, and an environmental quality—through the prism of expressive culture. In the works I examine, I show that struggles over quiet—often figured through efforts to generate, preserve, or disturb it and those who desire it—operate as a vehicle for broader struggles for sovereignty, self-determination, belonging, bodily autonomy, and political power. In some instances, an object of creative play and imagination, in others a lever of social control, these works offer a complex portrait of pleasures and pressures that are bound up in quotidian sonic scenes. Each chapter of the book thus stages a dynamic interplay between pleasure and pressure, illustrating the maxim that the Jamaican literary scholar Carolyn Cooper once taught us: "One culture's 'knowledge' is another's 'noise.'"[20]

This book offers three distinct interventions. First, I expand rich scholarly explorations of what Edwin C. Hill calls the "imperial ear" in studies of the construction of the Caribbean as an "imaginative geography." Calling for the expansion of our analyses of the colonial sensorium beyond the "imperial gaze" and into other sensory registers, Hill asks, "But what of the *imperial ear* and the 'hearing-man' of early travel texts? How do representations of sound inscribed in travel chronicles, ethnographies, and adventure narratives produce an imperial order for the valuable and meaningful mapping of the New World? How do written soundscapes lay the foundations for mythologies of black sound solidified in the twentieth century?"[21] Much of the vital and exciting scholarship on the study of Caribbean soundscapes has taken up these questions, drawing attention to the ways music, instruments, radio broadcasting, sound reproduction technologies, and even adornment, movement, and creole and patois discursive and performance registers became sites of policing and of social and political struggles for self-definition and creative sovereignty.[22] This study joins this chorus of scholarship by attending to a somewhat more elusive matter: sonic intensity. Loudness and quiet, and the capacity to modulate sonic intensity, was a key preoccupation of both colonial administrations in the anglophone Caribbean and the postindependence governments that followed. Attention to sonic pressure and intensity matters, in part, because it was variably perceived by the colonial elite as a form of unsanctioned sonic touch; a physiological and psychological attack; and a threat to familial, community, institutional, and state order. It was often the allegation of sonic intensity—loudness or noisiness—that colonials invoked to rationalize the use of force and justify hyperpolicing and expulsion from space.

Second, this book attends closely to the movement of the figure of the loud Black woman through the archives of Caribbean history and expressive cultures to elaborate how "loudness" came to operate as a signifier of Black gender and sexual deviancy. Decades of invaluable Black feminist scholarship on controlling images have opened a pathway for thinking about "control" through other sensory registers—such as how Black women hear ourselves and are heard. From the Combahee River Collective recounting that "we were told [. . .] to be quiet both for the sake of being 'ladylike' and to make us less objectionable in the eyes of white people," to Belinda Edmondson writing that "Black women, poor, peasant, black women in particular, were considered by both blacks and whites to be at odds with the Victorian ideal of quiet, subservient, maternal motherhood," to Audre Lorde's famous declaration "Your silence will not protect you," to Patricia Hill Collins citing the role of "bureaucratic hierarchies and techniques of surveillance" in "creating quiet, orderly, docile, and disciplined populations of Black women"—transnational Black feminist scholarship has many times invoked, examined, and challenged the specter of Black feminine loudness and elaborated on how these sonic stereotypes have been deployed to discipline Black women's bodies, creativity, and political capacity. Loudness, however, often appears as but one trope in a longer litany of antiblack and sexist rhetoric and controlling images. This book devotes its critical attention to the ways Black women and queer folks—and their expressive modes—both challenge and defiantly take up loudness as a marker of unruly gender and sexual expression.

Finally, this book poses an inquiry into sonic intensity as multimodal, not merely as a marker of aural intensity but simultaneously as one of visual, haptic, textual, and political intensity. Like other scholars of Caribbean sound, I take seriously the ways our vocabulary for describing sound bleeds into other registers; sonic markers like "loud" and "noise" can just as readily describe the sound of a voice as they can a sight, a smell, or the boldness of an idea. Yet the production of the Caribbean as either an idyllic quiet paradise or "the loudest place on earth" implied the management of cultural forms and political ideologies that could frustrate colonial administrations, economies, and social orders.

The Colonial Sensorium and the Making of "the Loudest Place on the Planet"

In the genre of the colonial travel narrative, the Caribbean was cast as a region where the codes of Western sonic etiquette failed, where the delicate aural sensibilities of white European and U.S. American travelers were routinely assailed. More, these condemnations were often cast in hyperbolic terms, casting the Caribbean as, quite literally in some accounts, the loudest place on the planet.[23] In 1962, in his travelogue *The Middle Passage: The Caribbean Revisited* (in which he made the now infamous declaration "History is built around creation and achievement, and nothing was created in the West Indies"), Trinidadian writer V. S. Naipaul wrote, "Port of Spain is the noisiest city in the world."[24] The region's alleged failure to govern the soundscape was intended to signal other kinds of failures to come, including and especially an inability for Caribbean people on the eve of independence to self-govern. Naipaul's move to cast Caribbean soundscapes and people as exceptional and dysfunctional was common in European and U.S. American travel writing in the decades prior to the publication of his work.

Though much of the Caribbean is now often associated with quiet, idyllic escapes from North American and European life, it was not always heard this way.[25] The "quiet" Caribbean is continually made; many times, it is the specter of Black noisiness—which serves as a synecdoche for other forms of Black unruliness—that routinely unmakes it. The story of the movement of the sign of "noise" in the Caribbean is a stubborn and persistent one. The region has a long history of being represented through colonial tropes of exceptionalism, which circulated through images and texts like travel narratives and fiction. The writers of these narratives were keen to shape how European and U.S. American audiences broadly sensed the Caribbean, how it looked, and notably, how it sounded.[26] These "early travel narratives," Edwin Hill Jr. underscores, "constitute primordial texts for the deep mythologies of New World sound and experience."[27] The "representations of sound" in these narratives worked to "produce an imperial order for the valuable and meaningful mapping of the New World."[28] In particular, sound operated as a crucial medium for normalizing exceptional and often pejorative ideas about Black sociality, political capacity, and cultural production. European and U.S. American travel writers, colonial administrators, and the local elite of the late nineteenth and early twentieth centuries would frequently couple their transparently antiblack descriptions of Caribbean people and spaces with complaints about the loudness or noisiness of cities, human voices, languages, technology, the environment, and even animals.[29]

European colonial expeditions to the so-called New World first sought to produce it as new by underscoring its sensory alterity: there, voyagers claimed to find people and lands both beautiful and "beastly," familiar and unfamiliar.[30] Foreign sights, sounds, smells, and tastes became the titillating stuff of myth, the popular subjects of colonial travel narratives and sketches. These sensational narratives and images caught in the duality of desire and disgust served as a powerful vehicle for producing the Americas. Primed by fantastical travel narratives, colonial explorers struggled to reconcile what they found in the Americas with what they "knew" about it from popular accounts.[31] By narrating nonwhite people and lands as sensory exceptions—as caught in a permanent state of deviancy from appropriate sensory norms—colonial expeditions, and later, administrations, justified regimes of white supremacist discipline, surveillance, and regulation.

The "colonial sensorium," a framework I invoke throughout the manuscript, is a name for the sensory norms—the ways of seeing, hearing, and feeling—that colonial regimes generated to normalize colonial occupation, dispossession, exploitation, and violence. A sense of Caribbean climates as desirable, even paradisiacal, and naturally rejuvenating can be just as useful for colonial administrations as a sense of the Caribbean climates as far too warm and therefore antithetical to the natural balance of European humoral constitutions. The former notion bolsters the tourism industry; the latter notion cemented the region in the minds of colonial travelers as hostile, as needing to be met with caution and force, and as needing to be subjected to order. In this way, the senses, which are often narrated as pre- or nonideological, are recruited in service of stabilizing colonial social and spatial norms. The extent to which the Caribbean was narrated as deviating from these sensory norms often depended on the writer, the audience, and the imperial aspirations and anxieties of the moment.

In nineteenth and early twentieth-century travel narratives, the hyperbolic loudness of the Caribbean was often attributed to the sound of the Black voice. Even more, Black women's voices specifically were most frequently identified as booming, piercing, panic-inducing, or otherwise aberrant. The U.S. American writer and editor Nathaniel Parker Willis's 1854 *Health Trip to the Tropics* dedicated a section of his travel narrative to describing the "vehement talking" of Virgin Islander women in St. Thomas.[32] "The *voice*," Willis declared emphatically, "seems to be the great escape valve for all manner of excitement, among the negroes."[33] Describing hearing the sounds of women in shock and mourning over the news of a baby's sudden death, Willis wrote, "I rushed to the window, this morning, thinking from the sudden screaming of one or two hundred women, that the town must have been cracked open by an earthquake. . . . I watched the negresses vociferating, like furies, at each other and with looks that I should have interpreted to indicate a quarrel between every two."[34] After a hotel staff member explained to Willis that "a new-born black baby had been found drowned in the harbor, and was laid out, for recognition, at the Police-office, a few doors above," Willis remained transfixed by the sonic spectacle of mourning, not on the tragedy of the newborn's death.[35] He remarked, "In any other population, it seems to me, the horror inspired by such a sight would have been expressed by a hush, or an undervoiced exchange of feeling. Here it made a clamor, pitched at the highest possible key. Turn over the philosophy of difference, at your leisure."[36] Texts like Willis's present serious challenges for the reader who seeks to read against the grain of his narrative: Virgin Islanders appear in his narrative as one-dimensional, as objects of fetish. He is an untrustworthy narrator.

By likening St. Thomian women to "furies," a reference to the fearsome and grotesque ancient Greek goddesses of vengeance known for punishing and torturing sinners, Willis tied what he heard as a scene of sonic cacophony to notions of aberrant femininity: it is not just loud but also hostile (prone to "quarrel" "at each other") and vengeful. Willis's preoccupation is with colonial sonic etiquette: the way these women express their feelings for the loss of the baby becomes a sign that they are not the right kinds of feeling beings. Deploying the logic of the colonial sensorium, Willis insisted that the right and suitable way to feel and express (feminine) mourning is in a "hush" and an "undervoiced" register. The right way to be in pain, he stressed, is *quietly*. It is not just a matter of loudness ("clamor") but also a matter of frequency ("pitched at the highest possible key"): they are mourning at the wrong volume and in the wrong key. Willis invoked common psychoacoustic associations between monstrous femininity and sustained high-pitch vocalizations: the mark of the (feminine) beast in popular culture is its tendency to shriek and generate unbearable, high-frequency vibrations that grate against or damage the listener's hearing and induce terror and panic. Willis noted that the volume and pitch of the women's mourning voices acted on him and induced movement and panic: he "rushes" to the window, fearing that a cataclysmic event—such as an "earthquake" that "cracks open" the town—has taken place. He is disappointed to find that all that has happened is that a Black baby has turned up dead; he dismisses St. Thomian women as hysterical. He missed the cataclysm right in front of him—the loss of Black life that the mourners insist on marking sonically as a disaster. One might read this as a struggle between the spectacular and the quotidian: for Willis, a spectacular event like an "earthquake" might have warranted their expressions of sonic shock, but the death of a Black baby, in his view, is all too quotidian.

Yet by crying out, we might read these women as refusing to accept the loss and the degradation of Black life as a routine feature of everyday life. Scholars of Black sound, slavery in the Atlantic World, and archival silence have underscored that the scream, an "elevating [disruption] of the verbal that take[s] the rich content of the object's/commodity's aurality outside the confines of meaning," can be understood as a valuable disruption of the archive's tendency to silence and normalize Black pain and death.[37] As Marisa Fuentes elegantly argues, "Enslaved women forced themselves into history with their screams—insisting that someone reckon with their battered bodies. Their pained and loud cries forced their torturers to confront their humanity even as it was being degraded."[38] These women "make strange" a scene that Willis aimed to normalize; they disturb the world order that Willis narrated. The colonial sensorium, then, reveals itself here as being as much about what one hears as it is about what one "unhears"; it is, in Willis's hands, a practice of withholding recognition of life-affirming expressive practices. They yell because their lives are precious, and because the baby's life was, and is, precious.

It matters that this event happened in the context of what Willis named a "health trip" to the West Indies. He traveled to the region for rest, recovery, rejuvenation, all of which were to happen to the soundtrack of the famous quiet of the Caribbean. In fact, the mythology of the Caribbean region as *terra nullius* settled by Europeans who longed for quiet frame his travel narrative. Of Bermuda, he writes, "Tradition says that the islands had no original population, but that Madoc, son of the Prince of Wales, 'got with him such men and women as desired to live in quietness,' and made the first settlement here. The 'desire' seems to have remained in tolerable force."[39] For Willis, then, the quiet of the region was always a speculative project of European wish-fulfillment in the region, one premised on the absence of an "original" population and designed to meet the needs of European travelers themselves.

The scene of mourning in St. Thomas, as conveyed through Willis's ears and pen, is not merely aberrant but enough to constitute a fundamental "philosophy of difference" along lines of race, gender, nation, and even humanity. This is the very gesture I seek to underscore: protests about noise in contexts like these often contain not merely a sonic complaint but a civilizational one. Travel narratives that described Caribbean soundscapes rarely recounted standalone sonic scenes but rather detailed exceptional and aberrant sonic spectacles to serve as evidence to support a racial, gendered, and sexual "philosophy of difference." This difference was often tethered specifically to Afro-Caribbean women's bodies and voices as the source of a civilizational divide. Though we may read their yells as "a rhetorical genre of the enslaved" that contains, in Saidiya Hartman's words, a "counter-history of the human," Willis suggests instead that their yells indeed make them *less* legible as human.[40] Yet travel writers like Willis nevertheless took it as the charge of a travel writer to render knowable that which was unruly, to narratively maintain the island's (and the region's) availability for a range of foreign ventures, including wellness ventures like his own, while still underscoring Black difference and exoticizing island geographies. "Noise," as Ronald Radano explains about the European travel narrative, "assumes a centrality in the discourse of European travel not to identify a resolute and distinct racial otherness. . . . Rather, it describes an other that reflects the ambiguity of the colonial relation."[41] Narrations of Caribbean noisiness in travel narratives did not function merely to condemn the region and Afro-Caribbean people as monstrous but to express the ambiguity of being (and wanting to be) in close proximity to that for which one holds contempt. Noise complaints, though they are often deployed in ways that repress and displace, often simultaneously express a bind of desire and disdain, of being both drawn to and repelled by disturbing sounds, people, and practices: "As a European category imposed on a wide world of sounding practices," Radano writes, "noise sought to render familiar an uncontainability, the cross-cultural power and significance of which arose from the very act of its naming."[42]

It is no surprise that such a philosophy of difference appears in the work of a white U.S. American travel writer working in the 1850s on the eve of the U.S. Civil War. Willis brought with him to the island the very philosophies of racial difference that he likely cultivated in the United States, in his home in New York where the famous Harriet Jacobs was simultaneously working for his family as a seamstress and composing *Incidents in the Life of a Slave Girl*, which would contest those philosophies of difference in the strongest terms. More, in this period, the Virgin Islands were still under Danish rule, though they would shortly be sold into U.S. ownership in 1917 as a bid to assuage fears of a growing German presence in the region during World War I. U.S. travel narratives, then, often had a hidden stake in representing islands that were not yet under formal U.S. ownership: they tended to magnify the Otherness, exoticism, and sometimes the dysfunction of these islands, making a subtle case for the alleged civilizing force that a U.S. imperial (or military) presence could have in these places. They mobilized the colonial sensorium in ways that helped, consciously or unconsciously, make a case for U.S. expansionism.

Black feminist approaches to silence, archival and otherwise, are essential to interpreting Black sound as it surfaces in archival records and African diasporic literary and filmic aesthetics. This body of scholarship has, in Jenny Sharpe's words, worked to "reveal silences not to be absences" and to reclaim "silence as a black female space of expression rather than one of negation."[43] It has underscored the importance of developing interpretive literacies that allow us to read beyond both the constraints of the archive and the affective constraints of life under slavery. In the context of the plantation where, as Joan Anim-Addo remarks, "the everyday pain of black life must be kept secret," Black affective expressions such as laughter, shouting, cries, and silence became dense repositories of feeling that remained opaque to the planter class and even to us as scholars of Black life.[44] These scholars underscore the importance of resisting reductive interpretations of Black sound and affect: it is not the case that silence or quiet represent inherently repressed conditions and loudness represents a liberated one. They indeed warn us away from such romances of agency in which we fetishize particular modes of heroic agential action that ignore the more complex ways enslaved people navigated their environments and appropriate figures in the archive in service of our own desires and ideals for Black political life. Silence—one expressive mode on the spectrum of what Tina Post calls "black modes of reserve"—often operates as a "nonverbal language," a nonnarrative form that speaks volumes, just as laughter or a scream might.[45]

This book attends to the production of the Caribbean region and diasporas in the late colonial and postindependence moments through tropes of sonic exceptionalism, often via calls for quiet as a crucial lever of colonial power. Although much of the Black feminist literature on silence concentrates on the archives of slavery, I am interested in the afterlives of these regimes of sonic surveillance in the postemancipation and postindependence periods in the region. I trace how colonial preoccupations with managing and repressing Black voices and expressive forms survived in the form of persistently pathologizing narratives about Black sonic exceptionalism and intensity. I also examine how these pathologizing rhetorics were scaled to become narratives about the nation, the region, and the diaspora writ large. At the same time, the region was being produced as a kind of earthly paradise where pristine nature and quiet relaxation could be experienced in abundance. I take my cue from Black feminist scholarship on the possibilities and dense meanings of silence by turning a critical eye to the life of quiet as a sensory and ideological production, rather than embedding it in romances of return to the original (and therefore better or more wholesome) state of nature.

The U.S. American travel writer Harry Franck exemplified this recourse to sonic exceptionalism as a sign of racial and regional dysfunction. He wrote frequently about the noisiness of the Caribbean in his infamously racist 1920 travel narrative *Roaming Through the West Indies*. In particular, his accounts of Cuba, Jamaica, Haiti, and the Dominican Republic (all of whom, with the exception of Jamaica, were under U.S. occupation during this period) are peppered with condemnations of their "noisiness." Of Havana, he wrote, "A deaf person would probably enjoy Havana more than those of acute hearing. I have often wondered why nature did not provide us with earlids as well as eyelids. A mere oversight, no doubt, that would not have been made had the Cuban capital existed when the first models of the human being were submitted. Havana may not hold the noise championship of the world, but at least little old New York is silent by comparison."[46] Franck's recourse to "nature" and the "first models of the human being" casts Havana outside of the "natural" timeline and processes of human development, as both a "world" exception and a human one. His own supposedly normative distress at the loudness of the city is juxtaposed against Cubans, who, in his words, "seem to thrive on noise" and who when "denied their beloved din" hasten to "[produce] another from their throats."[47] Franck waxed hyperbolic, going as far as to speculate that the Havana soundscape would have shifted the course of human evolution if it existed many millennia prior, that humankind would have evolved with "earlids" as well as eyelids. This casts Cuba not merely as a civilizational aberration but as an evolutionary anomaly.

Cuban women are consigned to a particular status of alterity in Franck's account. "There are no worse voices in the world," Franck argues, "than those of Cuban women. Whether it is due to the climate or to the custom of reciting chorus at school, they have a timbre that tortures the eardrums like the sharpening of a saw, and all day long they exercise them to the full capacity of their lungs."[48] Here again, we see the rhetoric of sensory exceptionalism: Cuban women's voices are not just repelling to Franck himself; rather, they are the "worst in the world." By tying his condemnations of the timbre and volume of the voice to both "climate" and "custom," Franck ties sensory qualities to other colonial narratives of Caribbean cultural and civilizational inferiority and dysfunction. He both reinvigorates old colonial notions about the supposedly deleterious effect of tropical climates on the personality and ideas of cultural inferiority. Thus, when Franck concludes that Cuban women's voices might only be described as "a free-for-all whirlwind of incomprehensible shrieking" (again, the trope of monstrous, "shrieking" femininity appears), it is clear that he is not merely making a subjective sensory claim but a civilizational one.

Franck's accounts of the loudness of Haiti and Haitians are even more egregious. Again, here, it is the sound of the Black voice that Franck hears with special contempt. Complaining of Haitians in the capital city of Port-au-Prince, he writes, "Their tongues are rarely silent, and frequent cackles of unrestrained laughter sound from the bundles beneath which their wooly heads are all but invariably buried."[49] More, he describes Haitians as lacking the sensory intelligence to appropriately interpret auditory cues. Describing his frustrations with driving through the capital, he writes, "The Haitian's hearing is acute enough, but his mind does not synchronize in its various faculties; he is aware of a disagreeable noise behind him, but that noise does not register as a warning of danger and a call for action [. . .] his psychology is that of the chicken, and in eight cases out of ten he darts across the road instead of withdrawing to the side of it."[50] Here, sonic descriptors ("cackles") are notably coupled with racial markers ("wooly heads") and colonial rhetoric about the supposed moral ("unrestrained"), intellectual ("his mind does not synchronize"), and psychological and biological ("his psychology is that of the chicken") inferiority of Black people.

His contemptuous construction of Haitians as sonic and aural others serves to normalize the quotidian violence of the U.S. occupation of Haiti. Immediately after claiming that Haitians react in ostensibly irrational ways to sonic signals of danger, he nonchalantly recounts a harrowing story of a U.S. American "estate manager" who hits a Haitian man with his car.[51] Though Franck concedes that the American driver tended to "drive a heavy car at a high rate of speed," he immediately qualifies that the driver is nevertheless "noted for his freedom from accidents." While driving "far out in the country" one afternoon, the American estate manager fails to honk to warn a Haitian pedestrian that he is approaching and strikes him with his car. Franck dispassionately blames the Haitian man for the accident, noting that he inexplicably "darted" into the path of the vehicle after being startled by its approach. According to Franck's account, the Haitian man only sustained "minor injuries" from a head-on collision with a speeding vehicle; rather, the cause of his death the following week is narrated as "blood poisoning caused by the native healer whom he insisted on having redress his almost healed wound."[52]

Examples like these proliferate throughout travel narratives in the nineteenth and twentieth centuries: from Archie Bell condemning the "boisterous and blatant yelling of half-savages" in Antigua,[53] to Harry La Tourette Foster describing the voices of Haitian market women as a "babble of voices quite meriting the description of 'deafening,'"[54] to Susan de Forest Day likening the sounds of Afro-Kittian schoolchildren's voices reciting their lessons to "the hum of insects," a "strange" "humming and [. . .] buzzing" sound that "take[s] possession of the hut,"[55] to Richard Henry Dana's complaints that Cubans "enfeeble the [Spanish] language" with the tone and pace of their voices which he describes as "thin and eager, very rapid, too much in the lips, and, withal, giving an impression of the passionate and the childish combined."[56] These narratives insisted that the region's sonic unruliness could be sourced to the Black body; the issue was insistently framed as a racial, gendered, and civilizational one.

The discourse of sonic exceptionalism here does political work for the United States: it advances the narrative that Caribbean people and spaces are out of control and uncivilized—socially, politically, economically, and psychologically, and that they are even evolutionarily dysfunctional and underdeveloped. In this way, it forwards the necessity of the supposedly corrective and civilizing presence of U.S. American businesspeople and the U.S. military. I began this project with an interest in sonic intensity (i.e., noise or loudness), but I later realized that my interest was in the power to call for the modulation of the soundscape, to subdue or intensify sounds at will. Just as colonial authorities in the Caribbean sought to organize and discipline people and landscapes, they also sought to generate "clean" soundscapes. A quiet soundscape became a sign of order, of effective colonial rule in the Caribbean, and the region's amenability to the economic and political agendas of Global North giants like the United States.

The colonial sensorium mobilizes white supremacist sensory norms to rationalize the intensification of oppressive regimes through surveillance, policing, displacement, and violence. The colonial sensorium is at work when underscoring the alleged fundamental sensory alterity of minoritized people enables and facilitates—through masking, intensifying, expediting, and refusing to redress—structural violence against them. Sometimes it takes the form of a travel writer complaining about the noisiness of a Caribbean city; other times, it takes the form of a state advertising campaign targeting the redressal of noise as a "chronic" national problem. What all these instances share in common is their targeted stigmatization of minoritized groups and the shielding of powerful state and corporate interests beneath the seemingly apolitical, mundane cover of sonic nuisance.

Thus far, I have talked about quiet primarily as a product of ideology, as a political question. More specifically, I am concerned with the ideological forces that produce quiet as an elite *aesthetic*. To discuss quiet as an aesthetic that has a racial, class, gender, sexual, and national politics is a means of calling into question the universality of quiet as an object of desire, of troubling the tethering together of quiet as a sensory experience and a social good. I query the innocence of what we really long for when we long for quiet: this work guides us through querying whether this longing is merely for a sensory experience, a psychic experience (i.e., finding "inner peace"), a sociopolitical experience (i.e., freedom from a particular kind of disturbing Other), or a combination of all these things. I do so to reveal how ideological structures can recruit us by making themselves felt as natural, noncontroversial, universal.

Though sound undeniably has a politics, it is also a matter of physics; it has a materiality. Sound is, as Caribbean sound studies scholar Julian Henriques explains, "an auditory vibration," "a mechanical process [. . .] that avoids being entirely bound up with language, notation, and representation."[57] The materiality of sound is essential to its politics: in many of the instances of noise complaint I catalog in the book, complainants make a case for the undesirability of a given set of sounds based on the physiological and psychological effects it has on their bodies. They are unable to sleep or to concentrate, and they feel violated by the vibrational "touch" of distant sound waves rattling their cupboards or rippling across their skin. Complainants tend to avoid explicit indexical discussions of sound that reveal the associations between sonic experiences (i.e., "quiet") and particular racialized bodies or cultural practices that produce or disrupt them. As such, this study must necessarily pass through the prism of the physics of sound, of its materiality, movement, and physiological and psychological effects, to reveal its politics.

There is a robust literature on quiet and silence as central to practices of meditation and mindfulness; it is essential, these texts urge, to find routine therapeutic respite from the "noise" of everyday life. From Thich Nhat Hanh to Anne Le Claire to Eckhart Tolle, these writers discuss "noise" as a kind of acute state of reactivity; lost in the strenuous and exacting busyness of everyday life, we lose contact with the beauty of life and the world around us. This takes its psychic and physiological toll: we become exhausted, fed up, and depleted. The call for quiet—for a pause, for rest, for mediative silence—is an invitation to heal, replenish, and restore ourselves precisely by temporarily wresting ourselves free from the grind of labor, from the busyness of our minds, from the cultural and moral imperative to be "productive." There is a version of this call in Black feminist popular writing, too, though it more often takes the form of calls for rest and self-care.[58] Though this book turns a critical eye to commonsense calls for quiet, it is not making a case against meditation, stillness, restfulness, or psychic rejuvenation, nor is it resisting the conclusions of scientists and scholars who underscore the benefits of restful quiet. Rather, I am curious about the ways quiet takes on a life as a marketable commodity, a force of physical and psychic rejuvenation, and as a luxe quality (and indeed entitlement) that, when tethered to certain scenes and people, generates a sense of exclusivity. I am tracing the implications of quiet as a sensory marker of order, exclusivity, and elite entitlement for those people and places routinely constructed as sensory deviants, sensory Others. To do so, I ask questions about the pursuit of quiet as a feature of well-being, as what Lauren Berlant might have called a "good-life genre," one that often elicits feelings of entitlement, fantasies of wholeness, and visions of a world without intrusion, conflict, or demands on our time and energy.[59]

I focus here on the ways quiet is seized upon as a privilege—even an entitlement or right—of the elite; this enables a strategic rhetorical conversion of what are otherwise infringements on the sovereignty of marginalized communities into self-protective reactions to alleged sonic harm. However, as Steve Goodman has outlined in his lyrical and principled analysis of "sonic warfare" and systemic efforts to generate "ecologies of fear," there is such a thing as sonic harm, though its coordinated force is directed not at the elite complainants I often catalog but rather at minoritized communities. The physiological and psychological effects that exposure to noise can have are so real, in fact, they are routinely deployed as weapons of war.[60]

Sound can and does harm; most often, it is marginalized communities who are targeted for sonic intimidation and harm. I am captivated by the fact that quiet is understood as a precious resource that can be seized by the powerful and withheld from the powerless. Quiet, in this sense, becomes yet another object of appropriation, that which the dispossessed are vulnerable to losing arbitrarily and without recourse. My attention to quiet as an elite entitlement, then, does not disavow the materiality of sonic harm nor the importance of quiet to our physical, mental, and emotional health; instead, it considers how certain people, places, and forms of cultural production are produced a priori as incompatible with quiet, as likely to disturb the peace, and as incapable of *being* disturbed and therefore targeted for preemptive action or whose quotidian social, cultural, and political expressions are hyperbolically cast as "harmful" and responded to with outsized shows of force.[61] Connectedly, however, I am compelled by the framing of the pursuit of quiet (especially as part of a regime of self-care) as a quest for a kind of justice; the making of a better world becomes entangled in the quest to pull away from the world.

Many of the texts I examine represent sound and its effects through language: often, I am analyzing a story about the physics and politics of sound and not the more dynamic, real-time vibrational propagation of sound. Henriques draws a critical distinction between an "auditory investigation" (or "thinking *through* sound") and an "investigation of audition" (or an inquiry into "how certain sounds are taken to indicate objects or events").[62] While my study tends toward the latter, I do so not to ignore the important advances in Caribbean literary and sound studies that push us beyond the merely indexical qualities of sound and toward sound as a mode of embodied theory. Instead, I seek to investigate the ways discourses about quiet often seek to obfuscate the indexical work of sound by representing sound as merely physiological, and therefore, nonideological. I focus my attention on the work of discourse to clear space for appreciating and examining the work of Caribbean writers, musicians, and everyday folks as sound theorists and artists who stage challenging disruptions to our sensory status quo and not merely as those lacking sonic etiquette.

The Feminist Aesthetics of Disturbance

Sonic policing—a subtle, yet effective mechanism of racial and spatial policing—works to naturalize elite claims to space and belonging while denaturalizing others. By tracing the sonic imaginations of Afro-Caribbean writers in this book, I call attention to the ways marginalized folks catalog these subtle forms of policing and yet still boldly claim the world as theirs.[63] To elaborate a "claim to the world" is distinct from underscoring resistance, although sometimes, the writers and characters I examine *do* explicitly resist, counter, or strike back against the violence of the state, the repression imposed by their families, and the surveillance of their neighbors. In addition to advocating for the dismantling of the structures that surveil them, writers and characters focus their political imaginations on imagining free worlds—practicing what George Lamming called "sovereignty of the imagination"—within the very conditions of constraint they struggle against.[64] In this way, these works of art illustrate something closer to what Aliyyah Abdur-Rahman calls "the black ecstatic" or "the black queer attachments, affective dispositions, political aspirations, and representational practices that punctuate the awful now with the joys and possibilities of the beyond."[65] These practices are distinguished by their immediacy; they seek to claim space in the world *now*, refusing to concede the present moment entirely to the pressures that otherwise shape their lives. The watchword of these practices might be "disturbance" rather than resistance: there is in these works of art a willingness to frustrate colonial order by refusing to adopt the subtle practices of sonic and social etiquette that are expected of them.

Many Black feminist and Caribbeanist scholars, myself included, have gravitated toward disturbance as a generative affect and effect and indeed an art of critique. As Mecca Jamilah Sullivan powerfully writes, "Black feminism takes pleasure in the studied art of disruption."[66] Sara Ahmed notes, "We learn about the feminist cause by the bother feminism causes; by how feminism comes up in public culture as a site of disturbance."[67] Susan Harewood theorizes "disturbance" as a key prism for understanding how Caribbean sound and performance intervene to reveal and refuse the sensory and rhetorical conversion of the region into a "paradise," which obscures the ways colonialism's ongoing legacies continue to create ever-intensifying forms of economic and political precarity for those living in the region. Harewood writes, "It is particularly important to examine the way colonial and postcolonial narratives produce a sound environment that converts some of the more disturbing noises of history into the more muted tones of Heritage [. . .] listening to the muted, though ever-present critique embedded in Caribbean performance might offer a way to come to terms with the disturbing noises of persistent coloniality."[68] Harewood's turn to the language of disturbance thus marks a specific kind of disruption of the colonial sensorium; it marks practices and ways of reading that trouble the notion of the region's amenability to Global North tourism and its dossier of sensory fantasies of the Caribbean. I, too, have entered this genealogy of theorizations of disturbance and the sensorium and have underscored the ways disturbance operates as a "vital affect of Black feminist creativity and knowledge-production."[69]

One elegant example of the feminist art and aesthetics of disturbance can be found in the Jamaican-American feminist writer, scholar, and activist June Jordan's writing, specifically in her meditations on the ways the colonial sensorium disrupted the potential for transnational feminist solidarities. In her renowned essay "Report from the Bahamas, 1982," a deeply personal and theoretically rich essay tracing how imperialism disrupts solidarities by transforming potential allies into "parties to a transaction designed to set us against each other,"[70] Jordan opens with a vignette rich in sensory detail. Describing the promotional materials for the Sheraton British Colonial, the hotel in the Bahamas where she was staying, Jordan was captivated by a photograph of a middle-aged Black waiter wading into the seawater to serve drinks to the hotel's patrons. She writes, "What intrigues me most about the picture is just this: while the Black man bears a tray full of "colorful" drinks above his left shoulder, both of his feet, shoes and trouserlegs, up to ten inches above his ankles, stand in the also "colorful" Caribbean salt water. He is so delighted to serve you he will wade into the water to bring you Banana Daiquiris while you float! More precisely, he will wade into the water, fully clothed, oblivious to the ruin of his shoes, his trousers, his health, and he will do it with a smile."[71]

Within Jordan's critique of the ad's reinvigoration of the antiblack image of the smiling Sambo, she draws particular attention to the word "colorful." Why is "colorful" framed in quotation marks? The use of quotation marks can be read on one hand as a gesture of disavowal: it marks language that comes from elsewhere, that does not belong to her. She is parroting the visual vocabulary of the photograph. On the other hand, the insertion of quotations constitutes a gesture of emphasis and of irony. It is a way of calling attention to a word with the aim of subversion—to cast doubt on the validity of the language, its object, or its source. The tray of tropical cocktails Jordan describes was likely colorful in a literal sense: flush with ombré yellow-blue or yellow-orange shades designed to emulate the shifting shades the eye might catch when tracing the ivory sands on the beach from shallow cerulean to its ultramarine depths, or while watching a Caribbean sunset drift from bright yellow to the saturated spread of blood orange. The scene depicted in the ad Jordan viewed was likely a cornucopia of color. Why, then, does Jordan cast doubt—not once but twice—on the word "colorful"?

Jordan does this to underscore the importance of sensory intensity and vibrancy to the production of the Caribbean as island paradise.[72] The Caribbean is a place where light's intensity, and the saturation, vibrancy, and variety of colors, is said to take on new proportions. As the narrative goes: No ocean blue is as clear, as unpolluted, as tranquil as that of the Caribbean Sea. No sun is as brilliant and unencumbered. Even the Black waiter is recruited into the parade of color, his brown skin as central to the scene as the vividly hued drinks he carries. We might also consider the ways "colorful" denotes that which is both "full of interest, excitement, and character" (i.e., a "colorful" personality) and that which is "disreputable, questionable, notorious" or even "vulgar and rude" (as in "colorful" language).[73] "Colorful" fuses the titillating with the taboo; it is reserved for that which is attractive *because* it is indecorous, conspicuous, or even obscene. The prospective patrons of the resort are intended to consume the scene of colorful drinks, sea, and waiter with pleasure because it latches onto ideas of the region, explicitly constructed and circulated through the medium of the senses, as the quintessential site of otherworldly, deviant sensory wonders and pleasures.

It is no mistake that Jordan, one of the most prolific and essential Afro-Caribbean-American feminist and queer writers of her generation, opens her famous essay about the obstacles facing—and radical potential of—transnational (and multiracial) feminist solidarities with reflections on the sensory vocabulary used to construct the Caribbean. By tying together ideas of Caribbean sensory exceptionalism to her larger critique of the ongoing legacies of colonialism in the region, Jordan names sense perception (vision, in this case) as both a crucial domain of imperial governance and a domain where solidarities either forge or fracture. Jordan admits the following about the Black waiter in the photo: "Every time I look at the photograph of that fool standing in the water with his shoes on I'm about to have a West Indian fit, even though I know he's no fool; he's a middle-aged Black man who needs a job and this is his job—pretending himself a servile ancillary to the pleasures of the rich."[74] The sight of the man offends Jordan, even as she grapples with her own relative economic privilege, with the fact that "compared to his options in life, I am a rich woman."[75]

The very visual scene that is intended to attract tourists to the region repulses Jordan; the lure of the colorful does not seduce her, and she does not see as she is supposed to see. Rather than taking pleasure in the photograph, imagining herself in it as the patron being served, dissociating from the dynamics of racial and economic exploitation that undergird the scene, Jordan registers disturbance. She is troubled by the image, angered; she is "about to have a West Indian fit," a fit that stands in juxtaposition to the coerced performance of joyful willingness of the Bahamian waiter. She is angry at him and for him. By registering disturbance, Jordan "makes strange" a scene that is otherwise intended to be felt as peaceful, inviting, and serene.[76]

Loud Black Women

Occupying a central place in my study are Afro-Caribbean women and femmes who are often cast in terms of sonic exceptionalism, as irreconcilable with quiet. Much U.S. Black feminist scholarship has long contested controlling images of Black women—as "mammies, matriarchs, welfare recipients, and hot mommas"—and pointed out how these images serve to "make racism, sexism, poverty, and other forms of social injustice appear to be natural, normal, and inevitable parts of everyday life."[77] Controlling images have the power to naturalize social injustice precisely because they take root in the zone of sense perception, and the senses are very often narrated as our pre- or nonideological link to nature and to reality itself. Vision, in particular, holds primacy of position as a truth-sense: to "see it with our own eyes" is to know the truth unequivocally. Yet in our emphasis on the visual realm—on "images"—we have historically overlooked the wide range of sensory regimes, including sound, in which racial meaning is made. "While vision remains a powerfully defining element of race," Jennifer Lynn Stoever writes, "scholars have yet to account for how other senses experience racialization and enact race feeling, both alone and in concert with sight."[78]

Black feminist analyses of controlling sounds instead require that we attend to the racial, gender, and sexual scripts that get tethered to sonic intensity. As Quashie offers, Blackness "is often described as expressive, dramatic, or loud."[79] These stereotypes are compounded by gender, sexuality, and nation. Historically imagined as loud, bombastic, belligerent, attitudinal, and disruptive, and therefore injurious even and especially to our own communities, Black women's voices and sounds are often subject to exacting scrutiny, efforts of modulation, fetishization, ridicule, discipline, and even appropriation.[80] For example, as Meina Yates-Richard elaborates, Black maternal screams and cries of pain are often mobilized in Black nationalist narrative as catalysts of Black masculine political rebirth, awakening, or consciousness-formation; Black women's sonorous and disturbing testimonies of pain appear as "the primordial ooze from which the black man arises, but must leave behind in order to claim a future for himself."[81]

There is a rich body of scholarship on antiblackness and listening, both on what Jennifer Stoever narrates as "the long historical entanglement between white supremacy and listening in the United States" and on what Mendi Obadike calls "sonic stereotypes of blackness" or "the ways in which sounds can carry reference to a mythic blackness that functions as a carrier for other ideas."[82] In particular, Black women's (singing) voices have served as an important locus of racial meaning-making in the United States. "The spectacle of the singing black woman," Farah Griffin reminds us, "often has been used to suggest a peacefully interracial version of America" or conversely to "signal a crisis in the spectacle of national unity."[83] Yet within this brilliant, ever-evolving body of work on Black sound, there has been less sustained scholarly attention accorded to the meanings of Black women's voices and sounds—and their imaginative potential—in their everyday context and outside of the context of performance. As Daphne Brooks underscores in her brilliant and capacious study of "a Black feminist intellectual history in sound," Black women artists "curate sonic performances that not only push the boundaries of musical experimentalism and invention but also produce daring and lyrical expressions of Blackness and womanhood that affirm the richness of their lifeworlds."[84] I am curious about how Black women's quotidian sonic practices and performances, those that are not necessarily explicitly claimed as artistic offerings, might serve as yet another useful archive of the ways Black women "affirm the richness of their lifeworlds" amidst routine sonic surveillance and stereotyping.

In the anglophone Caribbean, loudness has been invoked as a quality that is in direct conflict with the white supremacist protocols of Victorian gender norms and etiquettes and therefore routinely appeared as a sonic problem that shaped British colonial administrations and early Black nationalist ideologies in the Caribbean. The loudness of Afro-Caribbean women was invoked pejoratively in Victorian debates about Black West Indians' capacity for self-rule as a sign of the curious "inversion of gender characteristics" in the Caribbean. Where Black West Indian men were depicted as "lazy and docile" and thus fundamentally unfit to realize their intellectual, social, and political ambitions, Black West Indian women "were perceived to have the traits that Englishmen associated with men," notably that they were "hard workers, but loud and *aggressive*."[85] In other words, the loudness—and therefore the "aggressiveness"—of Black West Indian women was cited in part to underscore a deficiency in West Indian manhood and therefore in Black political capacity. In turn, early Caribbean nationalist politics, rhetoric, and literature sought to forward visions of noble West Indian male protagonists who were "male, of peasant origin" and accompanied by "brave and hardworking women" who were "auxiliar[ies] in his struggle for community."[86] These women were to occupy a supporting role, which included bearing children but excluded any explicit reference to sex or sexuality. Put simply, early Caribbean masculine nationalist ideologies forwarded the adoption of Victorian mores about normative gender roles as an integral part of anticolonial politics. If the nation was to achieve and sustain independence, Black West Indian women would have to literally and figuratively quiet down. The quieting of the too loud voice becomes part and parcel of the disciplining of (perceived) Black gender deviancy.

Loudness was (and is) frequently associated with Black sexual deviancy. The "loud" Black West Indian woman was often taken as a figure who was "aggressive," politically, relationally, and sexually. Where the quiet, demure voice indexed "appropriate" sexual modesty and passivity, the loud voice indexed open, uninhibited, and unruly sexual desire. Belinda Edmondson underscores the afterlives of such colonial regimes of sexual policing. Writing about Antiguan writer Jamaica Kincaid's *Lucy*, notably the protagonist's proclamation that "my whole upbringing had been devoted to preventing me from becoming a slut," Edmondson writes: "The meaning of 'slut' here takes on defiant connotations, not simply sexual but also a social defiance of the role of deferential womanhood. It is this role which 'decent,' 'respectable' black West Indian women—as opposed to loud, 'masculine,' black viragoes of the popular press—must continually be performing in relation to West Indian men."[87] Discourses about race, gender, sexuality, nation, and sound were inextricably bound together in the anglophone Caribbean.

These images of loud Black women as gender-deviant, sexual deviants, and saboteurs of Black social and political "progress" resonate not only in the Caribbean but in the United States, Canada, the United Kingdom, and elsewhere. The fact that these sonic simulacra circulate transnationally matters in part because they attune us to the fact that sonic stereotype, discipline, and etiquette are useful, durable, and effective tools of social coercion and control even across disparate geopolitical (neo)imperial, linguistic, and cultural contexts.

In much writing on racial, gender, and sexual stereotypes, visual, sonic, or otherwise, these tropes often appear in scholarship as narratives to be resisted and dismantled. We invoke the figure of the angry Black woman primarily to expose its "mythic" quality, to underscore that it is a white supremacist invention.[88] This is, of course, true, and any work that loosens the imaginative grip of these racial and cultural narratives is vital. Yet in the public discursive battle against these tropes, we sometimes overlook the curious forms of pleasure and power marginalized folks can forge within these scripts, the ways we sometimes occupy them—even boldly claim them—in ways that can radically undermine their very pejorative or demeaning force.

By pointing to the ways we occupy, claim, play with, and appropriate (sonic) stereotypes, I am not forwarding any reductive claims that stereotypes are somehow "good" for us. Instead, as Jennifer Nash argues, when we "move away from reproducing the good/bad debates around black female sexuality," we can "[make] space for theorizing, imagining, and inciting multiple forms of black female pleasures." Nash continues: "Popular culture is relentless in its reliance on stereotypes that can be hollow, tedious, violent, and humiliating. Instead, I am interested in how these admittedly limited stereotypes can also liberate sexual imaginations, and function as spaces in and through which black women name and articulate longings, pleasures, and desires."[89] Following Nash, I argue for the importance of examining moments when Black women artists claim ostensibly negative sonic stereotypes, such as loudness, as a crucial practice of Black social and political imagination.

The Jamaican-Canadian writer Makeda Silvera makes such a gesture in her germinal essay about the invisibility of Afro-Caribbean lesbians, noting that "loudness" became an important way for queer Afro-Jamaican women to both embrace gender and sexual nonconformity and to boldly assert claims to space and community in contexts where they faced the pressures of social isolation and exclusion. Recounting her grandmother's stories about queer women in their community, Silvera recalls that her grandmother never explicitly named their queerness but instead invoked their loudness as a stand-in for their queerness. Describing a queer woman named Miss Jones, her grandmother noted, "She was very loud. Very show-off. Always dressed in pants and man-shirt that she borrowed from her husband. . . . She always had her hair in a bob haircut, always barefoot and tending to her garden and her fruit trees. She tried to get me involved in that kind of life, but I said no."[90] Though Silvera's grandmother recounted these stories to try to dissuade Silvera from living openly as a queer woman, Silvera takes pleasure and comfort in the loudness of the queer woman her grandmother recalled as a cautionary tale. Silvera writes of Miss Cherry, another queer woman in her community: "I loved Cherry Rose's style. I loved her loudness, the way she challenged men in arguments, the bold way she laughed in their faces, the jingle of her gold bracelets. Her colorful and stylish way of dressing. She was full of wit; words came alive in her mouth."[91] For Silvera, Miss Cherry's loudness, the jingle of her gold bracelets, and her vivacious laugh become art forms, pleasurable invitations into community. Against her grandmother's efforts to narrate queerness through the lens of the eschatological and through the homophobic prism of the Biblical Sodom and Gomorrah myth, as destined for death, rejection, and isolation, Silvera hears Miss Cherry's joyful, playful, and defiant loudness as a life-affirming counternarrative: that queerness is indeed a site of exuberant, joyful, and pleasurable freedoms.

Sonic policing is not limited to Black women and femmes; it affects a wide cross-swath of marginalized people: racial minorities, immigrants, working class and poor people, and queer and trans folks, for instance. It echoes transnationally and across categories of oppression. Loudness, when attached to any number of marginal social positions, amplifies alterity. To be loud is one thing; to be loud, Black, and queer is another. The exact configuration of censure for loudness can vary based on the geometry of our oppression. The figures of the loud Black working-class immigrant and the loud Black fat femme are narrated as overlapping, yet distinct, genres of transgression.

Thus, although the book's provocations and arguments dwell with Black women and femmes, they are not—in Kaiama Glover's words—"in the end, rigidly gender-specific."[92] This means that my analyses of representations of Afro-Caribbean women's embodied sounds often implicate and open out into analyses of the lives and discursive frameworks used to describe people who are marginalized in different ways. By listening closely to how Black women and femmes are heard, we encounter complex matrices of oppression; yet we can also observe practices of freedom, community, solidarity, and autonomy. Through the book, then, I look closely at mundane conflicts over Black sound to query how antiblackness can pervade our commonsense notions of sonic etiquette and well-being. Yet the book also traces expressions of Black sonic creativity in the spirit of curiosity about what role sonic justice might play in ongoing struggles against colonialism and white supremacist capitalist heteropatriarchy and in how sound helps create livable worlds amidst the pressures of the here and now.[93]

The Afro-Caribbean (and the) World

This manuscript moves between geopolitical locales, from Kingston to New York City to Port of Spain to London. Some scholars name such a geographical and cultural configuration as the "circum-Caribbean," the "African diaspora," or both.[94] Krista Thompson explains that the benefit of such units of analysis are that they "[pry] open national, geographic, and disciplinary boundaries between places bound together by networks of people, goods, and visual performance practices."[95] More, they allow us to see how "disparate groups of people of African descent come to think of themselves as a transnational community."[96] It matters when scholars pair "circum-Caribbean" and "African diasporic": it is a way of specifying attention to the ways a transnational Black consciousness is being traced, practiced, imagined, or complicated throughout this broad border-transcending terrain we may call the Caribbean.

Rosamond King offers up the framework of the "Caribglobal" for thinking of the Caribbean and its diasporas in more dynamic and expansive relation than the words diaspora and transnational typically imply. "The transnational focus on mobility is relevant to the Caribbean," King writes, "but the lens too often focuses on those with the greatest mobility and the greatest access to the global North. The Caribglobal, however, is also concerned with people and phenomena that remain in and/or travel to the Caribbean," such as "large numbers of Haitians living in the Bahamas and the Dominican Republic, or of Dominicans living in Puerto Rico."[97] The Caribglobal represents another way of thinking beyond the artificial boundaries of the geopolitical nation state, which obscure the full complexity of movements and relationships that often shape Caribbean peoples' lives. In the lyrical words of Jamaican poet Kei Miller, "Straight lines on a map are decisions / made by men who knew nothing / of mountains or lakes or the spread / of aunts and uncles, or of language."[98] The "Caribbean" in the book's title is, accordingly, a geographically and politically expansive one, marked by mobilities within and out of the region.

However, the designation "Caribbean" cannot be taken for granted as an uncomplicated marker of identity. Speaking on a 2018 panel hosted by Barnard Center for Research on Women entitled Critical Caribbean Feminisms, the Jamaican writer and scholar Erna Brodber declared,

> I'm saying it for the first time openly. But to tell you the honest truth, I am more Black than Caribbean. And being Black, it means that I have to be involved with the United States of America. . . . The phrase I use is "the descendants of Africans enslaved in the New World." . . . The way I see it, if we are to rise up and do something, it's not the "Caribbean" which is a very mix-up mix-up place. It *has* to be, you *have* to understand yourself to be a descendant of Africans enslaved in the New World.[99]

Brodber echoed this sentiment earlier in an interview I conducted with her in 2015. When I asked her to discuss her consistent decision to frame her work in terms of the "African diaspora," rather than "creole Caribbean experiences and communities," she responded, "From a political point of view, 'creole' wants to forget where we're from and focus on what was made here in the Caribbean. And I think it's too early for that. I think, first of all, especially for the Afro-people, you have to look at where you're coming from first."[100]

The Tobagonian-Canadian poet M. NourbeSe Philip, conversely, has insisted at performances on being introduced specifically as a "Caribbean-Canadian poet." At a 2007 performance at the Bowery Poetry Club, the opening speaker introduced Philip to her audience as a "Canadian poet, novelist, playwright, essayist, short story writer, blender of genres and forms." Philip promptly corrected this and said, "I consider myself a *Caribbean*-Canadian poet, if you want to make a hyphen or a slash there. And there's a history and reasons for that."[101] Where Brodber expressed concern that monikers like "Caribbean" sometimes worked to obfuscate or undermine the essential political project of forging and sustaining transnational Black solidarities and connections, Philip—as a Tobagonian writer who lives in Canada—makes a point to index here how her Caribbeanness indelibly shapes her Canadianness. Philip—who has more frequently described herself and the scope of her work as "Afrosporic," "African Canadian," "African Caribbean," and "African Caribbean Canadian"—has long centered African descent in her framing of her work and approached the Caribbean with a political commitment to transnational Black solidarities.

As a transnational Black feminist scholar with deep investments in Caribbean literary studies—and the anticolonial political visions and commitments that informed the intellectual work of these writers—I, too, claim Caribbean, Black, and African diaspora as essential geographic and political markers of my work. Black describes both complex routes of African descent in the Americas, especially the Caribbean, and my own political commitment to a transnational analysis of the lives of, and connections between, people of African descent. Caribbean names a transnational terrain that includes and exceeds the geopolitical boundaries of the space we call the Caribbean. Having been born and raised in Flatbush, Brooklyn, by Saint Lucian parents, my experience of New York City was honed in a space that was itself profoundly Afro-Caribbean, a site of the ongoing practice and evolution of Caribbean culture, politics, and identity alongside, through, and inseparable from, African American and African history, politics, and cultural production.

The Caribbean is well-known for being a racially and ethnically heterogeneous region. Yet in spite of this heterogeneity (or indeed because of it), I, like Brodber, highlight and insist on the Blackness of the region. The gesture of "insistence" matters here: to claim the Caribbean as a Black space is to run up against a long history of scholarly counterclaims to the "hybridity" of the region, to risk accusations of ethnic flattening or erasure, and to graze against the painful ways "Black" has been deployed uniquely within the region and its diasporas as an insult, as a mark of social inferiority, of rudeness and "worthlessness," and as the warning sign of a certain kind of political rabble-rouser, ideologue, or malcontent destined for self-destruction. Yet this insistence is important; it is both a political and disciplinary choice. I follow Rinaldo Walcott who also insists,

> My thinking is based in the insistence that the anglophone Caribbean is in particular but not exclusively [. . .] a Black space despite, or in spite of, its multiracial and multicultural constitution. Blackness and Black people are or have become its foundational marker regardless of its demographics. Of course, my intervention goes against a significant body of scholarship that would argue an opposite position, and it is not my intention to call that scholarship into disrepute. I simply want to note that such scholarship is already shaped by the function of the institutional difference that Caribbean studies is supposed to mark as separate from Black studies [. . .] The distinction between the two studies means that much of our analysis on global Blackness wanes where it need not do so. The postslavery Caribbean is often disappeared behind the claim of pluralism, and the postslavery United States begins to appear, in some popular discourses, as the only postslavery society.[102]

To insist on the Blackness of the Caribbean is to move against the ways Caribbean studies and Black studies have sometimes been marked as institutionally and intellectually separate enterprises. My analyses follow the geographic imaginations of the writers I examine. For them, the work of documenting and dismantling colonialism's legacies in the Caribbean is a necessarily transnational project. This is because the conditions of life in the region continue to be shaped by a complex multinational web of actors who continue to battle for control over the region's natural and human resources, its land, its economy, and its cultural products.

On Archive

I am captivated by the social life of sounds. Several of the sonic events I catalog in this book are historical, but others are fictive, the curious inventions of artists, writers, and filmmakers. Some are scenes of what Carolyn Cooper might call "sound clash"—conflicts over the intensity, duration, or alleged dangers of sound. Others are scenes of pleasure and sonic possibility: a party, an inspired musical performance, or a moment of self-realization occurring against the backdrop of a recording. In all cases, sonic imagination is essential: how do sounds get embedded in dense webs of social meaning so affecting that two equally enthusiastic responses—calling the police, and entering into rapturous connection with one's body—might emerge from the same scene? More, what is the archive that allows us to ask and answer questions about sonic imagination? Why do questions about sonic imagination matter, and what kinds of insights and transformations can they lead us to?

Every book has intellectual forebears; here are some of the ways mine have answered these questions. Literary and Black sound studies scholar Mendi Obadike's influential *Low Fidelity: Stereotyped Blackness in the Field of*

Sound queries "sonic stereotypes of blackness," troubling the dominance of the visual field in our studies of racial stereotype. "Why do theorists who write about the social meanings of music often explore the cultural pleasures of the sounds they consider," Obadike queries, "but not the moments where the common readings of sounds are damaging, dehumanizing, reductive?"[103] She continues, "How can the conversations about stereotype that are so often cast solely in visual terms be expanded by what is known about habits of listening and social meanings of sound?"[104] Just as notorious visual caricatures of Black people were simulacra—representations with no grounding in an "original" figure or reality, but which nevertheless claimed to represent something "real" or essential about Blackness—sonic stereotype also relied on ideas of "mythic blackness," which were marked by the sense of a sound's "contrast with" or perceived deviation from white sound. Indeed, the evocative power of sound is so potent, Obadike argues, that we might speak of "acousmatic blackness," or the ways sound can call forth antiblack images, ideas, and affects even in the absence of Black people (for example, the use of an extradiegetic hip-hop soundtrack in television and film to mark a scene where criminal or otherwise illicit behavior is taking place). Sonic imagination, then, matters because it is just as fertile a repository of Blackness' meanings as the visual realm is, perhaps even more so. Obadike's archive included film, poetry, plays, novels, experimental sound, postcolonial theory, literary and cultural studies scholarship.

The textual remit of this book is similarly diverse. I gather a broad archive of sources in this book including fiction, poetry, essays, travel narrative, advertisements, policy statements, colonial correspondences, law, periodicals, and short film. Though these sources deploy different rhetorical and creative strategies, make varying kinds of claims to truth and historicity, and address different audiences, together they help us to see how debates about quiet operate as a battleground for other kinds of political investments. I am drawn to nonfiction historical and legal sources such as the colonial archive, periodicals, and travel writing because they are useful archives of how strange, anxious, contradictory, and uncertain colonial authorities and their rhetoric and ideologies indeed were. Although colonial rule is sometimes taken for granted as an eminently organized enterprise—a masterminded, well-oiled domination scheme—it is often "disorganized, uneven, plural" and even "incompetent" even as it is always deadly, pernicious, calculated, audacious, and mercenary.[105] When I turn to these sources, I do so in the spirit of "making strange" phobic rhetoric about Black sound; I point out its internal contradictions, scrutinize its rhetorical strategies, closely examine its historical and political milieu, and draw out its subtleties. I aim to be a shrewd and demanding reader of the colonial archive to reveal what interpretive possibilities emerge when the consensuses these texts work to naturalize fail.

I am drawn to expressive cultures like art, fiction, film, experimental poetry, essay, and quotidian speech for the ways they tend to highlight the perspectives of those being scrutinized or policed under regimes of sonic surveillance. Often those subjected to the unrelenting ear of sonic surveillance are reduced to anticommunal sources of nuisance in the grammar of noise complaints. Those writers and artists who explore what sounds mean to those accused of disrupting the peace refuse to merely pathologize those deemed noisy and instead demand that we expand our ethical imaginations so that we may probe the limits of our sense of community. I highlight art in an effort to gather as robust as possible a snapshot of what quotidian sonic creativity can look like. The analytical framework I bring to each of these works is informed by my background as a literary scholar: my readings of my sources often weave together postcolonial, feminist, queer, historicist, new critical, and critical race theory approaches.

Chapter Summaries

The chapters of this book each cohere around a single concept or principle that illustrates how sonic intensity—quietness or loudness—becomes central to particular political projects or imaginative exercises of political freedom. Moving from resonance, to aural privacy, to vibration, to subtlety, I examine how Caribbean people, women and queer folks in particular, get marked as sonic exceptions and how they (sometimes willfully, sometimes unwillingly) take up disturbance as a vital strategy and aesthetic of placemaking, self-sovereignty, and creativity.

In chapter 1, "Resonance," I examine the curious preoccupation that police, colonial administrators, and the local elite in 1930s Jamaica had with noise and the politics of resonance in Kingston and how mining those concerns reveals a much deeper set of anxieties about the material transformations that sex work, labor organizing, and anticolonial public discourse might produce on the island. The framing of the noise complaints themselves was also distinctly gendered: loud Caribbean women were viewed as threats to the social reputation of the island (with special emphasis on sex workers), whereas loud Caribbean men were regarded as threats to the political stability of Jamaica. In this chapter, I argue that authorities deployed a rhetorical strategy I refer to as "sensory rationalism," wherein they make what appear to be eminently reasonable, apolitical, and commonsense appeals for stricter policing and regulation of the soundscape to mask both the ideological dimensions of sonic policing (in the era of the 1930s when the British empire was eager to distinguish itself ideologically from the transparently white supremacist ideologies of Nazi Germany) and to disguise anxieties about the capacity of the British empire to withstand the fomenting labor riots of the period. I query the ways that an overemphasis on routine matters of sonic etiquette may have served as a strategy of rhetorical distraction, a way to tighten surveillance and policing without appearing alarmed while concealing anxiety and reactionary policing beneath ostensibly trifling, commonsense matters of etiquette. Although attention to colonial correspondences and periodicals in the archives offers insight into state efforts of noise management, Michelle Cliff's fiction offers insight into the lived impacts and afterlives of such programs of sonic surveillance, which operated on multiple scales, both domestic and national.

In chapter 2, "Aural Privacy," I walk through a transnational archive of noise clashes, moving from matters of neighborliness to questions of national belonging. Here, I highlight how sonic etiquette can be persistently invoked as a condition of belonging. Close attention to the dynamics of these clashes reveals the extent to which citations of Black sonic excess can harbor notions of Afro-Caribbean people as having a dysfunctional relationship to national regulations and mores around privacy and community, as always already impossible to live with. I approach the racialization of noise by considering how quiet gets converted into a rights object defined against minoritized peoples. If right-to-quiet discourse depends on the conversion of the soundscape into a white supremacist spatial jurisdictional territory where Black subjects are not legible as the subjects of rights, calls for quiet in this context serve as ways to govern Black movement and mobility—spatial, transnational, and economic. By performatively restaging the call for dispossession, whether or not calls for quiet are honored, complainants nevertheless work to reinvigorate doubts about Black entitlement to space and rights. Moving from noise clashes about aural privacy that first raise questions of neighborhood belonging, to those that map onto crises of national modernity, and finally of Caribbean regional belonging, I show how Black mobilities—whether literal (as with transnational migration), social (as with upward class mobility), metonymic (where the flow of the sounds of one's voice or music stands in for an embodied person or group), or symbolic (where certain sounds represent a way of bringing the sensory world of another nation onto domestic soil)—disrupt efforts to privatize the soundscape.

In chapter 3, "Vibration," I explore what becomes possible when we view so-called noisemakers' sonic practices through the lens of pleasure rather than through the prism of sonic injury. Here, I highlight the ways that debates over sonic etiquette often serve to produce noisemakers as antisocial and sadomasochistic and thereby unfit for inclusion within a local neighborhood or community. Moralizing antinoise discourse stresses the deleterious physiological, social, and psychological effects of noise and frames antinoise surveillance and policing as operating in the interests of public health and of the greater good. Another connected branch of this discourse, noise profiling, rhetorically casts noisemaking as a symptom of criminal behaviors to come. In this way, antinoise proponents couple public health concern with predictive policing to cast racial surveillance as rooted in a communal ethos and in a concern for the universal good. This, too, is an iteration of sensory rationalism that submerges antiblack and xenophobic logics beneath the ostensibly veil of health and communal well-being. Noise complaints, then, can operate as tools that facilitate historical and ongoing processes of Black displacement, exile, and gentrification. They can also disrupt efforts of placemaking amidst political, economic, and social pressures. In this chapter, I center the Afro-Caribbean institution of the blues party in 1980s London (one frequently met with noise complaints) and the infamous New Cross Massacre of 1981—an Afro-Caribbean house party that was cited for noise and then later firebombed, resulting in the deaths of fourteen teenagers. I do so both to elaborate the life-and-death stakes of noise citations for Afro-Caribbean communities in London and to show how Afro-Caribbean artists like Steven McQueen reclaim the blues party as an essential site of pleasure, community, and improvisation, against the grain of stigmatizing public discourse about blues parties as sites of criminality and violence.

In chapter 4, "Ultrasound, or Subtlety," I examine the racial, gender, and sexual politics of "subtlety" as a poetic value that is deployed in ways that include or exclude particular Afro-Caribbean artists from the halls of various Global North literary establishments. First, I catalog a series of stories of poetic anxiety where Afro-Caribbean women and queer poets like Kei Miller, Staceyann Chin, and M. NourbeSe Philip register anxiety, doubt, suspicion, and disturbance when standing before their audiences and when considering their places within British, Canadian, and U.S. literary establishments. I point to the ways quiet operates not only as a way to modulate the literal intensity of the voice but also as a strategy for disciplining Afro-Caribbean poetic voice on and off the page. I consider this alongside recent scholarship that has examined the limits of sound as a useful vocabulary for describing political subjectivities, desires, aspirations, and constraints. I consider the ways that sound (vis-à-vis maxims like "make your voice heard") comes to represent a specific set of liberal political fantasies, in which being perceived, sensed, understood, *heard, and seen* by those who wield structural privilege not only automatically produces a freer and more just future but also represents the apex and endpoint of racial justice struggles. I seek instead to catalog what we might learn from the work of Caribbean writers who maintain a stance of cautiousness toward the public sphere as a site of transformative possibility, who are at times uneasy about the audiences who may be attracted to their work. I consider ambivalence, anxiety, and suspicion to be uniquely generative Black feminist affective postures that can draw our attention to other sites and forms of meaningful political possibility.

This book queries what happens when stereotypes of loud Blackness meet fantasies of paradisiacal quiet in the Caribbean. Examining sites like local bars and restaurants, schools, the street, the stage, and the private home, I call attention to quiet as a pervasive colonial aesthetic of order, as a regime of political management, as a tool for segregating space, and as a mode of racial, gendered, and sexual surveillance that meaningfully shapes Caribbean life. Although the writers and artists I examine document the ways that sonic surveillance can sometime curtail creativity, dissent, and defiant pleasures, they also document the vital and everyday ways Caribbean people act as sound artists—and generate what Ashon Crawley calls "soundworlds"—in ways that willfully circumvent or otherwise destabilize efforts of sonic, spatial, and racial discipline.[106] Tourism ads, photographs, travel narratives, and resort promotional materials offer important insight into the ways the Caribbean was imaged for tourist consumption, but there are perhaps no greater archives of the meanings and quotidian impacts of quiet as an aesthetic ideal on Caribbean people than Caribbean art and writing itself.

Let us begin our journey now, then, into this rich archive.

1

Resonance

There is a haunting, recurring tale in the archive of Afro-Caribbean women's writing, especially those writers born, raised, and educated in the Caribbean in the 1950s and 1960s during the twilight of anglophone colonial rule. It is a tale of a peculiar colonial ritual that, as schoolgirls, they were compelled to join: the collective singing of the triumphant British colonial hymn "Rule, Britannia!" The renowned queer Jamaican novelist, poet, and essayist Michelle Cliff vividly recounts such a memory. Collective singing in this context was a coerced expression of colonial patriotism—a sonic "spectacle of imperial solidarity" and "community"—where Cliff painfully recalls hearing lyrics lauding colonial domination issuing forth from her and her classmates' mouths.[1] Sometimes the horror is in the lyrics of the songs; sometimes it lurks in the sound itself, even in what appears to be a seemingly benevolent scene of voices raised in unison. Cliff is not alone: other Afro-Caribbean and African diasporic women writers like M. NourbeSe Philip, Jamaica Kincaid, Andrea Levy, and Stella Dadzie tell the same story of registering disturbance at the experience of singing the song, of causing disturbance to the ritual of collective singing by refusing to sing.[2]

In Cliff's account, she remembers poignantly being led in the collective singing of the refrain of "Rule Britannia" in her colonial girls' school: "Rule Britannia / Britannia rules the waves / Britons never, never, never shall be slaves."[3] "Who among us," she retrospectively queries, "knew it was a sea chantey, sung by sailors plowing the Atlantic during the Middle Passage, cutting south into the Caribbean on the Windward Passage? Who realized those syllables, those notes, so brilliantly enthusiastic, emphatically spreading across the wake of a ship weighed down by its cargo?" She concludes, "None of us, of course. Which is one of the points of colonialism, of being colonized."[4]

In Cliff's account, there is a seemingly minor set of details about the sounds of the notes, which she describes as "brilliantly enthusiastic." She racks her brain to remember if there was "three-part harmony" in their singing.[5] Cliff juxtaposes the "harmony" of the notes with a series of horrifying images of the Middle Passage: enslaved men and women forced to eat and exercise on the top deck of a slave ship, the *speculum oris*—a tool "placed in the mouth to force the lips apart, to feed the recalcitrant slave," and the spread of "contagious melancholia" aboard the ship after an enslaved woman commits suicide.[6] Cliff parallels the historical use of the speculum oris with the induced collective singing of imperial anthems; just as the lips of the "recalcitrant slave" were forced apart to force feed them, the mouths of colonial schoolchildren were compelled open, forced to both enunciate and ingest imperial propaganda.

Cliff calls particular attention to the "harmony" and "enthusiastic" tenor of the notes themselves, which work on a sonic level to mask, or to reframe, the genocidal violence and sadism of the colonial project as a tale of civilizational triumph. "Rule, Britannia!" was most often played in G major, one of the most common keys in music, to convey a joyful, celebratory, triumphant, and majestic mood, in part through its use of a major scale and a 4/4 time signature (or common time, which is widely used in Western classical music). The closing line of the chorus—"Britons never, ever shall be slaves!"—draws to a symmetrical, harmonious lyrical and tonal resolution on the word "slaves," returning to the home chord of G major. I call attention to the key, chord progression, and time signature of the song to underscore that meaning is made in this anthem not merely lyrically but psychoacoustically: the key and time signature of the song suggest balance and harmony, implying that all is right with the world.

Yet Cliff registers disturbance at the "resonance" of these words, which she notes "we sang loudly," with "voices raised," "thinking the promise belonged to us."[7] Here, they were compelled and encouraged to sing loudly to ensure that their voices resonated. Yet as an adult, the memory of singing "Rule, Britannia!" haunts her, resonating because there is a tension between what the lyrics and melody declare aloud and what remains unspoken: Britons shall never be slaves, but their colonial subjects, apparently, shall. She was to sing to demonstrate that her body—and her voice—are those of a disciplined Jamaican schoolgirl; she was taught to evidence her discipline by fêting the promise of freedom that did not belong to her.

I am curious about the ways colonial administrations, curricula, and elite in the Caribbean (and throughout the British Empire) took an interest in matters of resonance. Of particular interest for colonial authorities was the resonance of the Black body and voice. By "resonance," I refer to the capacity to "cause (a sound) to be prolonged, echoed, or modified" or to cause a given space to be "filled with sound."[8] I simultaneously call forth another meaning of resonance as an emotional response, "to respond in a sympathetic or corresponding manner."[9] To declare that a person's words or actions resonate with us is to express that they have touched us, moved us emotionally, and that we are (willingly or unwillingly) *feeling with* others. "Resonance," Emily Lordi writes, names a "vibration between things, an elusive relationship that averts narratives of cause-and-effect but may be more diffuse and wide ranging for that."[10] Resonance, then, is both a property of sound and a relational experience.

I explore in this chapter the ways that colonial administrations in Jamaica viewed the control of resonance as a priority of colonial government and policing, both the resonances they compelled through rituals of imperial community such as collective singing, and those unsanctioned resonances they sought to suppress. The colonial elite often declared resonant sounds, such as the sounds that carried forth from bars, dancehalls, venues of sex work, and other sites of Afro-Jamaican sociality, to be criminally loud, and they sought to curtail Black sound through intensified and improvisatory policing. In colonial periodicals in the 1930s, elites complained about sleep deprivation, lamented the inefficacy of the police, and were scandalized by the illicit activities they (sometimes rightly) presumed to be happening under the cover of noise. They insisted that working-class Jamaicans lacked sonic etiquette and sourced much of the clamor to women's bodies and sexualities. They demanded "quiet." They articulated this demand as an eminently reasonable one, one devoid of ideological investments and a simple matter of etiquette.

Yet beneath their seemingly mundane calls for quiet lurked an unspoken and unspeakable preoccupation with Black women's bodies and sexualities as uniquely unruly, disturbing, and noisy. They complained about noise in Kingston to avoid talking explicitly about sex; yet their language for describing the "noise," and the Caribbean women who produced it, was sexually suggestive, even provocative. One writer complained in *The Daily Gleaner* that the noise problem in Kingston had "reached its climax of orgiastic horror."[11] The writer paints an evocative portrait of the soundscape, underscoring, "the howling in the streets of people who act as though they were semi-demons, by shouting and singing women in houses not far from the hotels in which they stay, but conversations carried on in the public thoroughfare by idle men or chauffeurs—or whomever they may be—from about eleven at night to three o'clock in the morning, by orchestras that play loudly and stridently all night, and by other such disturbances of human origin which effectually prevent from sleeping everybody except those who in desperation must resort to sleeping drugs."

The writer in distress turns to striking, descriptive language: *disturbances of human origin*. Where loud Afro-Caribbean women's voices appear in the colonial archive, allusions to social and sexual taboo are not far behind. This writer notes in passing, in parentheticals, that the "singing women" are "purveyors of parties lasting all night long (with or without nude dancing)."[12] The noise becomes a way to encode transgression against racial, gendered, and sexual colonial mores. Beyond transgression, however, these complaints offer a record of the ways Afro-Caribbean people made counterclaims to the world through their voices, through resonance. They were not merely compelled to passively adopt colonially sanctioned sensory frames. They routinely produced resonant disturbances that constituted for colonials a quotidian threat to colonial order, an unsanctioned form of vibrational touch. The mere fact that the colonial archive regularly features complaints about and prohibitions against Black sound (as far back as early nineteenth-century slave law in Jamaica, for example) is a sign of its seriousness and intractability as a problem.[13] Colonials did not merely touch, shape, and govern Afro-Caribbean people; they, too, were touched, shaped, disturbed, and transformed.

Here, in the writer's account, we get a very different kind of singing woman than the one Cliff provided. These singing women are imaged as animals ("howling") and even "semi-demons" who shamelessly signal their allegedly deviant sexual and social practices by taking up acoustic space at the wrong volume ("shouts"), the wrong times of day (forcing others to resort to "sleeping drugs"), the wrong places ("public thoroughfares"), and for unbearable durations ("eleven at night to three o'clock in the morning"). They resonate in unsanctioned ways; the writer demands that the police be "endowed with additional powers in this respect," that they be further empowered to prevent and suppress these "infernal noises."[14] The writer urges that quiet be restored to the streets to rehabilitate Kingston's "reputation" as a "fairly decent British West Indian capital" and to reclaim it from these unauthorized and condemnable "singing women."[15]

The political novelist Cliff's work, however, provides a counternarrative to that of the colonial archive: she reveals how the demand for quiet operated as a colonial technique for disciplining the Black body and imagination and managing the disruptive potential of anticolonial struggle.[16] Cliff attends to the ways resonance—and indeed "loudness"—served as metonyms not just for racial inferiority but gender and sexual deviancy as well. The "loud Black woman" was often presumed to be an embodiment of a wide range of social "ills" precisely because she (sometimes willfully, sometimes unintentionally) resonated with those who did not want to resonate with her. Yet Cliff's literary works—flush with scenes of sonic clash, sonic metaphors, and more—do far more than merely counter the propaganda of the colonial archive: they stage scenes of Black feminist and queer intimacy, pleasure, and political imagination that, though fleeting, take up meaningful space in novels where Afro-Caribbean women and queer characters are often haunted by unrelenting colonial and extrajudicial sonic surveillance. Cliff's works are temporally and geographically capacious (nonlinear and spanning multiple centuries and continents) and politically bold, and yet they are also strikingly subtle (even quiet), suggestive rather than explicit.

Cliff herself was an elusive personality who was rarely photographed; she recalls being deemed "quiet" as a young girl, writing, "I am reminded that a great compliment of my childhood was: 'She's such a quiet girl [. . .],' i.e., speechlessness as a quality—a behavior—held to be positive and encouraged in young girls. Therefore speechlessness is connected with being 'good.'"[17] Cliff was praised as a girl for containing herself sonically, for ensuring that she was "seen and not heard," as the sexist aphorism goes. More, Cliff underscores that quietness for women and girls was also taken as a sign of "chastity": a quiet woman was also a sexually disciplined one.[18] Quiet as a form of discipline extended even to her writing. Cliff repeatedly recounts across interviews a traumatic and violating incident during which her parents "broke open [her] drawer, took out and broke the lock on [her] diary, and read it"; later, they read the "intimate details" of her life recorded in her diary, including her feelings about menstruation and her meditations on being "in love with another girl," aloud in front of her relatives.[19] Cliff was thirteen years old at the time. "It was a silencing event," she reflects. "It silenced me for almost twenty years."[20] It was not until Cliff was thirty-one years old that she would write again, penning one of her landmark essays "Notes on Speechlessness" in 1977. In it, Cliff defined speechlessness as both "the inability to speak and the inability to reveal"; it is ultimately, she remarked, "to avoid real expression or revelation."[21] Her speechlessness manifested, she reflected, as much in her "withdrawal" and tendency to be "quiet" as much as it did in her use of "humor" and "chattering" as deflective mechanisms.[22] For Cliff, the moderation of her spoken voice and the repression of her writerly voice operated in tandem. She became, in her words, "shy and tongue-tied," in part because the contents of her diary were deemed sexually and sonically undisciplined and deviant.[23]

Cliff has been widely read and studied as a pivotal figure of the 1980s boom in Caribbean women's writing and an essential feminist and queer novelist, poet, and essayist who was a fixture of what Jafari Allen has called the "anthological generation."[24] Cliff's fiction and essays were widely featured in several landmark anthologies, studies, and collections of essays on Caribbean women writers in the 1990s such as Carole Boyce Davies and Elaine Savory Fido's *Out of the Kumbla* (1990), Pamela Mordecai and Betty Wilson's *Her True-True Name*, Evelyn O'Callaghan's *Woman Version* (1993), Myriam Chancy's *Searching for Safe Spaces* (1997), and Belinda Edmondson's *Making Men* (1999), to name a few.[25] More, she featured essays in several of the most renowned and beloved Black and woman-of-color feminist anthologies such as Barbara Smith's *Home Girls* (1983) and Gloria Anzaldúa's *Making Face, Making Soul/Haciendo Caras* (1990), and Cliff contributed both as a writer and editor to venues for lesbian and feminist scholarship and art, such as *Sinister Wisdom* and *Signs*.[26] The scope of Cliff's art and thought—like other Caribbean migrant and Caribbean-descended women writers of this vital period of Black women's literary production including Paule Marshall, Dionne Brand, Makeda Silvera, Jamaica Kincaid, and M. NourbeSe Philip—was insistently transnational. Though Cliff reflected on her relationship to Jamaica throughout her entire writerly career, her works were geographically expansive, often taking her characters to other sites of Caribbean diasporic life such as the United States and the United Kingdom. Of her relationship to place, Cliff remarked, "I grew up partly in the United States, I was educated in London, and I originated in Jamaica, so I can't limit myself to just one place."[27]

Central in Cliff's work, and in scholarship about Cliff, are paradoxes of place, irresolvable tensions between belonging and estrangement, attachment and alienation. Cliff once described her relationship to Jamaica as "a killing ambivalence."[28] Meditating on the possibility of return, she confessed, "I am afraid my place is at your side. I am afraid my place is in the hills."[29] Because Cliff was multiply marked as an outsider to the region because of her race, color, and queerness—and notably because of her relationship to feminist politics and art and as an expatriate writer living in diaspora rather than within the Caribbean region—her works posed vital, productive challenges to the way scholars marked the boundaries of the Caribbean and to fraught notions of Caribbean authenticity. Cliff's claim to Jamaica, and to Caribbeanness, troubled scholars and critics who viewed "authentic" West Indian cultural production as evincing a fundamentally "affirming" stance toward the region, as emerging from or entailing a return to Black, rural, peasant origins and as resistant to what were once (and sometimes still are) construed as extraregional Global North identity categories, political movements, and analytical frameworks such as feminism and queerness.[30] Belinda Edmondson's collective body of scholarship, in particular, has beautifully elaborated how contradictions of authenticity often revolve around crises of race, class, gender, sexuality, color, language, and place. Attempts at locating "real" Caribbean culture—a narrative venture that Edmondson argues represents an attempt to "re-masculinize" Caribbean space—are always already frustrated by the lived realities of the messy, multiple routes by which culture is produced.[31] Cliff could not, and did not, settle into an easeful sense of national belonging. She instead expressed a persistent sense of disturbance at the notion of national belonging; she routinely disturbed efforts to cohere an "authentic" Caribbean form, voice, and experience.

Although Cliff came to reject quiet as a performance of demure, disciplined femininity, what we do see in Cliff's writing are quiet, quotidian scenes of Black feminine and queer erotic agency that do not announce themselves as loud at all. The most impactful scenes in Cliff's oeuvre are often subtle, quiet, and tender. I read this as one way Cliff stages a disturbance to the ways quiet gets deployed as an elite aesthetic allowed only to those who accord with normative gender and sexual scripts. Cliff shows how Black women, femmes, and queer folks persistently carve out private spaces of intimacy, belonging, and interiority and yet still get produced as loud under colonial regimes of racial, gender, and sexual hypersurveillance. This matters because Black (feminine and queer) sexuality is so often produced as attention-seeking, as a spectacle, as willfully disruptive, and as aspiring to dominate the public sphere (as the complaints *Gleaner* writer show). Yet the reverse is far more often the case: Black feminine, queer, and trans people and sexualities are often compelled to disclose themselves, to make themselves public, to declare themselves, and to submit themselves for discipline and surveillance.

The colonial archive and periodicals offer up their own strategic narratives about resonance, quiet, and noise, but here I turn to literature for insight into the lived and felt effects of such formal and informal regimes of policing on Caribbean people and for signs of the ways they claimed the world anyway in spite of such policing.[32] Cliff's work magnifies the absurdity, neuroticism, and transparent antiblackness of the colonial officials' and homophobic publics' hyperbolic responses to quotidian sounds even as they compel loud, resonant declarations of colonial patriotism. Where the colonial archive sheds light on formal efforts to name and address the problem of noise, literature is helpful for calling attention to quotidian sites and informal strategies of navigating sonic policing. Cliff's oeuvre—including her 1984 novel *Abeng*, its 1987 sequel *No Telephone to Heaven*, and selections from her vast body of poetry and essays—offer special insight into how sonic governance operated as a mode of racial and spatial policing and helped sustain a sense of precarity for Caribbean people along lines of class, gender, color, and sexuality. Sometimes comical, sometimes horrifying, Cliff's literary stagings of scenes of sonic discipline denaturalize colonial mores of sonic etiquette that both literally and figuratively demand quiet of Black, queer, and working-class Jamaicans.

The chapter proceeds in two parts. In the first half of the chapter, I analyze an example of antinoise rhetoric in the late colonial period to expose how it deploys what I call "sensory rationalism" via literary and rhetorical devices—paralipsis and metaphor in particular—to encode its targeted references to race, gender, class, and sexuality; cast working-class Jamaicans as politically dysfunctional; and justify policing as the rational response to the presumed threat of their congregation. In the second half of the chapter, I turn to Cliff's writing, calling attention to the ways she exposes the uses of sonic policing as a technique for sustaining colonial racial, spatial, and temporal orders. In her work, Cliff "makes strange" colonial rituals of racial, sexual, and sonic discipline through her acts of sensory defiance and disruptive narration. Therefore, she carves out space for sensory strategies that, in Kara Keeling's elegant phrasing, "might support alternative forms of sociality, forms that are not necessarily predicated on familiar modes of exploitation and domination."[33]

Night Noises

Let us begin this story *in medias res*, in the middle of things. It is March 1934, and the streets of Kingston have boomed loudly for one night too many. The inspector general of the Jamaica Constabulary Forces in Kingston has written to the colonial secretary, urging that measures be taken to "effectively stop the present and most obnoxious nuisance of noise at night." The noise, he claims, is issuing forth from brothels and temperance bars where the "lower orders" congregate amidst the din of laughter, conversation, orchestras, gramophones, and radio-gramophones. He urges that these noises be banned after midnight. Pedestrian as his concerns seem, he is not alone. One month earlier, an editorial in the *Gleaner* had been published declaring that "Anyone who is unfortunate enough to live in a vicinity favoured by 'ladies of the life' are aware of how loudly the trumpets blow or the gramophones sound after night. . . . [I]n certain streets gramophones scream forth their raucous tunes until two or three o'clock in the morning, and loud orchestras keep a whole neighborhood awake, and nothing is done about it."[34] Another editorial complains and calls for an intensification of police surveillance: "For a week or so it was observed that the midnight and early morning noises in certain sections of Kingston had subsided and even entirely ceased. Now they are beginning again. That the police must have taken some action in the way of warning people to stop making the night a hideous torture to others is apparent; but what the average policeman evidently does not understand is that he must be constantly on the job and not rest content with sporadic activity induced by bitter complaints."[35]

The complaint—"nothing is done about it"—forwards the narrative that the so-called lower orders have become lawless, that colonial legislation and law enforcement are weak, and that the elite, embattled by noise and noisemakers, are left without recourse. They are outraged because, in their view, they have been stripped of their right to quiet. "Quiet," here, resonates in at least two ways: as "free[dom] from interference or annoyance" and, more subtly I argue, as an appeal to the legal framework of quiet enjoyment. As property owners, they are entitled to enjoy their property without disturbance; these night noises, then, have converted them into the victims of rights violations. Brothels and "ladies of the life"—sex workers—get special credit for making the nights unbearable. Who are these women allegedly turning Kingston into a "bawdy bedlam" at night? How did their "noises" work their way onto the top of the inspector general's to-do list?

Before this, a detour to an account of what the inspector general is and does, historically speaking. It is now 1865, and a Black Baptist deacon named Paul Bogle has organized a mass peasant-laborer resistance, the likes of which the British empire has seen time and time again, yet another flashpoint in a tradition of anticolonial struggle that is as old as empire.[36] After suffering widespread poverty, starvation, and criminally low wages; after being barred from formal representation through extravagant poll taxes; after formally appealing to the Crown for aid to no avail; after marching to the then capital of Spanish Town to meet with John Eyre, the lieutenant governor, and being summarily dismissed; and after peacefully protesting outside of the courthouse and being gunned down by a volunteer militia, the newly emancipated Jamaicans have set the courthouse ablaze and taken over Saint Thomas Parish. The Antiguan writer Jamaica Kincaid remarks saliently, "When I blow things up and make life generally unlivable for the criminal (is my life not unlivable, too?) the criminal is shocked, surprised."[37] And shocked and surprised they were. This came to be known as the Morant Bay Rebellion of 1865.

But what is the name for the extraordinary backlash, the "reign of terror" organized by Lieutenant Governor John Eyre in response?[38] In three days, Eyre's troops regain control of the parish and meet little resistance.[39] But he is hungry for blood and haunted by the success of the Haitian Revolution sixty years prior, so much so that his first official dispatch to Britain on October 20, 1865, is full of references to Haitians, making a point to report that "various Haytien refugees suspected of being mixed up with the leaders of the insurrection" had been apprehended.[40] (This, of course, is strategic; it is a preemptive attempt to persuade colonial officials in the metropole that the brutality of his reaction was warranted.) Eyre institutes martial law and employs government troops and Maroons to hunt down the rebels and indiscriminately slaughter Black people. All suspected organizers and leaders, including Paul Bogle and his brother Moses, are captured and hanged. After a month of martial law, hundreds are summarily executed, hundreds are imprisoned, hundreds more are brutalized, and nearly a thousand are displaced, their homes burned to the ground. Eyre deems this all necessary to "save the lives of the ladies"[41] of the island, even though no white women were harmed in the rebellion and even as he justifies violence against Jamaican women involved in the rebellion by remarking, "The women, as usual on such occasions, were even more brutal and barbarous than the men."[42]

The suppression of the rebellion and the extraordinary violence of empire, which sweetens their teas, stocks their tobacco pipes, and is woven into the fabric of their cotton garments—scandalizes segments of a British public an ocean away, a public who funds the very violence that stuns them. But, of course, there are also those who plainly defend Eyre's brutality, among them the so-called Eyre Defense Committee, which draws its members from many high-profile members of "the literary establishment," including Thomas Carlyle, Alfred Tennyson, Charles Dickens, and John Ruskin.[43] Dickens in particular, lauded by many then and now as a champion of the working class, responded to the irony of his opposition to this labor rebellion by summarily refusing any "platform-sympathy with the black—or the native, or the devil—afar off."[44] It is in response to this shock to the empire's system that the Crown establishes the Jamaica Constabulary Force under the direction of an inspector general. The charge of this police force is to ensure that mass mobilization of the Jamaican working class never occurs at this scale and with this efficacy again. The imperial response to the rebellion also takes hold in colonial curricula. As Cliff notes about the account of the rebellion circulated in colonial schools in the 1950s, nearly one century later, "She learned that there had been a freedmen's uprising at Morant Bay in 1865, led by Paul Bogle; but that this rebellion had been unwarranted and of little consequence, and that Bogle had been rightfully executed by the governor."[45]

It is 1934 again, and history is rhyming. Wages are low, poverty is widespread, and Jamaicans are routinely barred from political representation and land ownership. The laboring classes are organizing, and a yearslong unrest is fomenting across the British empire. Women are playing key roles in organizing, supporting, and participating in labor strikes, though many prominent labor leaders both overlook their contributions to the labor movement and refuse to recognize domestic work (which accounted for nearly one third of Jamaican women's labor) as a legitimate form of "labor."[46] Yet the inspector general of the constabulary forces—which were organized precisely to suppress such organizing—is concerned about noise and about brothels and sex laborers, loud laughter, conversation, and music at night. In an era of fomenting labor unrest, the armature of the state is directed toward sex work and the sounds and social spaces it generates, even as (or perhaps because) these laborers, many of whom are women, are working in trades that are not explicitly included in the unionization efforts of the period. Under closer scrutiny, concerns about noise, then, appear to operate as a proxy for another set of concerns: the threat of congregation, organizing, and Black sociality and political solidarities, and the countersurveillance capacities of sound and the informal and unregulated economies (i.e., sex work) signaled by those sounds. The noise marks spaces where—amidst enormous and punishing social, economic, and political repression—otherwise possibilities are being forged: ways of making ends meet, of speaking in chorus, of sustaining an anticolonial politics, and of being together. This is not a story about noise per se. It is a story about what political programs the discursive frame of "noisiness" seeks to veil, advance, or facilitate when deployed by colonial and state authorities, what these sounds represent for Caribbean people, and how these meanings coalesce around Black women's bodies in particular.

Here, we move through the archive of 1920s and 30s colonial correspondences, periodicals, and travel writing to tell a story about the political utility of narrating the Caribbean as a noisy or pathologically loud region. Oftentimes, I argue, both British and U.S. imperial travel writing and ephemera produced the Caribbean as a sonic aberration—and therefore a sonic problem—to depict the region as in need of stricter imperial interventions: from increased local policing to a more radical shift in the imperial guard (i.e., shifting from British imperial to U.S. imperial rule). This history matters in part because it helps demonstrate that the production of the Caribbean as a sonic exception served as yet another route through which "'the West' produces 'the Caribbean' as its other."[47] The famed Haitian historian and anthropologist Michel-Rolph Trouillot once called for scholars to "spell out [. . .] how the geography of imagination and the geography of management constantly intertwine to construct the management of imagination."[48] I answer this call by drawing into view how colonials imagined Caribbean soundscapes, and how their imaginings expressed and sought to manage various imperial ambitions and anxieties in the region, anxieties about both immediate and anticipated threats to the stability of imperial dominance.

Sensory Rationalism and the Narrative Work of "Failure"

Juridically speaking, complaints about noise in the colonial archive rarely amount to much. Antinoise laws are passed but are notoriously difficult to enforce. The matter of proof becomes troublesome: at what point does sound become illegal noise? At what decibel measures? Sustained for how long? From how many meters away must it be audible? And how does a layperson measure decibels and meters without special equipment? If the proof is purely experiential—being annoyed, disturbed, sleep-deprived, etc.—how does one distinguish a public nuisance from a matter of personal taste? How many people must complain for it to constitute a public nuisance? More, who is valued as a member of a recognized "public" that is vulnerable to disturbance?

Noise complaints appear in periodicals and colonial correspondences peppered with phrases like "everyone knows" and "anybody can hear," marking an assumed collectivity and upholding what I call a rhetoric of "sensory rationalism"—the veiling of targeted forms of racial, gender, class, and sexual surveillance and stigmatization behind a seemingly neutral, pedantic discussion of the senses as nonideological and universal. In the context of the study of sound in the Caribbean, this rhetoric depends heavily on the normalization of a white or creole elite bourgeois subject position, and vague invocations of collectivity—using pronouns and possessives like "everyone," "our," and "anyone"—to presume and advance a dominant common sense that marginalized groups "naturally" exceed or fall outside of the collective sensory (and political) standards and ideals of the nation.[49] A key function of sensory rationalism is to enable otherwise privileged classes to rhetorically assert a state of dispossession or embattlement—to claim that they are under assault or experiencing rights violations at the hands of marginalized groups. Sometimes it is couched in pedantic language about tone, volume, and duration; other times, it is plaintive and hyperbolic. In both cases, sensory rationalism is a strategic act of historical and political decontextualization and diversion, meant to mask calls for colonial violence beneath the seemingly reasonable, neutral, or even benevolent guise of concerns for the "public good."

Once noise complaints appear in colonial periodicals, their trace disappears. It is unclear what gets *done* in response to them. Or, it is unclear what gets done *in explicit response to them*, though it is clear that increased policing is what writers would like to see done. Indeed, the dominant narrative in colonial archives of the early twentieth century—and even later, in more contemporary rhetoric—is one of powerlessness: the police, the state administration, and the elite all claim to be overwhelmed by noise, perpetually unable to manage it. It is framed as a scourge that cannot be contained, a problem that exposes the limits of colonial governance. This is a part of why many scholars of the colonial sensorium view sound as a resistant sensory medium; it is difficult to delimit, to measure, to capture, to codify, and to suppress. It frustrated colonials, haunted them.

This scholarship on the ways that sound serves a key site for the preservation of Black cultural memory, a medium of communication that evades colonial surveillance, a route for forging and sustaining global Black solidarities, and a space to articulate resistance to colonial forms, mores, and epistemologies is essential to how I think about Caribbean people's relationship to sound.[50] I am also indebted to scholars who view Black sound as a site of contestation that was constantly subjected to efforts of colonial surveillance, suppression, and appropriation, even as it could never be fully mastered.[51] I celebrate the generative and subversive capacities of Black sound even as I am troubled by the ways colonial elites' narratives of the alleged failures of colonial governance—in this case, vis-à-vis their struggles to contain noise—nevertheless do work for empire.

When editorial writers in colonial periodicals complain about the intractability of noise as a social problem, they write to advocate for the intensification, expansion, and (perhaps most notably) improvisation of the policing apparatus. They construct a narrative of Black lawlessness, of Black failures of social and political etiquettes, and of the vulnerability of the elite, often in hyperbole, expressly to rationalize a "solution" that is extrajudicial and police-centered. By the late colonial period, those persons, activities, and industries that are condemned as the sources of noise are already targeted and restricted by a wide cross-swath of laws, including vagrancy laws, laws against religious expression, bans on horns, drums, and other sound reproduction technologies, and more. Noise complaints, then, appear not because there is no available juridical framework for condemning Caribbean people but as representation of a part of a collaborative effort between minor offense law, public discourse (in colonial periodicals), and the local elite to facilitate and justify the expansion of policing in ways that are more improvisatory, extrajudicial, and unbound by the formalities of law and procedure. In other words, these colonial narratives about being overwhelmed and powerless to contain noise are not innocent or transparently plaintive, and therefore, should not be taken at face value. They are narratives intended to intensify the policing of already hyperpoliced communities. More, these narratives and rhetorical strategies are also not confined to the era of colonial rule but recur in the postindependence period as well, signaling what Aaron Kamugisha refers to as "the coloniality of the present."[52]

I take my cue in part from prison abolitionist scholars and activists, like Mariame Kaba, who work to demystify and historicize the actual societal function of policing in practice as distinct from the "protect and serve" and "anticrime" narratives commonly deployed to justify their presence in communities. In a *New York Times* opinion piece entitled "Yes, We Mean Literally Abolish the Police," Kaba writes: "The first thing to point out is that police officers don't do what you think they do. They spend most of their time responding to noise complaints, issuing parking and traffic citations, and dealing with other noncriminal issues."[53] Though we are encouraged to view police as a safeguard against violent crime, Kaba reminds us that quotidian noncriminal issues, such as noise complaints, account for the majority of police work in communities. Yet as we know, routine traffic stops and house calls often become fatal encounters for Black people. Also, as I highlighted earlier, constabulary forces were often founded expressly to advance colonial efforts to suppress and surveil Caribbean communities and to protect the interests of the colonial elite. More, antiblack policing as a practice extends beyond formal law enforcement, security, or military personnel; it is enacted through a broad network of informal agents—teachers, neighbors, passersby—who attend to the quotidian work of sustaining the racial, gendered, and sexual hierarchies of public space.

My attention to noise is energized by an interest in elucidating how minor offenses, public "nuisance," and quotidian disputes over sonic etiquette become essential mechanisms for justifying and normalizing hyperpolicing and sustaining a sense of precarity—the knowledge that at any moment, state violence and other institutional forms of antiblack, sexist, queerphobic, and transphobic discipline may be arbitrarily enacted. It is the very sense of the triviality of minor complaints that permits their operation as mechanisms for sustaining and intensifying policing while allowing them to masquerade as innocent, neutral, objective, commonsense matters of public good that require no further scrutiny. In the colonial and postindependence Caribbean, local officials and elites did not merely aspire toward spectacular demonstrations of colonial power; they sought to preside over seemingly trifling matters of etiquette, comportment, leisure, and more to contain and constrict the possibilities of disruptive forms of sociality and political solidarity. It is this low, quotidian hum of colonial governance and its afterlives that I trace throughout the book. I draw the register of "minor" offense into view—through the entry point of the noise complaint—to elucidate the ways it seeks to serve as an alibi for the intensification of policing and the retrenchment of colonial hierarchies in spaces and moments when those hierarchies are being contested. I also underscore minor policing to highlight the importance of the ways Afro-Caribbean people strike back against such policing by claiming the world in their own minor, quotidian ways.

A "Paradise for Prostitutes"

There is an open secret about the colonial archive's strange preoccupation with noise in the late colonial period: often, "noise" was a euphemism for sex. In a 1934 editorial in the *Gleaner*, one writer makes it plain: "Unquestionably Kingston has become a paradise for prostitutes. These have progressed so far that one or two of them are said to have introduced here the entirely nude dancing."[54] The writer then conspicuously pivots: "But this is not what we want to deal with in this article; what immediately concerns us is the amount of noise that these people are permitted to make between the hours of eleven and three o'clock at night."[55] The writer's turn to paralipsis—a rhetorical device in which a speaker calls attention to a subject precisely by denying their intent to discuss it—serves to convey that he does, in fact, want to "deal with" sex work, exotic dancers, and other trades and forms of entertainment, and not merely—or even primarily—the problem of noise in and of itself.

The writer seems scandalized by the fact that these so-called ladies of the life and their zones of labor have the gall to announce themselves acoustically. He expects them to conduct their affairs at a whisper, lest what is done aloud be mistaken for being allowed. However, he skirts past potential accusations of moral puritanism by emphasizing instead the hours (11 P.M.–3 A.M.) during which the noise should be contained. This is an example of how the rhetoric of sensory rationalism enabled the colonial elite to level targeted critiques at specific groups while attempting to inoculate themselves against accusations of racism. The writer does not outright say the noise is illegal; rather, he calls for the police to be endowed with the power to circumvent "the technicalities of the law relating to 'noisy assemblies,'" which require that "two private householders [...] prove that the noise complained of can be heard at such and such a distance.... Which means such a great deal of trouble and annoyance to people already in their beds."[56] In the writer's view, the law—somehow too "technical"—gets in the way of policing, which he believes must be improvisatory and discretionary to be effective. In the writer's words, "The police should be empowered to take the initiative," though he quickly qualifies that "no one wants police tyranny in this country: we are not keen on developing along German lines."[57] By shrouding his claims in seemingly pedantic concerns about times of day and the technicalities of reporting noise complaints, the writer tempers and rationalizes his opening complaints about the declining moral character of the island at the hands of Jamaican sex workers. Most notably, however, the writer manages to call attention to what they view as deviant Black gender and sexual practices while simultaneously refusing to speak about them. The article renders Black sex work specifically, and Black sexuality broadly, unspeakable even as it casts it as unbearably noisy and disruptive. This twoness of Black femme sexuality as both unspeakable and irresistible, as both disturbingly sonorous and silenced, is the throughline that binds the archival and literary sources in this chapter. I ask how quiet as an acoustic and social value sometimes subtly casts Black femme bodies and sexualities as inherently noisy, disruptive, or otherwise in need of regulation. As a means to respond to this, I theorize what I might call Black gender and sexual sonorities. Here, I name the ways that deviant sounds, volumes, and timbres get discursively tethered to Black women, femmes, and queer and trans folks in ways that facilitate and rationalize the quotidian policing of our bodies and sexualities.

By the early twentieth century, sex workers in the Caribbean were routinely invoked as the embodiment of societal ills. Kamala Kempadoo describes this historical juncture in terms of the emergence of a "rational" and medicalized rhetoric of racial, gendered, and class-based moral superiority: "The emergence in Europe in the mid-nineteenth century of social studies, in conjunction with an increasingly rationalized medical science and a burgeoning middle-class morality, produced assumptions about the socially 'evil' and 'diseased' nature of prostitution, with special emphasis on the 'inherent' promiscuous, immoral, and unclean character of working-class women and nonwhite peoples who did not, or refused to, adhere to European bourgeois family norms and ideals."[58] The *Gleaner* writer's sensory rationalism tethers itself to an existing rhetoric of medicalization, both of which work to normalize ideas of white racial superiority, cleanliness, and morality. (The writer, in fact, opens the piece with a reference to the "popular" supposition that "venereal disease" abounds in Jamaica, a belief even he concedes is specious.)[59] The flourishing of sex work in the Caribbean—a response to the uneven forms of economic scarcity and labor insecurity of the 1930s—risked exacerbating Jamaica's reputation as a site where the codes of "civilized" sexual conduct faltered. The burden of this declining morality was heaped on sex workers themselves and on Black women's allegedly unruly sexuality, not on the sex workers' clientele, who were very often white Global North tourists, foreign military officers, and members of the local white and creole elite. In many cases, as Hilary Beckles has shown, unmarried white women in the colonial Caribbean made a living by directing the sex trade. Beckles explains: "White women's businesses were concentrated in the informal sector, especially in those areas that bordered on the illicit and illegal as defined by white male officials. In most Caribbean societies, prostitution was illegal, but white women made a thriving business from the rental of black and coloured women for sexual services in the port towns."[60] Yet the symbolic burden of sexual deviancy rested disproportionately on enslaved women, not on the white elites who recruited them into—and economically relied on—their sex work. On the part of the colonial elite, this anxiety about sexuality was, of course, primarily tied up with a concern about the steady decline in their social prestige as white and creole elites as Jamaicans pushed for fair wages, enfranchisement, political representation, and independence from Britain.

As Yasmin Tambieh points out, the battle to position Caribbean nations as "modern" has involved measuring their "'moral' location [. . .] vis-à-vis the metropolitan centers of the North Atlantic."[61] Yet the sex worker's body also became "a site around which nationalist and feminist struggles were framed, as well as a basis for working-class Caribbean women to contest ruling-class hegemony."[62] Complaints about the noisiness of the districts where sex workers labor, then, are likely not at all about a "reasonable" or otherwise neutral concern about noise at night, but about what their bodies, their work, and the social spaces they generated represented politically. Sex workers were dually policed for the ways they were seen to produce the colony's social and moral ills and for the ways they served as what Tao Leigh Goffe calls "extracolonial conduits of sociality and creativity," as well as capital.[63]

The *Gleaner* writer claims that the noise prevents "anyone in the vicinity," within earshot, from sleeping. But he also notes that there are those who are drawn to, rather than repelled by, the noisiness of sex workers' zones of labor. As he sees it, the noise "encourages another class of nuisance, the men who assemble at street corners or within garages to discuss the topics of the day at night-time at the top of their voices."[64] These men, the writer bemoans, "desire to transform an open thoroughfare into a drawing room [. . .] but the drawing room range of tone is certainly not that adopted by these street or garage conversationalists."[65] In other words, where one finds noise, one finds illicit sex *and* disruptive political discourse. Codependent narratives of sexual, sonic, political, and moral excess and dysfunction are discursively clustered here, producing broad categories of persons who are cast as disruptive to the "public good." Caribbean women's bodies and sexual practices in particular are singled out as sites of reproduction for these clusters of disruptive subjects and politics. Caribbean masculine bodies, voices, and sonorities are targeted, too, condemned as the sources of political disruption; their discussions of the "topics of the day" constitute both a sonic and political nuisance and source of anxiety. It is the metaphor of the "drawing room"—a space historically associated with discussions of politics and rituals of social intercourse targeted toward cultivating and shoring up class-based allegiances among the white British aristocracy—that divulges that the writer is indeed concerned about what kinds of political debates and class solidarities might emerge from the "garage" or the "street corner" rather than the drawing room. He calls them "garage conversationalists" diminutively, as if eager to stress the informality, the gaucheness of these debates.

Notice here how the condemnation of the gathering and the discourse is masked through the rhetoric of sensory rationalism, through a seemingly pedestrian and ostensibly reasonable concern about "tone." He insists that it is not the fact that they are engaging in "social intercourse" and political discourse but the volume at which they are doing so. Political anxiety is masked with a concern about proper sonic etiquettes. Here, the drawing room works to normalize a white male British aristocratic tradition of political discourse that was, in one sense, neatly contained in private space—that did not spill out into the streets either sonically or in the form of mass mobilization and protest. (Because, of course, ruling class politics already pervaded the streets.) The drawing room also encodes gender ideals as much as it does race and class ideals. As Roshanak Kheshti reminds us, the space of the drawing room was specifically tailored to white bourgeois women, who in the Victorian era "performed [their] genteel status" through piano performances, and later in the twentieth century—with the emergence of automated sound reproduction technologies like the player piano and the gramophone—performed their status through genteel forms of listening. There is a racialized and gendered repertoire of sounds and aural practices that mark and reify the politics of the drawing room. To invoke it as the standard of sociality and political discourse in the context of 1930s Jamaica is to insist upon the maintenance of racial, gendered, and class hierarchies at a moment when those orders were being sharply contested by Caribbean labor leaders, activists, political theorists, and artists.

The *Gleaner* writer invokes the drawing room and its attendant race, gender, and class codes of conduct to cast Jamaicans as politically, socially, and sexually dysfunctional in a moment when the labor rebellions of the period were "creat[ing] conditions for a new political dispensation and a rearrangement of social relations between colonizer and colonized."[66] He both deploys sensory rationalism to mask his comments as being apolitical and includes coded references to race, class, and gender that his intended audience of white and creole bourgeois elite readers would recognize without requiring explicit elaboration. Yet close attention to his chosen metaphors and rhetorical strategies betray that he anxiously recognizes what is happening on street corners and in garages as a set of social rituals meant to cultivate and sustain a collective politics, to shore up solidarities that are anticolonial and that are deliberately not organized under the sign of the "drawing room."

Finally, colonial vagrancy laws in this period already unambiguously condemned sex work, and criminal law prohibited the management of brothels and the solicitation of sex labor. The 1902 Vagrancy Law classified "common prostitutes" who "wander[ed] in any public place" or solicited clients—along with practitioners of obeah, people engaged in public gambling, and those who sought to "gather alms" or "obtain charitable contribution" via "false or fraudulent pretense," among other persons—as "idle and disorderly persons" who were liable to imprisonment. (Lawmakers, of course, saw no irony in charging these persons engaging in efforts of self-sustenance in the face of enormous economic pressure and scarcity with "idleness.") Why not, then, argue for the vagrancy laws to be enforced? Why argue instead (or additionally) for noise law enforcement to be adjusted, loosened to evade its "technicalities"?

Antinoise and antivagrancy rhetoric, legislation, and law enforcement share much in common. Caribbean feminist legal scholars Janeille Zorina Matthews and Tracy Robinson have argued for closer attention to the durability and efficacy of "the body of laws governing minor offenses that [...] are applied to police the poor and socially excluded."[67] Writing about vagrancy laws in particular, they argue, "These broadly and vaguely worded colonial criminal laws have become indispensable in constructing gender non-conforming and transgressive persons as modern vagrants in the Caribbean."[68] These supple and enduring legal discourses, then, are "deployed to police *prevailing* gender expectations and anxieties and to demarcate citizenship."[69] Even when minor offense charges cannot be adequately proven or upheld, they nevertheless empower the police to conduct arbitrary stops and arrests; to detain alleged offenders for days, exposing them to abuse at the hands of police and loss of wages due to missed work; and to exact public humiliation, among other punishments. They enable the police to attach criminality to, and thus create and sustain targeted environments of precarity for, the poor and working classes, gender non-conforming people, sexual minorities, and women, whether or not a legal transgression is indeed taking place. In other words, the law sometimes achieves its intended end not through prosecution of offenses, but through the *pursuit* of alleged offenders (whether or not they have committed a crime), that is, through surveillance and stigmatization, the relentless bearing down of the scrutinizing gaze of law enforcement, colonial officials, and antiblack public discourse in supposed anticipation of offenses. In 1993, Ruth Wilson Gilmore makes this very point about the policing of public space in Los Angeles, writing, "The police allow the Sunday Venice Beach exhibitionists to hang out, but constantly remind them, through high profile presence, busts, arrests 'under suspicion of,' random identification checks, and general harassment, that license to pass can be revoked at any time."[70] She remarks poignantly, "Los Angeles streets are effectively closed, though they seem open to the inexperienced eye."[71]

There is overlap between the groups that tend to be targeted by noise and vagrancy laws: "the poor and homeless, especially in urban areas, female sex workers, and religious dissidents, such as practitioners of obeah, Spiritual Baptists and Rastafari."[72] The primary functions, then, of minor offense laws, law enforcement, and public discourses are to uphold colonial racial, gender, class, and sexual hierarchies and norms by sustaining environments of precarity for marginalized communities and to justify an ongoing police presence in these communities—a force whose role is to surveil and terrorize people, spaces, and activities that might constitute or mobilize resistive solidarities and "otherwise" possibilities for living and being amidst conditions of enormous social and economic pressure.

Sonic etiquette and excess—markers assigned along lines of race, class, gender, and sexuality—became one way to draw distinctions between the colonial body politic and its unruly Others. Issued from the wrong location and the wrong bodies, loudness came to mark nonconformity, criminality, the illicit, that which disrupted colonial order. Here, I am not only concerned with the ways Black sound and acoustics are policed and stigmatized within law and public discourse. I am more pointedly interested in how the vocabularies and structures of meaning that colonial regimes used to organize the soundscape into permissible and impermissible sound radiated outward and availed themselves to other rhetorics of racial, gendered, and sexual policing of the body, of labor, of clothing, of gender, and of sexual identities and practices. Loudness, in colonial rhetoric, was synesthetic and multimodal: it was at once a marker of aural, visual, and legal transgression. More, sonic markers get freighted with moral meaning. Loud women are not just loud, especially when they are Black; they are also cast as sexually excessive, agents of chaos, threats to the body politic, and unworthy of the protections of law. The *Gleaner* editorial exemplifies how this happens: by embedding critiques of sonic excess within repudiations of other alleged moral ills, such as illicit sexual practices. Noise complaints, then, operate not only as the *cover for*, but are also *coeval with*, concerns about sexuality. Sexual, sonic, racial, and political subjectivity were viewed by colonial authorities as intertwined concepts.

The Low Hum of Sonic Discipline

Where the colonial archive and minor offense law and law enforcement deploy the rhetoric of sensory rationalism as a politically neutral matter of "public good," Cliff exposes the surveillance and suppression of Black sound as a colonial technique for the gendered disciplining of the body, sexuality, the imagination, and historical and political consciousness. The discourse of sensory rationalism seeks to obscure the relations of power that routinely produce Afro-Caribbean women and femmes as the sources of sonic excesses that require containment; Cliff situates nearly all her references to sound within a sustained critique of the ongoing social, economic, and epistemological violence of colonialism's legacies in Jamaica.

The fundamental "problem" of both *Abeng* (1984) and *No Telephone to Heaven* (1987), Cliff's acclaimed duology of novels, might be distilled into this: Clare Savage, the novel's protagonist, does not see the world the way she is supposed to. She is not proud of the things she is supposed to be proud of (namely, her white patrilineal lineage; she is the descendant of a slaveowning British puisne justice). She is not intrigued by the right things. She hears one thing when she is supposed to hear another. Her sensory training is not going as planned, and as a result, she is not being properly socialized. When her father proudly takes her to see the ruins of her great-great-grandfather's former home—the "great house"—she sees the house instead as "so small," "broken down," "dingy and mindful of the past."[73] Rather than instilling in her a sense of racial superiority and pride, the house "carried over to her a sense of great disappointment—maybe of great sadness. It was a dry and dusty place—not a place of her dreams."[74] Despite her family's, teachers', and friends' efforts, Clare is turning out to be a problem. She is continually disturbed by her world—by the racism, colorism, classism, and homophobia of her world, spanning the 1950s to 1980s in Jamaica, the United Kingdom, and the United States. She cannot rest until she finds others who are disturbed, too. The tones of the novels are uneasy, melancholy, marked by a routine, insistent dissonance between her budding self-realization and the norms of her world, which she finds strange and unacceptable.

In this sense, I read *Abeng* and *No Telephone* as narrating problems of sensory rationalism, or more specifically, cracks and failures in its imposition. These novels make exceedingly strange a world that is said to be eminently rational—"the way things are"—even if brutal and disappointing. The act of narration, then, is an exercise in the art of feminist disturbance. Cliff once wrote of the real people, places, and experiences that inspired the semi-autobiographical *Abeng*: "I don't have to have an imagination. All I have to do is record things. It's as if Bertha Rochester was next door."[75] By insisting defiantly that it is not *imagination* that produces the extraordinary events of her novels but a faithful *recording* of reality itself, Cliff underscores the importance of narration—of the way we tell stories about our world—as a strategy for disrupting the normalization of violence. Reality is not reasonable in Cliff's works. It is absurd and unsettling, even more so because of the ostensible quiet acquiescence of the characters around Clare. The absurdity—the injustice—is denied any extended discursive space in the narrative. Instead, it registers most powerfully in the realm of the senses as a sound, sight, taste, smell, or feeling that stubbornly stands against the grain of the official history, the accepted common sense, the "usual activity of life" that Clare is expected to take for granted.[76] I trace, then, the ways Clare stubbornly claims the world as hers by acting—feeling—askance of what is expected of her. This produces her as an insistent disturbance, impossible to fully discipline. Her quiet refusal to feel the way she is supposed to, in turn, releases her "from the normativity of intuition" and makes her "available for alternative ordinaries." Her disruptive feelings and perceptions enable her to "harbor viable alternatives to white bourgeoisie North American common sense"; they energize her search for other ways of being in the world.[77]

Cliff understands sound as yet another terrain—much like the natural landscape, the body, and sexuality—that was jointly subjected to the early disciplinary and organizing efforts of colonial surveyors. Thus, many of her references to sound are situated within a broader narrative project of imagining a return to pre-Colonial time, a timespace she envisions as containing essential imaginative resources to energize anticolonial struggle. In her poem "Colonial Girl," the narrator declares her longing to be "wild," envisioning a return to a "more ancient / pre-Columbian / pre-Contact / growth / Edenic underbrush / unyielding / thick as a woman's thatch."[78] Cliff envisions a divine natural ordering—Eden—in contrast to the imposed orders and cultivated flora and fauna of "post-Contact" colonial rule. By declaring a desire to become "wild," the narrator searches for a way to reclaim and preserve who she is—or might be—before or outside of the ruptures and remakings characteristic of colonial rule.

This longing is a response to the young narrator's trauma after her parents discover she is queer and forbid her from seeing the girl she loves. She recounts this as a kind of quiet, unspoken violence, writing, "The word was not spoken / I was told to forget everything / I would never see her again"[79] Her parents refuse to explicitly acknowledge her queerness by "speaking the word" themselves; rather, they violate the narrator's privacy and read her diary aloud and then recode her expression of her sexuality as a passing phase: "They rifled my hiding place / ransacked my words / read me aloud / on the / verandah / under the impossible sun / my father / uttering / 'When you're twenty we'll laugh about this.'"[80] Meanwhile, her young lover "ended up in the bush / at a school where such things were / taken very seriously / severely," where "she was watched / for signs."[81] Here, Cliff highlights the quiet imposition of sexual order in colonial Jamaica, without requiring a single explicit verbal command being exchanged between the informal agents of policing, sited in the family home and the colonial school. The reading of her diary "aloud" represents not only an unwanted amplification of, but also a fundamental distortion of, her innermost thoughts; the reading aloud is a ritual that inaugurates her and her lover's subjection to intensified scrutiny, where henceforth they will be "watched for signs." Even as they are punished, the matter of queer intimacy remains unspeakable. When the narrator, overwhelmed by sadness at the loss of her lover, withdraws to the library in her school to cry, she finds herself "weeping / violently / against spines of biology / running into history."[82] By staging the narrator colliding with biology textbooks in the library, a space famous for its strict sonic culture of quiet, Cliff calls our attention to the ways racist and homophobic scientific discourses were wielded to discipline Black women's bodies and sexualities. The biology textbooks hearken to the homophobic common sense that was often used to ridicule and stigmatize queer intimacy between women. The queer Afro-Jamaican writer Makeda Silvera describes how such common sense was circulated in a "whisper" during her childhood. Silvera writes, "Tales of women secretly having sex, joining at the genitals, and being taken to the hospital to be 'cut' apart were told in the schoolyard. Invariably one of the women would die.... Such stories always generated much talking and speculation from 'Bwoy dem kinda gal naasti sah!' to some wise old woman saying, 'But dis can happen, after two shutpan can join'—meaning identical objects cannot go into the other. The act of loving someone of the same sex was sinful, abnormal—something to hide."[83] In the library, Cliff's narrator cannot grieve without being obstructed by these discourses, without literally and figuratively colliding with them. In Cliff's framing, the sonic exercises of oppression are evidenced by the silent sexual surveillance regime of "watching for signs" and the obstructions of the biology textbooks in quiet library space. In the late colonial period in which the poem is set, textbooks do the quiet, quotidian work of racial, spatial, and sexual policing. The narrator copes, then, by imagining a time before the imposition of such constraints.

Similarly, in Cliff's novel *Abeng*, Jamaican history does not begin with the violence of Spanish arrival and the dawn of the Columbian era; instead, origins are marked in geological time. The first lines of the novel read: "The island rose and sank. Twice. During periods in which history was recorded by indentations on rock and shell. This is a book about the time which followed on that time. As the island became a place where people lived. Indians. Africans. Europeans."[84] By marking time in this way, Cliff disrupts what Gerald Horne might call the "creation myth" of settler colonialism by calling attention to the *before* of not only colonial time but human history.[85] Elsewhere, in her 1993 novel *Free Enterprise*, Cliff tells the fictional story of Annie, a Jamaican woman who joins the plot to execute John Brown's 1859 Raid on Harper's Ferry. Amidst the story of the events leading up to the raid, Annie imagines the soundscape of the Caribbean in the time of the original Carib and Arawak inhabitants of the islands on the eve of European invasion: "Cinnamon men carved flutes from the bones of their enemies. They were the musicians. They were the navigators.

The men had a secret dialect with which to plan war. Cinnamon men cried into battle at midnight, blowing their war conches, smeared with white powder made from the claws of wildcats, swinging their war clubs over their heads in wide arcs. The island sang with their noise."[86] The narrator continues: "Can you imagine all these sounds? Cinnamon men smeared white crying into battle in the middle of a tropical night. Flute songs. The carving of stone. Turtle song. Language."[87] Here, noise is tied to the will to resist domination. By imagining the sounds of war—especially the blowing of the "war conch," an important icon in the visual and sonic repertoire of anticolonial struggle—in the context of a novel about an antislavery rebellion, Cliff narrates anticolonial revolt as a long tradition that precedes and withstands the onslaught of colonial rule and resists colonial efforts of historical erasure. She stresses the availability of access to empowering or liberatory visions of the past through the imaginative pathway of the senses, sound in particular. Cliff's approach represents a departure from what Aaron Kamugisha describes as "the constant language of doubt" that is often attached to the Caribbean's momentum toward social, political, and economic transformation in the aftermath of the Grenada Revolution.[88] Instead, Cliff stresses the "unyielding" growth of the "underbrush," a terrain of radical potential that is insistent and never loses its potential to reemerge.

Cliff's novel *Abeng*, in its very title, highlights the crucial role of sound in the ongoing liberation strategies and struggles of Jamaicans. The abeng, named after the Akan word for "horn," is a cow's horn that was famously used by Jamaican Maroons as a tool of communication. As Cliff explains in the opening of the novel, the instrument was "used by the Maroon armies to pass their messages and reach one another." The abeng's history as a tool of anticolonial resistance has made it an attractive moniker, symbol, and metaphor in Caribbean anticolonial art and writing. For example, the *Abeng* newspaper—a leftist, pan-Africanist, and anticapitalist publication that emerged in Jamaica in 1969—took the abeng as its titular moniker and symbol. As the editors remark in "Why Abeng," an introductory article in the newspaper's first issue: "The intention is that this newspaper will have 'a particular call' for each and every Jamaican. We hope that each and every Jamaican will answer the summons. . . . This newspaper is to be an instrument similar in function to what we are told the Abeng was to the Maroons."[89] Just as the newspaper's aim was to serve as a consciousness-raising tool that scrutinized the endurance of colonialism's legacies in Jamaica, the protagonist of Cliff's *Abeng*, a young Jamaican girl, comes into consciousness of the continued hold of colonial ideologies of race, gender, color, class, and sexuality in late colonial and postindependence Jamaica.

Set in the late colonial period of 1950s Jamaica, *Abeng* narrates the coming-of-age account of a queer light-skinned Jamaican girl, Clare Savage, who is born into a creole elite family who lost their wealth generations ago. As the narrator writes, the Savages are "no longer threatening" to some because of their poverty; yet to others, "because of the family name and general coloration, their arrogance was still a force, a power once specific, now abstract."[90] Clare's father, named "Boy Savage," discourages Clare from regarding herself as Black, instead regaling her with tales of her paternal great-grandfather, a white British puisne justice sent to Jamaica by the Crown in 1829 and from whom the family inherited the "Savage" name.[91] As Belinda Edmondson writes of the character's naming, "The name represents a locus of struggle over identity.... 'Clare' represents, obviously, the 'light' of European ancestry, and yet from *Abeng* we learn that Clare is named after a black mother, a maid, who saves her mother's life—the sign of good, therefore, is black.... 'Savage' is an illustrious Jamaican name, and yet, as the name implies, it carries with it a barbaric history. Thus even *within* the paradox of the name are concealed paradoxes."[92] Despite Boy's ardent attempts to raise Clare to adopt the ideals of the creole elite and embrace a love for European languages and classical literature, she instead inherits her mother's love for and identification with Jamaica and embraces her Blackness and queerness.

Clare's journey to racial, sexual, and political consciousness as a young girl is catalyzed when she witnesses disruptions to the quotidian idioms and authorizing rituals of colonial administration take the shape of problems of acoustical resonance. In one scene, Clare recalls attending her father's middle-class church and watching a Scottish schoolteacher struggle comically to play Presbyterian hymns at a harpsichord while leading the congregation in song. The narrator writes, "The instrument had never adjusted to the climate.... There was a gravelly tinkle in its voice, far more than a harpsichord is supposed to have, and it was easily drowned out by the passing traffic, the voices of the congregation, the pair of croaking lizards who lived behind the cross of Godwood, sounding a double bass in the wrong tempo, as the schoolteacher tinkled out the prelude."[93] The harpsichord, a centerpiece of seventeenth and eighteenth-century baroque music, appears here as a curiously outdated icon of colonial dominance; its outdatedness is at once a nod to the ways the Caribbean gets framed as a space exempt from modernity and a parody of the absurdity of efforts to impose British sonic and classical musical norms in Jamaica. Even though it is clear that the harpsichord is "not meant even in the most perfect of climatic conditions to accompany a hundred voices," the schoolteacher chastises the congregation for singing too loudly, "advis[ing] the congregation to tone down their singing, to consider the nuances of harmony and quiet—but this didn't work."[94] What is a problem of the instrument's unsuitability for the context into which it has been transplanted is instead projected onto the congregation, who is assumed to lack an appreciation for the "nuance" of musical dynamics. Ironically, however, the harpsichord—unlike the piano—is itself unable to express dynamic shifts: because of the plucking mechanism by which it emits sound, the volume of the note remains the same regardless of the force applied to its keys. In spite of the absurdity of the schoolteacher's demands, the narrator highlights how this effort at sonic discipline naturalizes British environmental and sonic norms and destabilizes the congregation's view of the island: "They had always thought their island climate a gift; the harpsichord told them different."[95]

In yet another climactic scene, Clare recalls an incident in her predominantly white British colonial school where her Jamaican classmate Doreen has an epileptic seizure during a class assembly during their collective singing of a hymn. Even though Doreen is described in the novel as a genius who excels in both academics and sports, her dark skin and working-class background make her the subject of increased surveillance by the school's white headmistress. After Doreen unexpectedly falls to the ground seizing, the headmistress, instead of moving to help her, attempts to mask the noises of Doreen's seizure by singing even louder. The language of the scene depicts Doreen as posing a kind of acoustic challenge that the headmistress is determined to quell: "The headmistress sang louder, as if to convey to the girls that they must not stop, must work to cover the sound of Doreen's skull and face hitting against rock, and the low groans coming from inside her. But the voices of the other girls, which had thinned considerably in volume could not mask the noise—and the headmistress's spindly second soprano moved forward almost in a solo, with only small support from the other mistresses."[96] Shortly after this episode, the headmistress promptly determines that Doreen is unfit for the school, takes her scholarship away, and asks her, to her grandmother's distress, to leave the school.

What is it about this seizure that elicits this degree of punishment? In her nonfiction essay "If I Could Write This in Fire, I Would Write This in Fire," Cliff reveals that this scene was inspired by an actual event she witnessed in her own colonial school in Jamaica. Cliff remarks: "Were the other women unable to touch this girl because of her darkness? I think so now. . . . Then, we usually excused that kind of behavior by saying they [the schoolteachers] were 'ladies.'"[97] In the novel, when Clare asks her mother why the nuns did not help Doreen, her mother explains that epilepsy is viewed as a communicable sickness, running parallel to the "congenital defects of poverty [and] color."[98] Here, the intertwinement of the discourses of medical rationalism and sensory rationalism intervenes: both the Black body and Black sound are depicted as bacteriological, as vectors of communicable disease. The attempt to cover the sound of Doreen's seizure, then, is rooted in an understanding of Black sound as a pollutant to an otherwise "clean" white colonial soundscape. By singing louder, the headmistress asserts acoustic dominance as a way of combating Doreen's unexpected and unintended acoustic assertion of presence. We may also recall the chapter's opening vignette where Cliff recalls being compelled to sing "Rule, Britannia!" as a schoolgirl. If this hymn—or one like it—is the one that Doreen's seizure disrupts, we might infer that Doreen is punished for staging a disruption to a crucial ritual of colonial sonic socialization.

In *Abeng,* Clare's schoolteacher harshly punishes her Black classmate's acoustic assertion of presence; in *No Telephone to Heaven*, the sequel to *Abeng*, the now adult Clare witnesses a different kind of antiblack acoustic violence, one that goes uncontested by both her professor and classmates. In this novel, Clare moves to London and temporarily enrolls in a graduate program for renaissance art. During one of her seminars, a noisy protest led by the white supremacist, fascist, far-right National Front party marches past the building where her class is being held yelling racial epithets and chanting, "KEEP BRITAIN WHITE!"[99] Cliff describes the noisiness of the protest, emphasizing how the sounds of their chants "invade" the classroom: "Chants. Shouts. Noise slamming against the glass of the well-appointed, high-ceilinged room. . . . The voices rose and invaded the room further, forcing the professor to raise his voice, in anachronistic disdain cursing the 'blasted miners.'"[100] Clare's professor lapses into a "high pitched ramble" in an attempt to drown out the chants, "but the outside jargon smashed clear through his words, louder, louder."[101] Clare experiences the sound as a force, imagining "glass breaking, flying" in response to the shouts.[102]

Even as the protest so clearly produces a disturbance for the students and professor, they largely experience it as an aural disturbance—an annoyance—rather than a political or ideological disturbance that requires any corrective action. When Clare later discusses the protest with a white classmate, her classmate denounces it as a "bloody rabble" and a "racket" but cannot seem to understand why Clare experienced it as "dangerous" and "upset[ting] on another level."[103] Instead, citing Clare's "thinned" blood—making casual recourse to the white supremacist common sense of blood quantum logics to informally measure Clare's degree of proximity to Blackness and indigeneity (despite Clare's insistence on citing both her Black and Carib ancestry)—her classmate responds dismissively, "You needn't take it personally. . . . [Y]ou're hardly the sort they were ranting on about.'"[104] This moment of sonic and political disturbance, which her peers readily code as quotidian—as merely a "racket"—prompts Clare's decision to leave her graduate program and return to Jamaica. Upon her return, she joins a revolutionary, anti-imperialist organization of guerrilla fighters whose goal is to disrupt, among other things, the Jamaican state's authorization of foreign bauxite mining, the industrial waste from which contaminates the soil in nearby farming villages. During her entry interview for the organization, Clare declares to the woman running the organization, "I owe my allegiance to the place my grandmother made."[105]

Abeng attends to the endurance of colonial institutions and ideologies in the late colonial period of the 1950s; *No Telephone to Heaven* tracks the shift to neoliberal models of exploitation and dispossession even in the aftermath of *de jure* independence. *No Telephone to Heaven*, however, culminates tragically in

Clare's and her comrades' assassination at the hands of the Jamaican state as they prepare to launch an attack on the set of a U.S. American film set. Having been sold out by one of their comrades, Clare notes mournfully that the "soft signal of the abeng," which would have marked the beginning of their attack, has been submerged beneath the "noise" of military gunfire.[106] The final page of the novel lapses out of prose and into a stream of onomatopoeic sound phrases, such as "cutacoo," "piju," and "cwaah." Cliff herself explains the novel's ending this way:

> [Clare] ends her life literally burned into the landscape of Jamaica, as one of a small band of guerrillas engaged in a symbolic act of revolution. While essentially tragic, I see it and planned it as an ending that completes the circle, actually triangle, of the character's life. In her death she has achieved complete identification with her homeland. . . . Clare Savage is burned into the landscape with gunfire, but she is also enveloped in the deep green of the hills and the delicate intricacy of birdsong. Her death occurs at the moment she relinquishes human language, when the cries of birds are no longer translated by her into signifiers of human history, her own and her people's, but become pure sound, the same music heard by the Arawak and Carib.[107]

Thus, Cliff tracks sound both as a contested medium of anticolonial struggle and as a zone that far exceeds the bounds of human language and history. "Pure sound" for Cliff represents a return to an ideal and ethical relationship to land and other life forms, one not governed by the drive toward ownership and hierarchical subjugation but about a symbiosis between life forms.

Conclusion

This chapter moves ambitiously through time and space: from Cliff's meditations on precolonial time to the 1930s period of the labor riots in the anglophone Caribbean, to the 1950s late colonial period of Michelle Cliff's childhood, to the 1980s period of Clare Savage's adulthood; it also moves geographically from Jamaica to London and back. This is in part because Cliff's narrative style is planetary and capacious, often weaving together disparate moments and places in history. To think with her is to surrender to the boundarylessness of her historical, geographical, and political imagination. Yet as the opening vignette on colonial anthems illustrates, Jamaica and London are geographies that are always tethered. Regimes of colonial sonic discipline ensured that the presence of empire was acutely felt whether Jamaicans were in the Caribbean or in London. The singing of colonial anthems demonstrates how important it was for Britain to be in Jamaica, even as it began to mount organized resistance to the presence of Jamaicans in Britain. (I dwell more on this era—the state and social backlash against West Indians in Britain and the importance of anti-noise rhetoric as a vehicle of that backlash—in chapter 3.) We can observe much of the same rhetoric of sensory rationalism and calls for increased policing recurring in the contemporary moment, both in the language of the law and in public discourse complaining about the inefficacy of the law.

Although here I examine resonance as an arena of colonial discipline in Jamaica, these examples of sonic policing draw into view other ways that Caribbean bodies, sounds, movements, and sexualities are stigmatized and cast as unlawful: through the rhetorical emphasis on private property as that which grants one a "right" to other kinds of privacy—namely, aural privacy. In the chapter that follows, Black resonance persists as an object of scrutiny, but instead, complainants experiment with carving out segments of the soundscape that might be privatized, subjected to the rule of private property. Let us follow how the movements of these sounds, and the people who make them, are policed and how Caribbean artists imagine beyond the conceptualization of sound as property.

2

Aural Privacy

In 2015, in a now infamous Facebook post, Jamaican model, socialite, and YouTube lifestyle vlogger Jodi "Jinx" Stewart-Henriques, also known to some as the wife of famed dancehall musician Sean Paul, complained about her "neighbor from hell." Jinx, a Brown Jamaican woman, had recently moved into Norbrook, a wealthy, "uptown" (or elite) neighborhood in Kingston known for its million-dollar properties and its roster of famous residents, including former Jamaican prime minister Edward Seaga and reggae artist Shaggy.[1] Her neighbor, she claimed, threw seemingly endless parties that stretched well into the early morning hours, rode dirt bikes through the neighborhood, talked too loudly, and yelled. Fed up, she took to social media. Her "horrible neighbor" and his "nasty behaviour" had made her desperate to move.[2] She—like the complainants in the previous chapter—mourned the inefficacy of the police, noting that they refused to intervene to put a stop to the noise; she—like the complainants in the previous chapter—turned instead to the court of public opinion. According to one report, another neighbor anonymously supported Jinx's claims, noting that the person in question had "shattered the calm" of what was otherwise a "nice neighborhood."[3] "Between the bikes, loud, horrid music, parties and screams," Jinx wrote, "I honestly wish he would go back to where he came from." Her neighbor's sonic practices—his ostensible lack of sonic etiquette—had marked him in her mind as an outsider, as a "stranger-neighbour," as someone who had infiltrated the place she calls home.[4]

As it turns out, the "neighbor from hell" Jinx so fervently denounced was Jamaican Olympic sprinter and eight-time gold medalist Usain Bolt. Jamaican poet and essayist Kei Miller writes about this incident satirically: "Poor brown lady. She had taken him as just another country boy—the kind of boy she had learned her whole life that she should be able to talk down to and reprimand. She did not take him for who he had become, a man beloved around the world, the decorated Olympian, Usain Bolt."[5] Here, Miller highlights the clash of two genres of belonging; national iconicity (Bolt) runs up against the national elite (Jinx). The Caribbean literary and cultural studies scholar Carolyn Cooper writes with similar sarcasm, "There was a time when dancehall DJs lived in downtown ghettoes. And they knew their place. No moving uptown into supposedly exclusive neighborhoods and bringing their blasted noise to upset nice and decent people.... Once upon a time you could buy protection from unwanted neighbors. Not anymore."[6] More, Cooper draws a parallel between Bolt's predicament and Bob Marley's own move from Trench Town to a more upscale neighborhood in his iconic home at 56 Hope Road. Of Marley's famous line "I want to disturb my neighbor" from his 1980 track "Bad Card," Cooper writes, "In response to those who wanted to keep him [Marley] in his place and out of theirs, Marley launched a full-scale sonic assault."[7] Both Miller and Cooper expose through satire the ways efforts to curtail spatial, racial, gender, and class mobilities are thinly veiled within the grammar of the noise complaint, which encodes complex entanglements between antiblackness, classism, and sound—both surrounding genres of music and stereotypes about the Black subject's alleged lack of sonic etiquette. Conversely, "disturbance" appears in Marley's lyrics as a strategy of space-claiming, a bulwark against these forms of neighborly policing.

The backlash to Jinx's comments was extraordinary and transnational. She promptly issued an apology, admitting that her comments were "unwarranted" and "highly inappropriate." She continued, "Although I am and have been frustrated by the disturbances, I should have dealt with this in a more private and civil manner."[8] I find noteworthy the way "privacy" and "civility" appear jointly here as the antidote to, and the inverse of, her neighbor's "disturbances," his noisiness. Racism, colorism, and classism become sublimated within the vague language of the "unwarranted" and "highly inappropriate"; notably, she apologized for a breach of etiquette, for failing to be "appropriate," not for insisting that Bolt does not belong in Norbrook (that he should "go back to where he came from"). By citing privacy and civility as the appropriate principles of repair in the event of a noise disturbance, she evades reckoning with race, color, gender, and class while simultaneously producing herself as a respectable sonic subject, one who knows the appropriate ways to deal with "disturbances." Jinx's performance of respectability—her insistence on privacy and civility and her display of a kind of demure self-reflexivity ("I should have dealt with this")—is indeed a sonic performance of racialized gender. If, as Belinda Edmondson notes, "Black working class [Caribbean] women were usually described as loud, lewd, and not respectable" and respectable middle-class Black femininity depended on "creat[ing] notable and distinct differences in habit, speech, and style," then Jinx's insistence on the inappropriateness of her brash complaint is a means of signaling her intimacy with, and awareness of, the codes of respectable middle-class feminine speech and habits of thought.[9]

Jinx's complaints about Bolt's presence are part of a regime of racial, gender, class, and color policing. Of his experience moving into Norbrook, Bolt recalled that he "had issues with a few of the lighter-skinned people."[10] Bolt recalled a neighbor, a lawyer, who warned him when he moved in to "be careful; they don't like to see young people strive."[11] Because of his experiences with the relentless surveillance and policing of his neighbors, Bolt rushed to build his own home and move elsewhere. Meditating on the "strong badmind" of his neighbors, Bolt reportedly explained, "A lot of them, because dem go school and work years and years fi reach, and me jus come up and because of sports mi get everything, dem nuh happy."[12] Bolt offered that his neighbors sublimated their deeper frustrations about the possibilities for Black upward mobility (outside of the carefully circumscribed route of access to elite education and job opportunities) into vague anxieties about neighborliness. Here, Bolt's assessment of his neighbors' frustrations converges with Carolyn Cooper's earlier satirical analysis: the vigilante policing of his neighbors, which exercises itself in part through sonic surveillance and demands for quiet, functions as a deterrent to and a guard against forms of racial, spatial, and class mobility.[13]

I am interested in the ways "quiet" can be taken both as a fundamental acoustic property of private space—of the home, in particular—and as a fragile elite entitlement, one that is often endangered when the wrong kind of person is allowed into or near a community. In this way, demands for quiet can double as strategies to curtail Black movement, whether spatial movements into or through communities or symbolic efforts to connect with birth or ancestral homelands. Disturbances to the dominance of quiet become occasions to discursively perform and reify notions of racial, gender, and sexual belonging, to draw hard lines between those who exist under the protection of the police—and even of the nation—and those who do not. More broadly, noise control (or the lack thereof) is routinely invoked as a civilizational litmus test, as a way to measure the relative functionality (or indeed dysfunction) of a neighborhood, a city, or a nation. Many times, these calls for quiet, which often simultaneously operate as calls for racialized surveillance, repression, and displacement, are cast as just by framing sonic disturbance as both a rights violation and an infraction against a communal ethos. In particular, complainants underscore their right to aural privacy (as property owners and as residents) while noting that noisiness represents a more fundamental failure of community and of belonging.

"Privacy," in both its common conversational and legal interpretations, denotes a "state or condition of being alone, undisturbed, or free from public attention, as a matter of choice or right."[14] Equally important is its meaning as a state of "seclusion" or as a "freedom from interference or intrusion." Privacy, then, sits in tension with disturbance's meaning as an "interruption" of a "settled condition," as an unsettling force. Privacy is intended to provide protection from disturbance, to grant the right of control over the objects and territories considered to be under one's jurisdiction. Although the right to privacy can apply to a range of things, such as one's body, data, and expression, the home is one territory where one's privacy is considered a right. To insist on aural privacy, then, is to make a claim to the soundscape as an extension of one's private property, to forward that one should be able to curate the sounds that flow into one's home.

In what follows, I walk through a transnational archive of noise clashes, moving from matters of neighborliness to questions of national belonging. It is perhaps most explicit in these cases the ways that sonic etiquette can be persistently invoked as a condition of belonging. More, close attention to the dynamics of these clashes reveals the extent to which citations of Black sonic excess can also traffic in notions of Afro-Caribbean people as having a dysfunctional relationship to national regulations and mores around privacy and community, as always already impossible to live with.[15] I approach the racialization of noise by considering how quiet gets converted into a rights-object defined against minoritized peoples. I examine the undercurrents of the rights discourse of antinoise proponents not to dismiss noise altogether as a source of physiological and psychological harm but to point to how these discourses of harm both draw on histories of, and become complicit in the continuation of, ongoing processes of Black dispossession and displacement. It is also notable that the ways class and race shape one's likelihood of being exposed to extreme industrial noise or the explicit uses of noise as a technology of torture or warfare—which do occur and are primarily directed against minoritized people—are rarely the objects of critique for right-to-quiet proponents.[16] Instead, noise complainants primarily highlight forms of sonic nuisance and elevate them to the milieu of constitutional or civil rights violations often to enact cultural, social, racial, and economic forms of policing. These forms of elevation, in turn, obscure and help to extend systemic, historical processes of cultural suppression and civic exclusion. By pointing to Black people as the sources of noise or as emblems of a sonically primitive past that must be regulated by the modern technology of noise control, they also trouble racial, economic, and national Others as belonging and protected members of a national body politic. If right-to-quiet discourse depends on the conversion of the soundscape into a white supremacist spatial jurisdictional territory where Black subjects are not legible as the subjects of rights, calls for quiet in this context serve as ways to govern Black movement and mobility—spatial, transnational, and economic. By performatively restaging the call for dispossession, whether or not calls for quiet are honored, complainants nevertheless work to reinvigorate doubts about Black entitlement to space and rights.

A central component of the work of this chapter is to assemble a transnational and transmedial archive with which to map the significance of demands for sonic etiquette and aural privacy at various scales. I move from noise clashes about aural privacy that first raise questions of neighborhood belonging, to those that map onto crises of national modernity, and finally of Caribbean regional belonging. In each instance, Black mobilities—whether literal (as with transnational migration), social (as with upward class mobility), metonymic (where the flow of the sounds of one's voice or music stands in for an embodied person or group), or symbolic (where certain sounds represent a way of bringing the sensory world of another nation onto domestic soil)—disrupt efforts to privatize the soundscape.

Neighborhood Belonging | Marcus Garvey Park

On July 6, 2008, the *New York Times* ran an article titled "An Old Sound in Harlem Draws New Neighbors' Ire" covering a dispute between a black drummers' circle in Marcus Garvey Park in Harlem and the residents of a nearby, newly erected luxury co-op. It matters that we begin our inquiry in a park in Harlem that bears the name of the famous Jamaican pan-Africanist thinker, writer, and activist and national hero Marcus Garvey. The very name of the park underscores forms of Black mobility and self-determination that Garvey insisted upon in his lifetime; it is also haunted by the United States' unrelenting surveillance of Garvey and his eventual imprisonment and deportation in 1927.[17] The drummers, who are African-American, African, and Caribbean, had been playing in the park every Saturday since 1969, often closing their sessions between 9 and 10 P.M. When the co-op was erected a few years prior, however, new residents, most of whom were "young white professionals," began filing noise complaints against the drummers' circle. When police officers approached the drummers' circle in response to the complaints, and demanded that the drumming stop, the drummers refused, citing their decades-long tradition of playing in the park. In response, the officers called for backup, bringing nine officers to the scene,[18] and surrounded the circle in a tense impasse until, about a half hour later, the officers left.[19] As Khadijah White points out in her compelling study of the incident, the de-escalation likely occurred both because of the efforts of the Marcus Garvey Park Alliance, who intervened with the local police precinct during the incident, and because many members of the audience were recording the scene on their cellphones.[20] Ultimately, the drummers' circle was allowed to continue to convene in the park but only after being relocated twice within the park to distance them from the co-op.

Several periodicals surveyed residents of the building for their perspectives on the incident, despite the president of the co-op board's urging to avoid speaking to the press. Residents overwhelmingly qualified that they did not resent the group's longstanding presence in the park, nor did they dislike the drumming itself, nor were they "united against the drummers"; indeed, as one anonymously surveyed resident noted: "Many of us think it is important to respect the drummers' rights as residents of Harlem, and as musicians who are an important part of the Mount Morris community and who are practicing something they feel passionate about."[21] Instead, one resident emphasized that it was the volume, duration, and "inescapability" of the drumming that was disturbing. In an article about the incident, resident Beth Ross declared: "African drumming is wonderful for the first four hours, but after that, it's pure, unadulterated noise. . . . It was like a huge boom box in the living room, the bedroom, the kitchen. You had no way to escape except to leave the apartment."[22] Another resident, who sounds strikingly like Ross, was quoted anonymously in a *New York Times* article: "Everything, after four hours—even if it's Mozart—is pure, unadulterated noise."[23] The turn to the universalizing discursive repertoire of colorblindness (i.e., any kind of music would have elicited the same response) itself, of course, betrays any attempt to disavow the racial dynamics that structure social relations between new white residents of a gentrifying Black neighborhood. Yet more compelling for my purposes is the account of spatial infiltration and trespass via noise that she offers: the sound was one she wanted to "escape," yet it suffused every room in the house and threatened to chase her out of her home. Once the sound became *noise*, it became an agent; it developed the capacity to threaten, surround, violate, and evict her.

It is not insignificant that Ross likens the sound of the drumming to a "huge boom box," a technology associated overwhelmingly with Black cultural production, hip-hop in particular, and its ethos of open confrontation with institutional racism. It also matters that the boom box is "huge"; this operates to magnify the already perceived excess of the boom box itself, which is inextricable from notions of Black physical and sonic excess. The naming of sound amplification and reproduction technologies can appear as a substitute for explicitly naming Black subjects (who can be then obliquely and more subtly condemned through the criminalization of these objects). As such, what Ross describes as an inescapable boombox that materializes in every room of her home and chases her out relies on a racial imaginative repertoire that imagines Blackness as a supernatural terror, threat, and toxin that requires unceasing and extraordinary measures of containment.

The *New York Times* coverage of the case quotes Donald Williams, the then president of the Mount Morris Park Community Improvement Association, who explained that although the drummers are a vital part of the neighborhood, "The residents have said, 'We have the right to live here too, and the right to have some *aural privacy*,' and they do."[24] The unwanted sound of the drumming here unexpectedly takes on the character and gravity of a constitutional and civil rights violation, specifically as both a violation of property rights and the right to privacy. This construction of "aural privacy" relies on the conversion of the soundscape into an extension of the zone of private property rights and of bodily integrity. The sound of drumming that infiltrates Ross's home is unacceptable in part because the dominion of her private property extends into the soundscape surrounding her co-op unit. The drummers, then, are discursively accused of trespassing, both aural and physical.

The first half of the discursive construction is also notable: "We have the right to live here too." This statement operates on at least two interconnected levels, both of which are reactions to the rights-claims being made by the drummers' circle and their supporters. First, the residents here subtly invoke their property rights as justification for their presence in the neighborhood. This becomes necessary precisely because of the threat of what Khadijah White describes as the drummers' counterclaims to "racial belongingness." White defines belongingness as "ownership of and entitlement to a space that can challenge existing property-based claims and is communicated through physical, aural, and temporal iconography and display."[25] The drummers themselves, Black residents, and Black nonresidents of the community make claims of belonging to Harlem that are rooted in Harlem's historical importance as a "Black Mecca."[26]

The residents, however, tap into a notion of economic rights that Patricia Williams unpacks in *The Alchemy of Race and Rights*: "The discussion of economic rights and civil liberties usually assumes at least two things—that equal protection guarantees equality of opportunity 'blindly' for the benefit of those market actors who have exercised rational choices in wealth-maximizing ways; and that those who make irrational non-profit motivated choices have chosen, and therefore deserve, to be poor."[27] The co-op residents, in the midst of media reportage of the incident as an example of gentrification and racial displacement, push against this notion by suggesting instead that their ability to pay for property in the neighborhood itself is evidence not only of their right to be there but of their position as ideal "market actors" who should not be punished for their "wealth-maximizing" savvy. The ultimate goal of this discourse, of course, is to imply that whatever forms of Black displacement result as a function of their presence in the neighborhood are perhaps tragic but not unjust.

Next, however, this turn to "rights"—specifically to a "right to live here too"—responds to Black claims to space precisely by appropriating them. The "too" here situates the residents as the figures whose claims to space have been initially challenged; their invocation of rights here reads as a counterclaim meant to fend off an unjust attempt to evict them from the neighborhood. This obscures the fact that the initial contest to belonging originated with the co-op residents and was directed toward the drummers' circle; the claims to racial belongingness put forth by the drummers' circle were, in fact, defenses against this initial act. Yet as the co-op residents' claims are articulated, they are the constituency under attack; they are the ones who seek the racial harmony of an integrated neighborhood; they just want to be here, too. This requires a broad reenvisioning of the privileged subjects of rights as those who are equally, if not more, vulnerable to rights violations.[28]

Further, according to the account of the Harlem drummers' circle case offered by *Workers' World*, one attendee of the drummers' circle explained, "This is about dignity and consideration of others. For many people who come [to the drum circle] this is their only mechanism. For many they don't have the luxury to go to the Islands or the Hamptons."[29] Yet another attendee is quoted in the Associated Press's coverage of the case as noting, "People come and drum for spiritual reasons—and to get away from the hustle and bustle." Finally, a musician in the drumming circle explained, "Some of these drums are prayed over, blessed in Africa. And if a policeman comes over and put his hands on the drums, it'll be over."[30] According to these accounts, then, the drumming constituted for Black diasporic musicians and attendees a form of physical, psychological, and spiritual mobility. It was a way to leverage aural and cultural forms to enact a kind of voyage to an ancestral and birth home, in spite of financial limitations, national boundaries, and the conditions of exile. Perhaps more alarmingly for the co-op residents, it was also a way of bringing to the shores of the United States a range of Caribbean and Western African aural-cultural repertoires of the outside of the market logics of commodification and capital accumulation; it represents Black refusal of the limits of the geopolitical nation-state. In other words, the drummers are making a claim to their belonging in the United States expressly through a practice that articulates their belonging elsewhere and their memory of and longing for another kind of home. Those issuing the complaints work to curtail Black mobility even as they are loath to see (and hear) them stay in place.

The core discursive impulse of the co-op residents—who are eager to avoid accusations of racism and gentrification—is to construe themselves as the victims of rights violations.[31] This is curious on a number of fronts: the longtime Black residents of the neighborhood, not them, are facing the danger of displacement due to the forces of gentrification emblematized by the luxury co-op; it is the drumming circle, not them, that has experienced police surveillance, intrusion, and forcible relocation. Perhaps most illustratively, it is on behalf of the co-op residents that the police mobilize in overwhelming force, on the brink of what may have quickly and easily escalated into an all-too-familiar scene of antiblack police brutality. In practice, and contrary to the residents' claims, they are already the privileged subjects of rights.[32]

The soundscape, then—especially as it becomes a contested, hybrid spatial-sonic rights territory—becomes a site where the familiar racist imagery of innocent, pure, civilized whiteness under threat of wild, bestial, uncontainable blackness gets redeployed in sometimes subtle, other times overt ways. This turn to rights discourse, however, hinges itself on drawing attachments between the flexible signifier of quiet and whiteness; quiet is not only the originary, rightful state of the soundscape that gets polluted through noise; it is a constructed rights-object that is susceptible to theft and violation by nonwhite subjects. The sign that the aural privacy of the co-op residents is being honored is a quiet soundscape, free of sonic markers of Blackness.

Here, quiet takes on meaning as the aural marker of not just social and legal order but as a fundamental feature of domestic organization. Brandon LaBelle explains that the spatial identity of a site that we call "home" often depends on curating the space in a way that reflects and meets the physical, psychological, and emotional needs of its residents, including the need for quiet. The making of a home, LaBelle notes, often entails a yearning for "auditory clarity, where order is equated with quiet, and the maintenance of domestic life with audible regulation."[33] The power to regulate the soundscape of the home is often taken as a fundamental feature of homemaking. This is not merely about sound itself but about broader concerns about escaping the bind of the social. "To come home," LaBelle explains, "is to seek refuge, however consciously, from the uncontrollable flows of noise and the harangue of the exterior. Following the movements of this domestic imaginary, the home is heard as a set of signals whose disruption suggests breakdown, neglect, or invasion."[34] The value of "quiet environments" can be so pronounced that "silence might be heard as the very basis for individual freedom."[35] Complaints about noise here tap into another element of sensory rationalism: demands for quiet reflect a set of values around belonging and the home, the dominant common sense that one's home is—or should be—devoid of the disturbing aural presence of the Other, and that those who belong should have the power to regulate and moderate the soundscape in accordance with their values and their desired relationship to the social.

In public discourse and organized resistance to the vaguely defined phenomenon of noise, quiet is often mobilized as a stolen object of desire whose unjust theft stands as a sign of a kind of dispossession. Right-to-quiet and antinoise organizations and activists, in particular, are key engineers and arbiters of the presentation of quiet as a civil, constitutional, and human rights object. Indeed, the Chapel Hill–based organization Noise Free America once posted a video recording the sounds of the Harlem drummers' circle on their website as an example of unjust forms of noise the organization condemns.[36] Situated largely among examples of industrial noise such as car horns, loud pipes, motorcycles, and leaf blowers, the citation of the Harlem drummers' circle appears as an outlier in this ostensibly objective, apolitical list of noise sources. Yet the organization's name alone declares an aspirational reach toward a version of the United States where sources of noise—including the Afro-diasporic drummers in Marcus Garvey Park and the communities and cultural practices they represent—are appropriately subdued, regulated, and more rigorously subject to the rule of law. Rights discourse, then, intervenes to reimagine privileged subjects as those vulnerable to rights violations, often to reinscribe Black people and their cultural practices as threats to the body politic, nation, and world.

Noise, Property, and Citizenship

Although noise opponents and right-to-quiet organizations often struggle with the public perception that noise complaints are petty, priggish, and curmudgeonly, noise complaints often signal deeper conflicts of race, class, gender, and nation, most notably when those complaints are leveled against members of marginalized communities. By elevating their complaints to the milieu of the rights violation, complainants claim a state of injury. Doing so not only obscures the differential structural power dynamics between complainants and the accused but also justifies the incursions of law enforcement into already heavily policed communities on behalf of the aggrieved complainants. Especially common in antinoise discourse is the imagery of home invasion where noise ruptures concentration, interrupts sleep patterns, and threatens to evict residents from their homes or even drive them out of their neighborhoods. The invocation of the private home in this context is strategic; it rests on a certain presumed equivalency between rights-bearing citizens and property holders. It also works to extend the domain of private property beyond the physical limits of the property itself and often into public spaces such as parks, as we see in the Harlem drummer's circle case. Paying special attention to these property- and privacy-based notions of the soundscape, I explore how noise complaints often become furtive sites for reifying colonial and property-based narratives of citizenship.

The exclusive narratives of citizenship and belonging, however, are site-specific and tap into local dynamics of race, class, gender, and nation; the language of noise complaints varies with geographical and historical contexts. Where the defensive language of noise complainants in the Harlem drummers circle case explicitly took on the antiblack imagery of Black threat and alterity, noise complaints in the context of the Caribbean tend to take up, instead, the language of civilization, development, and citizenship. Noisemakers in this latter context are accused of obstructing Caribbean nations' efforts toward development and upward mobility on the global stage according to Western "civilizational" norms. Quiet, then, appears in this context as a horizon of civilizational possibility.

Though the local dynamics of race and class are distinct here, the language of civilization nevertheless conjures older narratives of Black and Indigenous savagery that framed the colonial project as a "civilizing mission." Furthermore, in the Tobagonian-Canadian poet M. NoubeSe Philip's examinations of critiques of Carnival in the Caribbean, she highlights the alliances between the white elite and "creole middle class" (to which Jodi "Jinx" Stewart-Henriques belongs), the latter of whom tend to frame their arguments in terms of morality and respectability.[37] In both cases, complainants conjure a subject of rights who is under attack but stop short of explicitly naming the alleged attacker. Instead, they turn to imagery, discourse, objects, and discourses of rights and property ownership that have historically animated and justified Black dispossession. In other words, though local social, economic, and political dynamics differ between contexts, these cases are united by their antiblack discursive repertoires.

Take, for example, the way the now defunct website TT Citizens Against Noise shaped its agenda around advocacy for quiet as a "basic right" due to citizens. Notably, however, this site's discourse describes poor noise law enforcement as a civilizational and developmental problem: "In every civilized country in the world, loud music and other forms of noise pollution are not tolerated by the law, because law enforcement recognizes the basic right of an individual to exist in an atmosphere of peace and quiet. In T&T, we no longer enjoy these rights. We live as hostages in our own homes, while we continue to work hard and serve our country. This is simply not acceptable."[38] The failure to control noise here is perceived as a failure of the Caribbean postcolonial state to live up to Western standards of civilization, development, and modernity; the state's capacity to claim membership in a democratic, rights-based mode of governance is at stake. The pointed reference to "every civilized country in the world" is a thinly veiled reference to Global North nations like the United States, Canada, and the United Kingdom where noise legislation is imagined to be more stringent, effective, and enforceable because the rule of law is presumed to be more potent in these places. A 2010 op-ed in the *Trinidad and Tobago Guardian* titled "How to Control Noise from Bars, Restaurants" makes this reference explicit: "In 'civilized' countries where citizens respect the rights of others, there are well-established laws to regulate noise levels, especially in residential areas. These laws are vigorously enforced. In Canada, the United States, the United Kingdom, and in most other European countries, there are laws to regulate the opening and closing hours for bars, pubs, restaurants, and dancehalls."[39] In a 2013 anonymous letter to the *Guardian* titled "Noise and Inconsideration Are Our Culture," the writer declares, "Politicians talk about T&T becoming a developed country. But what kind of uncivilized, sick society are we living in that citizens and animals can be subjected to such harsh, cruel and unusual punishment without any hope of redress from the authorities?"[40] The title of the letter riffs on a 2001 series of press ads released by the Trinidad and Tobago Environmental Management Authority (EMA), which bore the slogan, "Remember, music is our culture, noise is NOT!," an ad campaign I will return to later in the chapter. Both the letter and the press ads position noise, and those who produce it, as antithetical to civilization, music, and culture.

A nation's capacity to control "noise"—and by extension its capacity to govern the groups who produce it—is here upheld as a mark of civilization. Upholding Global North nations as civilization's standard-bearers remains untroubled. This line of argument deliberately invokes the specters of colonial rule in the Caribbean and its attendant discourse of Black civilizational dysfunction that intensified after emancipation: the state's capacity to control noise curiously becomes converted into a gauge of modern (read: Western) statehood, a test of Caribbean states'—and by extension (Afro-)Caribbean peoples'—capacity for and right to sovereignty. This discursive move draws a distinction between a vague universal "we"—the modern subjects of rights—and aural others who constitute a threat to those rights. Further, antinoise discourse tends to define noise through negation, as unwanted sound. It is impossible then to point to any coherent definition of quiet; rather, quiet only comes into view as a lost object of desire. In this context, quiet is confined in time, consigned either to a romanticized past or a modern, "civilized" future. The term, then, beyond calling for the immediate cessation of anything that might be described as noise, becomes a repository of fears of Black excess and barbarity.

Next, present in the TT Citizens Against Noise statement is the imagery of home invasion, where the complainants are "hostages in [their] own homes," pointedly as they "continue to work hard and serve [their] country."[41] The unit of the home, notably their "own homes," discursively positions complainants as property owners; thus, property ownership becomes the legitimizing grounds not only for the complaint but for the complainants' status as citizens as positioned against the illegitimate belonging of noisemakers. To cite property ownership as that which legitimizes one's citizenship and belonging invokes the colonial history of property ownership as a construct that functioned in large part to undermine and supersede other kinds of claims, for example, Indigenous peoples' claims to land and enslaved Africans' claims to their bodies, families, and labor.[42]

Black feminist scholars throughout the diaspora have long elaborated and problematized property relations under colonialism and slavery. As Hortense Spillers explains, African kinship structures necessarily needed to be disrupted in order to legitimize the master's claim to slaves as property: "Certainly if 'kinship' were possible, the property relations would be undermined, since the offspring would then 'belong' to a mother and a father."[43] Property relations in the context of slavery worked to anticipate and undermine counterclaims of self-possession. One of the markers of the colonial discourse of property ownership, then, is that it is strategically deployed to undermine a preexisting claim to space and belonging; they are intended to effect dispossession. Noise complainants who cite their property ownership status as the legitimizing grounds of their status as rights-bearing citizens do so to anticipate and supersede noisemakers' claims to sonic, and indeed national, space and belonging.

M. Jacqui Alexander highlights in her examinations of heterosexualization and the postcolonial state how the colonial Caribbean state established links between "ownership of property, colonial respectability, manliness, and rights of political representation." She points to the ways the state's discourse of "protection" illustrates "the state's desire to own the popular narrative of struggle, to convert it into a hegemonic narrative of deliverance, to be seen as initiated *only* by itself as a benign patriarch."[44] Alexander's work clarifies how the specific combination of references to property ownership and citizenship and appeals to a benevolent, "protective" state characterizes colonial narratives of citizenship. To invoke such a narrative in calls for noise control is telling: complainants who are claiming a state of vulnerability to rights violation ironically ground their appeals in a decidedly colonial discourse of privileged citizenship.

The use of the term "hostage" sets up clear poles of criminality and victimhood where noisemakers are perpetrators whose actions unambiguously require serious and forceful intervention by law enforcement. The characterization of the antinoise "we" as patriots who "serve their country" additionally establishes yet another distinction between rightful citizens and national Others. Rightful citizens are those who faithfully take up the charges of productivity (through hard work) and "service" to their country; it is implied, then, that noisemakers neither work hard nor serve the country but instead leech off the state and the labors of proper citizens—a familiar racist narrative of Black laziness, fraudulence, and craftiness. The complaint does little to problematize the premium placed on hard work, productivity, and service in the face of systemic barriers to economic opportunities, political representation, and social justice.

Curiously, many noise complaints in the Caribbean often revolve around classed sites of sociality and labor—bars, dancehalls, churches, and carnival most frequently. Thus, this characterization of noisemakers in these places masks the fact that they are indeed often laborers, though their hours, conditions, and sometimes less formalized exchanges of capital differ from what is typical for wage workers in the daytime economy. A hierarchy of "real" work—work that bears the right kind of fruit for the nation—is sustained in the complaint. More importantly, the nation is invoked as an object of loyalty, and citizenship and its attendant rights are framed as privileges earned by those who demonstrate the proper loyalty to the state. Conversely, noisemakers are framed as undeserving of the protections of the state. As the complaint makes a case for rights violation, it implies that rights are earned, not owed, and that noise complainants' rights precede those of accused noisemakers.

The conversion of the soundscape into an extension of private property serves to radically expand the domain of the home in ways that permit complainants to police social and cultural practices that occur at a remove from residential areas in public space or industrial zones. The sudden August 2018 cancellation of Carnival Kingdom—an outdoor concert that has become a centerpiece of Caribana, or Toronto Carnival, and which was to be headlined by Trinidadian soca artist Machel Montano—only two hours before the event was slated to begin stands as an example of this. Although the city of Vaughan vaguely attributed the cancellation to the organizers' failure to "comply with the terms of the permit," news coverage and frustrated would-be attendees speculated that residential noise complaints about other Caribana events—and general antipathy toward Caribbean expressive cultures—were to blame for the cancellation, even though the event was slated to take place in an industrial, rather than residential, area.[45] The satirical publication *The Beaverton* published a piece titled "Caribana to be Replaced by 'Scotiabank Celebration of Noise Complaints,'" satirizing the consistency with which Caribana events have been targeted, disrupted, or shut down by noise complainants.[46]

By converting sound into an extension of private property and framing themselves as a metonym for a broader body of rights-bearing citizens who are under threat, the complainants in the Harlem drummers' circle and Caribana cases and TT Citizens Against Noise make possible rights-based claims for legal regulation and law enforcement intervention. They frame themselves as victims of assault, trespass, and of denial of access to the "basic" (read: universal) right of an "atmosphere of peace and quiet." What might otherwise be understood as a nuisance is elevated to the milieu of a human rights violation. This turn to rights discourse is unique for the ways it both reimagines those who are the privileged subjects of rights as those who have been stripped of their rights and makes unspoken assumptions about to whom the soundscape rightfully belongs, assumptions that I argue are rooted in inherited colonial hierarchies of race, gender, sexuality, respectability, and citizenship.

Crucial here are the ways noise complaints serve as furtive vehicles for policing Black cultural practices and social spaces. Freighted with the racialized vocabulary of rights, property, and citizenship, the language of these complaints represents a sustained refusal to accept particular spaces and practices as legitimately cultural, as crucial to the social fabric of the nation; they are instead understood as unbelonging and in need of regulation or suppression. Although noise laws across nations are notoriously difficult to enforce, noise complaints, antinoise discourse, and the police presence tasked with responding to complaints nevertheless act as persistent reminders that Black cultural production and sociality are regarded as suspicious, scandalous, and antagonistic. Even as complainants often mourn the lack of decisive enforcement, the reminder of unbelonging is itself a crucial, historical, and pernicious mechanism of noise control as a technology of antiblack surveillance and repression.

Writing about Caribana in Toronto in 2001, Philip explains in her essay "Black W/Holes: A History of Brief Time" that carnival is consistently policed on the grounds that "a collectivity of black bodies [. . .] is always seen as a potential source of trouble."[47] She explains how much of this policing and harassment occurs under the veil of legalism, through the withholding of permits and funding:

> The white fathers control the space through which these black bodies will move and will to move: virtually every year the police flex their collective muscle and threaten to withhold permits and licenses. The white fathers reaffirm their supremacy by portraying the African organizers as being unable to manage money. Proof being the debt the organizers have incurred. No mention is ever made of the monies the province annually pours into European-based arts such as the opera, the ballet, the symphony, the Art Gallery of Ontario and the Royal Ontario Museum. None of which generates the financial returns which Caribana does. . . . But within this space allowed to African people, to black bodies, there must be a ritual scourging of those who will not be allowed to be all over the place. And ritual obeisance to those who are, indeed, all over the place.[48]

Philip's language of "ritual scourging" and "ritual obeisance" is especially useful for marking the ways seemingly trivial, procedural minutiae of permits function as reminders of Black unbelonging in Canada, even in the instances when Caribana is permitted to proceed. Noise complaints surrounding Black social and cultural practices function similarly by circulating colonial discourse of civilization, citizenship, and property that have long been used as grounds to deny Black subjects the access to rights and to membership within the body politic.

From colonial bans on the drum to late colonial prohibitions against noise in bars and dancehalls, the suppression of noise as a colonial management technique has been nearly ubiquitous throughout the Caribbean and elsewhere in the diaspora. These antinoise provisions have served as a surveillance mechanism, authorizing officials to enter Black social spaces, investigate them, and suppress the sources of noise. This impulse to surveil is rooted in fears of Black mass mobilization and the forms of social, political, and economic empowerment and transformation that become possible in Black social spaces. In other words, the targeting of Black social spaces via noise complaints, legislation, and law enforcement must be examined as legacy of slavery and colonialism.

Philip makes this connection explicit in her essay "Jammin' Still," writing, "Those of us who come from cultures that have been riven by colonialism understand its destructive impact: wherever they conquered and/or unsettled, colonial powers disregarded Indigenous and local traditions and practice [. . .] trampling or forbidding them as they did the drum in Trinidad."[49] She explicitly links such colonial tactics of suppression to ongoing programs of surveillance, criminalization, and repression of contemporary Afro-diasporic music and dance, during carnival in particular.[50]

Noise and Caribbean Regional Belonging

In February 2012, the Trinidad and Tobago EMA launched a campaign—the first of its kind—targeting the "chronic issue of Noise."[51] The campaign inaugurated a twenty-four-hour "pilot noise hotline," where complainants could call in and have their complaints forwarded to the nearest patrol officer, and included the publication of a "noise FAQ booklet."[52] The most extensive branch of the campaign, however, was a sweeping public awareness and advertising program, including "ads via press, radio, TV, movie theatre advertising. . . . AdNet ads located at various locations across T&T, water taxi ads, bus stop shelters, [and] e-billboard advertising via multiple website ads and through social media."[53] Who did this preponderance of advertisements target? Who is the public that needs to be educated about noise? Though the 2012 EMA annual report explicitly notes that they would target "event promoters and venue owners," the scope of the ad campaign suggests something more ambitious—aiming at those who might patronize, or be sympathetic to, these local events.[54] In other words, this ad campaign is an exercise in persuasion; it is an exercise in converting spaces and practices that might otherwise be experienced as desirable into sites that elicit caution.

The campaign adopted a striking slogan: "Music is our Culture, Noise is Not." The slogan again raised questions of audience: who is the public that needs to be educated about the difference between music and noise, between culture and the lack thereof? The very assertion that "culture" must be taught from above, not lived and practiced from below, is a colonial rationale. The recourse to such logic suggests that the target audience includes those who are not themselves considered part of the local elite but nevertheless live under their relentless scrutiny: always being measured, assessed, and watched for signs in the yawning gray space of ambiguous national belonging. Alexander's words about the ways the state "coheres" its power through "the kinds of symbolic boundaries it draws around sexual difference" as well as racial, gender, and class difference, come to mind here.[55] By fastening debates about sound's "appropriate" measures to ideas about what can properly be considered "our culture," the ad erects one such symbolic boundary. The production and receptive embrace of sounds that are read as noise can exile some from the collective "our" that defines the nation and its cultural production. Bodies marked as unbelonging or ambiguously belonging—those bodies marked with racial, gender, class, and sexual alterity—can offer "reassurances" of their alignment with the nation by maintaining the proper volume.[56]

Debates about noise, then, do not just index subjective attitudes toward sound but are deployed to mark forms of belonging and alterity. As Edmondson writes: "Noise is not merely sound. A cultural and ideological concept, it is the audial representation of the enslaved, the working class, the immigrant, the Other."[57] And for whom must these policed bodies demonstrate such measured, constrained performances of sonic subjectivity? The fact that this must be litigated in the public sphere in the first place is a sign, in Alexander's words, of how particular "bodies are offered up [. . .] in an internal struggle for legitimation in which [. . .] postcolonial states are currently engulfed."[58] Despite what we know about the ideological dimensions of noise, as scholars like Edmondson, Cooper, Alejandra Bronfman, and others have brilliantly outlined, noise complainants tend to perform a kind of political innocence, to anticipate anticolonial analyses of the discourse of noisiness with counterassertions of common sense: it's *just* inconsiderate to be awoken in the middle of the night by the sounds of music; it's *just* unreasonable to play music at certain volumes; it's *only natural* (indeed medically recommended) to resist exposure to sounds at a certain volume. Here, I again call forth for scrutiny the ways that sensory rationalism relies on a "common sense" aesthetic to deter critical analysis. The rich bibliography on Caribbean sound and vernacular that this book joins is interested in the task of extracting claims about noise from the realm of common sense, of "Nature," and to resituate them within a longer colonial history. More, I illustrate how the state, through ad campaigns like these, sometimes embraces such forms of common sense in ways that reify colonial norms and forestall the radical potential of other kinds of critiques: of empire, labor conditions, the uneven distribution of wealth, gentrification, and displacement, and even the limits of political speech.

The EMA ad campaign included a triptych of commercials, each warning of the dangers of noisemaking and noise exposure. The EMA ads themselves are tonally cautionary and forbidding. In each ad, ominous music plays in the background as a narrator warns of the dangers of noise emission. In the first ad, the narrator remarks, "Promoters! Are you planning an event? If your noise is excessive, you can be shut down!"[59] A black-and-white graphic depicting hundreds of hands raised in revelry streams in the background, with some hands displaying the devil horns gesture, others with middle fingers raised, and still others displaying finger guns, shaka signs, and peace signs. This strange mélange of gestures curiously gives the sense of a countercultural crowd of Others by drawing on a repertoire of images that reference cultural, musical, and political movements that originate outside of the Caribbean region. The graphic registers the ways music operates as, in Faith Smith's words, "a site of contestation over who may speak for, indeed who may be counted part of, the constituency designated [. . .] 'Caribbean people.'"[60] While the narrator warns the event promoter, the graphic tells a story about those who patronize noisy events, who consume and take delight in noise: they are counter or subcultural rather than properly cultural. They are, indeed, not authentically Caribbean. The slogan then intervenes to drive the message home: "Music is our culture, noise is not!" This is a message about cultural and national insiders and outsiders, those who belong and those who do not.

In the second ad, stock images of vulnerable and adversely affected parties scroll across the screen: a sleeping baby, an elderly Black man lying in bed with his fingers pressed against his forehead, a dog, a Black woman squinting in pain with her fingers poised to her temples, and a sleepless white woman lying in bed while forlornly watching a nearby clock that shows the time as 3:55 A.M. As the images scroll, the narrator explains: "Noise can have serious effects on babies, the elderly, at-risk patients, and pets. It can cause migraines, irritability, hearing loss, and sleep deprivation."[61] Here, another two-pronged narrative appears: admonitions about the adverse health risks posed by noise are coupled with a moralizing appeal to the audience to protect the most vulnerable members of society. Noisemakers and revelers are produced here as those who harm the helpless, who take advantage of the already vulnerable. To be noisy here is to be, at best, inconsiderate, and at worst, sociopathic.

These vulnerable parties, however, are represented by what appear to be stock photos; nothing marks them as distinctively Trinbagonian or Caribbean. More, the figures represented in the photos traverse categories of race, color, gender, age, and species. By conjuring women, children, the infirm and elderly, and (small) pets as the images of vulnerability, the ad mobilizes a set of feminized emblems that are both vulnerable to masculine aggression and in need of masculine protection. In this way, the drama between noisemakers and noise complainants is subtly presented as a battle between noble and ignoble masculinities: those who protect the vulnerable and those who prey on them. The slogan, which hearkens to national culture, suggests that this is more precisely a struggle between nationalist masculinity (law-abiding, respectful, and respectable, moderate in volume, protective) and those who would compromise the nation-building project (criminal, loud, abusive, uncouth). Feminized subjects appear as passive, in need of state protection against disorderly noisemakers. Although the graphic seems to disavow that the primary victims of noisemaking in Trinidad and Tobago are themselves Trinbagonian, the slogan nevertheless castigates Trinbagonians for generating and patronizing those practices and establishments that blur the boundaries between music and noise.

In the final ad, the narrative becomes explicitly punitive, highlighting the rule of law. As a string of titles of various legal acts and ordinances scrolls across the screen, the narrator declares, "Noisemakers beware! Excessive noise is against the law. Did you know that apart from the noise pollution control rules, there are over ten pieces of legislation under which noise can be addressed? Any officer of the police service can take action against noise pollution."[62] Noisemakers here are represented as criminal, and a vision of the ubiquity and comprehensiveness of the legal apparatus that can justify punishment is pulled into view. The ad conveys that noise grants police carte blanche to "take action" in whatever way they see fit; it warns that there is virtually no protection under law against police harassment for noisemakers. (This, in spite of routine criticism in the *Guardian* by noise complainants who conversely claim that in practice, noise legislation, the EMA, and the police are "toothless" in their enforcement of antinoise policies and standards.)[63] Here, the rule of law props up a discourse of criminality: noisemaking as a criminal act, noise as that which breeds criminality, noisemakers as those who are protected neither by the law nor the police but who are viewed as those who threaten the rule of law. When the slogan appears here—"music is our culture, noise is not"—it demonstrates a discursive effort to align cultural expression at the proper volumes with the rights and protections of citizenship. To exceed the noise standards is to relinquish these protections and to become the targets of law enforcement.

This triptych of ads works to tether respectable volume to citizenship and national belonging. Yet in its emphasis on event promoters and attendees, the EMA ads conceal something else. The 2012 EMA annual report notes another key source of noise pollution in Trinidad and Tobago that receives considerably less attention: quarrying, or mining operations. As the report details, quarrying represents a significant threat to biodiversity "principally through the removal of large tracts of forest, through pollution of waterways, and through noise pollution."[64] Although it is clear that quarrying represents a far greater existential threat to the island because, in the report's words, it "pushes the ecosystem beyond its limits of regeneration," there is no mention of quarrying in the literature on noise nor any mention of public awareness campaigns that are calling attention to the severe, overlapping threats that quarrying poses to the environment, including but not limited to, noise pollution.[65] Ideas of social and cultural pollution are highlighted while corporate polluters are anonymized and shielded. My work's aim is not to dismiss noise as a source of nuisance or to deny its potential deleterious impacts, though I do underscore that noise is far less often condemned as a scourge when it disproportionately affects minoritized people or when the parties responsible for producing it are local elite, state, military, or corporate entities. Rather, my aim is to examine the moments when efforts to police the soundscape serve as vehicles for reifying colonial hierarchies and codes of conduct and for diverting attention away from processes of antiblack displacement, exploitation, expropriation, and surveillance.

The conundrums raised by this ad campaign might be traced to the very origin story of the EMA itself. Decades prior, in June 1992, the United Nations Conference on Environment and Development (UNCED), or the "Earth

Summit," took place in Rio de Janeiro. This summit convened with the aim of "focus[ing] on the impact of human socio-economic activities on the environment."[66] At the same time as the UN summit, a separate Global Forum of NGOs was being simultaneously held in Rio, "bringing together an unprecedented number of NGO representatives, who presented their own vision of the world's future in relation to the environment and socio-economic development."[67] Much critical scholarship on the predatory functions of NGOs throughout the Black world—including and especially in the Caribbean region and across the African continent—has highlighted how these organizations tend to align with state, business, and international donor interests rather than "aiding" local communities. "International NGOs," in Jemima Pierre's words, "do not change the prevailing power relations that place African states at the bottom of the global economic order and its populations at the bottom of the global division of labor."[68] It is telling, then, that this 1992 UNCED summit, which itself emphasizes "development," synchronizes with the development agenda of a conglomerate of international NGOs: the UN, in fact, weaves the NGO forum into its own official narrative of the conference's agenda to produce a "new blueprint for international action on environmental and development issues."[69]

It was at this 1992 summit, during which member nations were urged to make "sustainable development" a national priority, that Trinidad and Tobago committed to establishing the EMA. Before this moment, environmental management affairs in Trinidad and Tobago were highly decentralized, resulting in "a patchwork of approximately forty (40) pieces of legislation addressing various aspects of environmental management and some twenty-eight (28) government agencies involved in carrying out the associated functions and activities."[70] The establishment of the EMA, funded by a World Bank start-up loan, was upheld as representative of the government's "intention to foster and encourage ecologically sustainable development."[71] Yet Pierre argues we must be cautious when the language of "development" appears. As Pierre explains, the "vernaculars of development orthodoxy"—a "racial vernacular" that "thrives on the construction of a notion of fundamental African racial difference (and white Western normativity) while rendering the unequal institutional and material relations of resource extraction, among other things, through terms that sediment cultural narratives of this presumed African inferiority"—serve to "undermine the [. . .] state's sovereignty and encourage dependence on Western agencies."[72] The fact that the founding of the EMA was tied to the assumption of World Bank debt is illustrative of such a dynamic. More, Rajendra Ramlogan critiques the EMA's "minimalist approach to promoting public participation," noting the general scarcity of opportunities for the public to shape the EMA's policies and operations, particularly around the issuance of permits.[73] Curiously, however, Ramlogan finds one "strange" exception to this rule: "With respect to noise, there is provision for public participation in the granting of a permit for the emission of noise. . . . The right of the public to comment on the granting of permits for the emission of noise is commendable but somewhat strange in light of lack of similar rights with respect to the granting of other permits."[74]

Why, then, is noise the only realm in which the EMA invites public commentary and participation in the permit-granting process? I suggest that noise regulation serves as a useful site for inviting public participation because of the ways it lends itself to the transmutation of discussions of environmental degradation at the hands of state and corporate actors into debates about individual etiquette and national belonging. This "exception" points us to another way of thinking about the soundscape that this book examines—the uses of sound as a repertoire of metaphors for political speech and subjectivity (i.e., "speaking out" and "making your voice heard"). The case of the EMA's unique approach to noise demonstrates how certain invitations to speak out—to participate in state- or corporate-approved forms of liberal political discourse—can shield from public inquiry other kinds of structural threats and dangers (i.e., quarrying) that would demand accountability from corporate and state actors rather than individuals. In this sense, an invitation by the elite for minoritized folks to "make their voices heard," coupled with corporate and state declarations of commitments to "listen," can, in and of itself, stall meaningful structural changes rather than advance them. (I examine this question at greater length in chapter 4.)

The EMA's noise campaign focuses on individual etiquette, generalizations about the risks of exposure to noise, and distinctions between noise and culture, on insisting, in effect, that noise is not Trinidadian. But who was making the case that noise is inherently Trinbagonian in the first place? To whom is this campaign responding? On one hand, the ad may be read as anticipating those Trinbagonians who argue in support of the sonic practices and spaces being restricted under the banner of noise abatement. On the other hand, it gestures toward an existing colonial discourse about Caribbean sensory exceptionalism—Caribbean people, space, and cultural practices as being unusually loud—that is inseparable from broader white supremacist claims about Caribbean primitivism, exoticism, and alterity. Even as the ad campaign heaps the responsibility on Trinidadians themselves to moderate their volume, and their behavior more broadly, it also inadvertently indexes a long history of resistance to this pressure to adhere to colonial codes of etiquette, sonic and otherwise, which have been used as methods of cultural repression and surveillance.

A central concern of this book has been tracing how and why debates, complaints, and defenses of Caribbean sound both conceal and reveal deeper concerns about—and visions of—political capacity, belonging, and self-determination. How might we begin to hear and embrace the soundtrack of free futures proffered by the practices of Caribbean people and artists? The book begins with the claim that the power to shape the senses is the power to make worlds. I close this chapter with the invitation to allow the volume, pitch, and duration of taboo sonic practices to transform us, to touch us, to linger and resonate with us.

Conclusion

This work offers an account of precisely how the soundscape becomes discursively constructed as an antiblack territory by describing one particular and curious conversion that enables racialized calls for quiet and endows them with moral authority: the conversion of the soundscape into an extension of the zone of private property. I point to the ways the discourse of private property redeploys and sustains colonial notions of property relations that seek to create rigid racial, classed, and gendered divides between belonging citizens who are the deserving subjects of rights and those who need regulation and policing, who are threats to the body politic.

Here, I highlight that the regulation of the soundscape is, in equal measures, a profoundly sonic and spatial problem that produces new forms of discursive and representational antiblackness. When Black people are reprimanded or punished for noisiness, censure often arrives in the form of law enforcement's intrusion into, and Black expulsion from, space. To be deemed noisy is to have one's right to occupy space, and one's suitability for inclusion in an imagined collectivity, challenged. This is not merely symbolic or imaginative but rather, such sonic vocabularies are a feature of the way law itself narrates disputes over property ownership. For example, a lawsuit that is designed to clarify and authenticate rightful ownership of property is referred to as a suit to "quiet title." "Quiet" here expresses a will to settle, resolve, or repress any disputes over the title to a property. The implication here is that property ownership as an absolute logic of dominion is disrupted and agitated, becomes noisy, when questions of rightful ownership arise. The notion of quiet as a fundamental state of order, then, is deeply embedded in the logics of property.[75]

The crime of noisiness is framed often as an unjust or unlawful disruption of an otherwise orderly, civilized soundscape—it is an assault on quiet. Yet quiet gets framed as a hybrid spatial-sonic zone that Black subjects are forced to occupy as a condition of belonging, access, safety, and citizenship but which is simultaneously coded as antithetical to Black being and expression. "Noise" and "quiet" in this usage are converted into distinct, though complementary, territories that exclude and are defined against Black subjects. Thus, white colonial spatial logics suffuse debates about the soundscape in ways that actively invigorate and extend centuries-long processes of Black displacement. This work seeks to expose how the strategic turn to the ostensibly neutral, democratic zone of the soundscape is meant to inhibit and deter analyses of this occupational impulse.

Caribbean writers and artists alike, on the other hand, depict the chaotic and disruptive potential of unruly sound—what is framed as "noisemaking" by right-to-quiet proponents—as an important decolonial strategy that resists colonial deployments of and demands for quiet as a requisite marker of respectability, national belonging, citizenship, and modernity. Yet decolonial thought and struggle in the Caribbean was and is never merely about inverting colonial forms or reactively negating them (i.e., embracing noisemaking because it is the perceived opposite of quiet). Instead, it describes a complex process of, in George Lamming's words, "struggling to move away from being a regional platform for alien enterprise to being a region for itself, with the sovereign right to define its own reality and order its own priorities."[76] Thus, Caribbean artists' visions for what a decolonized soundscape might sound like are not bound by colonial binaries that situate noise and the absence thereof as antitheses.

In the first two chapters of this book, the Caribbean people, practices, and spaces deemed noisy and targeted by the discourse of aural privacy are being *produced* as disrupters of quiet. They are not, in any particular way, trying to disturb others even as they are not shy about taking up sonic space. What happens, though, when Caribbean people and art do actually seek to produce disturbances? How do we theorize instances when sonic intensity is deliberately generated not only in ways that disturb others but which generate pleasure for willing listeners? Noise, often condemned for being a source of physiological and psychological harm, is sometimes embraced and enjoyed by artists precisely because it overwhelms, surrounds, even hurts. In what follows, we meet the artists for whom the pleasures and pains of sonic intensity are deeply entangled.

3

Vibration

Martha Trenton, the Afro-Jamaican protagonist of Steve McQueen's 2020 short film *Lovers Rock*, has a naughty secret. She has been engaging in—if Hollywood is to be believed—the quintessential young adult act of rebellion: she routinely sneaks out of the house (through her second-story window, no less) when her parents believe she has settled in for the night. The reason for her nightly excursions is simple: she is determined to go to a party that her parents would never allow her to attend.[1] It is 1980 in London; the film opens at night with only the dim glow of streetlights and the headlights of two passing overground trains illuminating the scene. The ambient noises of the trains matter here: Martha uses this sonic cover to mask her quiet grunts as she first tosses her shoes and purse out of her bedroom window and then shimmies down the drainpipe to reach the ground in the backyard of her parents' home.

This is a clever and studied sonic subterfuge: Martha knows precisely when these concurrent trains will pass, how much sonic cover they can provide, and for how long. (In fact, Martha repeats this very ritual in reverse at the end of the film.) She is a student of the soundscape. Her ritual is fluid and practiced: the trains appear to provide her with no more than thirty seconds of cover. Yet in that time, Martha has left her window ajar, descended to the ground, slipped on her heels, and begun clicking calmly down the sidewalk in a biscuit-colored trench coat with her beautifully coiffed press and curl framing her silhouetted face. This is not Martha's first rodeo. She moves with the ginger precision of a person who is accustomed to being surveilled, who knows those who surveil her better than they know her.

Spoiler: Martha never gets caught—not, at least, during the one-night escapade the film covers. To sympathetic viewers, this may be a relief: we can assume, as is often the case with this narrative trope, that if (or, more typically when) the young adult is caught in the act, there will be hell to pay. In Martha's case, the threat of hell may be somewhat more literal: she is the daughter of strict Christian Afro-Jamaican parents of the Windrush generation. They would almost certainly condemn the house party that she is hurrying to as a den of sin. Another spoiler: Martha has probably for some time now been delightfully indulging in all the things her parents have likely been trying to keep her away from: secular music, sensuous dancing, drinking, smoking, flirting, erotic touch, heady kissing, and more.

Let us cut ahead to the halfway point of the film, to the moment for which she has been waiting: a luxurious, sensuous scene of intimate dancing at a blues party. In this scene—perhaps the most famous scene in the film—the walls are sweating. An extreme close-up of the wallpaper, awash in warm yellow gold lighting, shows tiny droplets of condensation trailing gradually. Throngs of Afro-Caribbean partygoers packed in a modest living room-turned-dancefloor sway sensually to Janet Kay's iconic 1979 lovers rock ballad "Silly Games." The scene is especially seductive because of how slowly they wine, how closely they touch. Martha and Franklyn, the film's central lovers, dance with foreheads pressed to one another. The space between them is lost in the film's play of shadow: it is difficult to tell where Martha ends and Franklyn begins. They are not alone: other pairs dance just as closely and sensually. Some dance alone, lost in revelry. The walls are sweating because the room itself has become a body; it glistens with pleasurable exertion. It, too, has come alive as a sensual being responding to the intimacy of the scene in its interior.

There is no dialogue and no meaningful distinction between diegetic and extradiegetic sound; as a result, viewers, too, momentarily can feel themselves a part of the scene. After the song runs its course, the emcee gradually quiets the track, and we hear the partygoers pick up where the recording left off: they now collectively sing Kay's "Silly Games," swaying to its slow, steady rhythm and pensive lyrics. The partygoers are no longer simply dancing to the record; they have become it. This durational scene of singing and dancing runs nearly ten minutes, a sequence that reportedly was not scripted to last that long, but "unfolded naturally during the filming."[2] This—in this room framed by stacks of booming speakers—is a scene of sonic intensity that pleases and transforms rather than harms.

This chapter explores what I read as a radical artistic claim, which also operates as a strategic discursive disruption: that sonic intensity is valuable and pleasurable because (not in spite of the fact that) it can elicit certain painful, uncomfortable, or illicit sensations. Public health experts caution against prolonged exposure to noise, noting that it can generate certain negative physiological sensations or effects—ringing in the ears, tachycardia, and feeling disoriented or overwhelmed. Antinoise rhetoric often cites these risks of physiological and psychological damage—such as hearing loss, cardiovascular disease, sleep deprivation, anxiety, and depression—as justification for calls to repress the people, communities, technologies, and genres of sound that are marked as disturbing. Yet these calls for noise control often extend beyond the medical and into the moral and ideological. The moralization of sound has various iterations: criminalization (noisemaking is a precursor to criminal activity), financial risk analysis (noise may risk lowering property values in an entire neighborhood), altruism (noise is a sign of antisocial proclivities), and health and wellness (noise is detrimental to one's physical and psychological health). If, however, the pain of noise (health and wellness discourse) can be experienced as pleasurable, even transcendent and vital to one's thriving, we can challenge how certain antinoise proponents imagine a healthy, sustainable, normative, and indeed moral life. We can release the presumption, as Saba Mahmood urges, "that secular reason and morality exhaust the forms of valuable human flourishings."[3] For marginalized communities living under acute social, economic, and political pressure, curating experiences of sonic intensity may operate as a form of release, a lifeline, and a survival and thriving strategy.

Many critics were drawn to the scene of sensual dancing in *Lovers Rock* because it serves as a metonym for what they see as the film's overall emphasis on freedom, pleasure, and exuberance, a departure from what many critics have described as Black British director Steve McQueen's affinity for the body in pain. In K. Austin Collins's words, the film invites viewers to lose themselves in "radiant sound and communal feelings."[4] The film's long durational shots of singing, dancing, and music devoid of dialogue entice viewers by pulling them into the visceral pleasures of feeling and moving to music. Though many critics laud the film as joyous and pleasurable, Collins remarks that it is "not without darkness."[5] This scene of joyous dancing and revelry has, he notes, "a startling tail—an encroachment of male violence that had been hinted at all along and with which we learn our heroine, Martha, is painfully familiar."[6] Shortly after this scene, Martha will leave the party to discover—and forestall—an attempted sexual assault. The assailant is an attendee of the party who, only a few frames earlier, was dancing sensually (and consensually) with the woman he later tries to assault. Put simply, the film refuses to omit pain from its narration of liberatory, transcendent pleasures.

Lovers Rock tethers together pleasure and pain, possibility and danger in its narration of the "blues party"—a house party where entry fees were levied and food and alcohol were sold—as a crucial site of possibility and a mainstay of Black British social and political life in postwar Britain.[7] McQueen himself, discussing the film with Paul Gilroy, insisted that *Lovers Rock* was fundamentally "futuristic" and at its core about the forging of "possibilities."[8] Gilroy, too, has elsewhere identified the "blues dances" as one of several essential postwar Black British institutions that "confound any Eurocentric idea of where the line dividing politics and culture should fall."[9] If indeed the party is a site where characters articulate different social and political possibilities for themselves, I give an account in this chapter of the kinds of possibilities it opens up for them (for us), and how they (we) use sound—typically loud, booming sound—as a crucial instrument of transformation. The film's cast of characters routinely use resonant veils of sound to reshape their environments and themselves, to generate a sense of possibility. This book is dedicated in part to tracking how Afro-Caribbean diasporic communities use sound to reorganize the world. This is not hyperbole. The sounds of our environments routinely compel us to behave in certain ways, to feel certain things, to motivate actions or to prohibit them.[10] Sound is explicitly, consciously mobilized by institutions and civilians alike to produce these effects. When characters in *Lovers Rock* manipulate and curate their sonic environments by playing loud music, they are enabling new, pleasurable possibilities by modulating affect, by supplanting and challenging the existing sonic directives and sociocultural imperatives associated with both public and private space—the streets of London as well as the home.

Lovers Rock is a film that demands an analysis of the sensorium. In an interview with Dennis Lim, the then director of programming for the New York Film Festival, McQueen remarked: "*Lovers Rock* was, for me, about every single sense: the taste, the smell, the sound, the feel. . . . It was about a certain kind of aesthetic, a certain kind of Black aesthetic, if you will: a joy, a release."[11] *Lovers Rock* is part of *Small Axe*, an anthology of short films directed by McQueen; many of the films in the series explicitly depict key, high-profile events and figures that were crucial to the story of Black British life from the 1960s to the 1980s. *Lovers Rock* is the outlier in this series. It is not a history; it is evocative rather than strictly narrative, intended to arouse the senses. Reviewers of the film routinely note that *Lovers Rock* moves audiences sensually, making them want to dance and sing, and even—as Paul Gilroy notes in his commentary on the film—enabling viewers to smell the food being cooked in the kitchen.[12] Though sound serves as an entry point to my analysis of the film, it is inextricable from other sensory registers. Sound is vitally linked to the entire sensorium and to the feeling of "possibility" that McQueen stresses in the film. I read McQueen's choice to underscore the sensorium and offer us an account of the complex embodied pleasures and possibilities of the blues party—rather than magnifying the ambient threat of antiblack violence that marked postwar Britain—as a deliberate choice to tell a different kind of story of Afro-Caribbean life. It goes against the grain of a certain kind of "dominant reading" or representational trope—"black migrants as *a problem*"—that has defined much of the media about this period.[13]

Blues parties were much maligned and pathologized by politicians, police, and civilians alike and were frequently the target of noise complaints that offered police a premise to "raid and shut down" these events.[14] Yet rather than offering a straightforward recuperation of the blues party by inverting the representational tropes typically assigned to it—by scripting it as safe rather than dangerous, as a site of communal harmony rather than discord—the film instead embraces the complex and sometimes contradictory landscape of pleasure and pain, cooperation and conflict that is essential to any representation that captures the "oppositional forces out of which radical social transformation might be generated."[15] Martha accesses new freedoms and contends with new dangers at the party. She is surrounded by a community of like-minded partygoers who contend with similar social, political, and economic pressures, but they do not always contend with them harmoniously or collegially. In some moments, they sway together in thrall to the booming music; in others, they antagonize, attack, confront, and negotiate with one another. In other words, the film celebrates the blues party not by defensively sanitizing it but by boldly insisting on its complexity.

I am drawn to the scenes depicted in *Lovers Rock* not only because they offer a counterdiscourse to what was readily condemned by neighbors, politicians, and police officers as dangerous "noise" but because the counterdiscourse the film proffers does not disavow sonic force. The crew in the film concedes that their sound system is indeed very loud (that is the mark of their success). In *Lovers Rock*, when the sound system crew finally finishes setting up the stacks of powerful speakers that will provide the sonic backdrop of the party and they roar to life, the powerful bass notes rumbling audibly even on the floor above them, the sound system crew croons in delight, one of their members yelling, "Whaaa! Sound ah *big*!" Sonic force is rendered desirable rather than fearsome, visually, sonically, and discursively.

Pleasure offers us a new way of asking and answering questions about what sounds mean and what their effects are. To foreground pleasure is to center the sensory world of the alleged noisemaker and not the complainant. Attention to pleasure, of course, does not attempt to resolve matters of disturbance or even pain. The discourse of sonic injury—central to many noise complaints—presumes, among other things, a dynamic in which an antisocial or sociopathic noisemaker has harmed an innocent, passive complainant. In this way, the grammar of the noise complaint requires, at least on the discursive level, a social disavowal of the noisemaker and their sounds. It obscures what these sonic practices *do* for alleged noisemakers; it renders inconsequential the kinds of creativity, thriving, coping, affirmation, and vitality that a wall of sound can generate. As such, in many cases, the convention of neighborly noise complaints can inhibit our ability to generate a situated analysis of what we are hearing and, therefore, what actions we might take in the pursuit of a community that values, rather than devalues, those figures Sara Ahmed calls "stranger-neighbors."[16] In this way, my approach to sound aligns with a foundational feminist principle Saba Mahmood once elaborated: "In order for us to be able to judge, in a morally and politically informed way, even those practices we consider objectionable, it is important to take into consideration the desires, motivations, commitments, and aspirations of the people to whom these practices are important."[17]

When we are not debating about whether sounds constitute noise, what else can we say about them? For one, it frees us to explore the complex pleasures (and pains) of sonic force rather than merely highlighting its well-documented dangers. To hold pleasure and pain as necessarily connected rather than conflicting can, as Mireille Miller-Young's thoughtful and field-transforming work has shown, serve as a way to "explode assumptions about what constitutes proper gendering of, and appropriate pleasure and pain for, the black body" in order to show that "social power is changeable and that racialized sexuality can be toyed with."[18] As Jennifer Nash underscores, it is essential for us to consider Black women's pleasure outside of the binary constraints of agency/liberation and good/bad and instead attend to the complex and sometimes surprising ways pleasure emerges at the nexus of liberation and constraint.[19] Here, I highlight how attention to scripts about sensory pleasure and pain (pleasure *as/in* pain) can offer us an alternative to sensory rationalism's moralizing bind without disavowing the risks of such pleasures.

Steve McQueen

Perhaps best known for his critically acclaimed yet controversial[20] 2013 film, *12 Years a Slave*, an adaptation of Solomon Northup's 1853 slave narrative, McQueen, the London-born son of Grenadian and Barbadian immigrants, rose to international prominence in the late 2000s with the release of his 2008 film *Hunger*, which depicted the 1981 hunger strike that resulted in the death of Irish anticolonial activist and IRA (Irish Republican Army) member Bobby Sands only one month after he was elected to Parliament.[21] Shortly afterward in 2011, McQueen was appointed a Commander of the Order of the British Empire for "services to the visual arts," and in 2013, he became the first Black filmmaker to win an Academy Award for Best Picture for *12 Years a Slave*.[22] His films *Shame* (2011), a psychological drama about a man battling sex addiction, and *Widows* (2018), a heist thriller about four women who execute a heist that their deceased husbands—professional thieves—planned before their untimely deaths, were also both released to critical acclaim.

While McQueen was experiencing a meteoric rise to fame for his feature-length films, he was simultaneously developing an anthology short film series called *Small Axe*, which would not be released until November 2020. The series, which McQueen began developing ten years prior in 2010, focuses on stories of Afro-Caribbean life in London from the 1960s to the 1980s, highlighting what scholars and historians generally refer to as the Windrush generation and their descendants. The Windrush generation—after the passenger liner HMT *Empire Windrush* that transported over one thousand Jamaican migrants to London in 1948—names a massive, decades-long, postwar wave of Caribbean migration to London in search of better economic prospects. Following the passage of the 1948 British Nationality Act, which granted limited citizenship status to British colonial subjects, including the right to live and work in the United Kingdom, and in response to the postwar economic downturn, Caribbean people sought to resettle in London in the hopes they would be able to find work and better support their families.[23]

McQueen's parents both belong to this generation, which has been the subject of countless literary, filmic, and musical treatments. Stories of the Windrush generation and their descendants often call attention to how antiblack racism, economic pressure, and anti-immigration sentiment and public policy created hostile, and routinely deadly, environments for Afro-Caribbean people in the United Kingdom (particularly London) in this period, from employment discrimination to the passage of vagrancy laws (or "sus laws") targeting Black youth for arbitrary stops and searches to increasing incidents of racial hate crimes.

This period was formative to the forefathers of the discipline of cultural studies, which gathered steam as an intellectual approach and institutional formation in the 1950s and 1960s. Cultural studies was spearheaded by British Marxist academics including Caribbean intellectual giants Stuart Hall and Paul Gilroy (a friend and former professor of McQueen's) and others such as the founding Centre for Contemporary Cultural Studies (CCCS) director Richard Hoggart, Raymond Williams (of *Keywords* fame), and Dick Hebdige (of *Subculture* fame). The discipline combines cultural analysis and political economy, producing accounts of how both everyday cultural practices and mass cultural phenomena operate as important sites for the fortification, elucidation, and defiance of social, political, and economic arrangements of power. The CCCS at the University of Birmingham (from which the eponymous "Birmingham School" of cultural studies scholars takes its name) became the first cultural studies program to be housed at an academic institution, though it would face several challenges to its existence, including program restructuring and, ultimately, defunding. The sharp rightward shift in British politics in the aftermath of Windrush—reaching a spectacular zenith with Margaret Thatcher's rise to power—became a particular object of concern for cultural studies scholars. Indeed, it was Hall who popularized the term "Thatcherism," the language we now use to refer to the neoliberal, socially conservative policies characteristic of this period in the United Kingdom.

Nearly all of the five short films in Steve McQueen's anthology series *Small Axe*[24] explicitly address the harmful impact of this era on Afro-Caribbean communities in London, often taking as their subjects the historical events and figures representative of flashpoints in this history, such as the Mangrove Nine, novelist Alex Wheatle, and the Black British police officer Leroy Logan. The short film *Lovers Rock*, however, is an outlier in the anthology. It is the only film that relegates antiblack racial tension to the margins of the film; it is the only film that scripts a Black woman as its protagonist. Where the other films in the series center on weighty stories of antiblack violence, educational discrimination, and protest (all of which are based on true events), *Lovers Rock* tells the story of an Afro-Caribbean blues party in London in 1980. Sensuous, indulgent, and gleeful, with a sinister edge that surfaces but does not dominate the film, *Lovers Rock* is often discussed as a sharp departure from what one critic described as the "abjection some of us have come to expect of McQueen's work."[25] *Lovers Rock* is largely pleasure-centric and celebratory.

McQueen boasts an extensive career as an installation artist, photographer, visual and sound artist, and short filmmaker that predates his celebrated feature-length films. As scholars of his work have urged, close attention to this earlier work is essential for contextualizing his later feature films.[26] For instance, it is essential to point out that *Small Axe* was not McQueen's first foray into exploring the experiences of Caribbean people living under the longue durée of colonial rule. For instance, his 2002 installation *Carib's Leap/Western Deep* (2002) juxtaposes an "homage to [Grenada's] indigenous Caribs, who in 1651 leapt to their death rather than surrender to the invading French" with footage of the "hot, noisy depths of a South African goldmine," thus "liken[ing] modern mining conditions to a historical act of genocide."[27] More, McQueen's oeuvre demonstrates a longstanding interest in racialized sexuality and the sensual body: his ten-minute silent video installation *Bear* (1993) featured two nude Black men (one of whom is McQueen himself) cast in shadow circling one another and occasionally tussling, sometimes playfully and other times confrontationally, before breaking away again. The film offers, in the words of one writer, "a strange, quiet interplay which tip-toes between tenderness, flirtation, agitation, conflict, and longing."[28] The ambiguity of the encounter is essential to the film's power: it demands a reckoning both with the concurrent scripts of sexual desire and threat that viewers vest in Black masculine bodies and with the opacity of these figures' desires for and doubts about one another.

As Pumla Dineo Gqola writes (vis-à-vis an engagement with Jessica Horn's work), "The body is the primary avenue for [. . .] control, as well as the vehicle used to escape and resist."[29] Rather than seeing McQueen's body of work as evidence of an affinity for suffering, I propose that we understand his oeuvre instead as invested in reminding us of the power of the body as an extraordinary vehicle for transforming the world (or, indeed, for maintaining a status quo). This is especially important to me as a scholar of the sensorium—as someone who tracks the role of curating and shaping the senses as a critical strategy of domination and invaluable avenue of liberation.

There are many rich visual, dialogic, haptic, and other details of *Lovers Rock* that are worth unpacking at length. For this chapter, however, I will luxuriate in analyses of the soundscape. I will organize my analyses by focusing attention on several rich sites and scenes of sonic sociality in the film. In each of these instances, I show how characters create pleasurable, healing soundscapes that make it possible for characters to come to terms with their traumas. Sometimes it is the precise trauma of intimate partner violence, and other times, it is a more inchoate set of traumas that have to do with alienation from homeland and community, that have to do with enduring living with the "weather" of escalating antiblack and anti-immigrant sentiment and violence in 1980s London.[30] In many cases, the scenes I highlight reimagine as pleasurable and healing those very scenes of noisemaking that have long been framed in public discourse as antisocial, disruptive, and violent.

Mercury Sound

The sonic architect of the blues party in the film is the sound system crew who collectively name themselves "Mercury Sound." Two key figures in Mercury Sound drive the party: the emcee, Samson, and the selector, Parker B. These characters—alongside fellow crew members Lizard and Skinner—labor together to transform the front room of a single-family home into a dancefloor flush with stacks of powerful speakers. They take turns vigilantly guarding the sound equipment van as others unload the heavy speakers one by one as a duo of young white men look on from across the street disapprovingly, threateningly. The precious sound equipment that will create the soundscape of the party must be guarded against interference, just as the party itself will need to be guarded later.

The scenes of sound equipment setup are an audio cornucopia of quotidian sounds but are largely free of dialogue: wire cutters snipping gingerly, footsteps on a creaky wooden floor, lighters flickering on and off, amps plugging in, long ropes of sound wire being unraveled, the delicate click of a record being mounted on the turntable, a call from across the room to "tape it [the sound wire] down!", and finally, climactically, the first heavy bass notes of a reggae tune churning to life on the speakers. The moment the music begins, one crew member declares celebratorily, "Sound ah *big*!" That the sound is "big"—loud, booming, bold, substantial, pervasive—is the sign of its success. The scale of the sound is proportional to the size of the collective, the "massive," who will enjoy it.[31] We get a sense of its resonant potential when we cut to a scene upstairs where Cee Cee, the birthday girl, gets dressed for the party; even upstairs, the bass notes rumble prominently and clearly in the background.

Mercury Sound is tasked with the conveyance of at least one key message: that partygoers may find safe harbor amidst their careful curation and stewardship of sound. Improvising on the mic before the party starts, Samson riffs a few lines that we will hear echoed throughout the night. He declares, "Mercury Sound bring the vibes each and every time."[32] He plays with the double meaning of vibe as both the oscillation of a sound wave and as the oscillation of molecules at the level of human cellular structure, the control and manipulation of which is believed by some spiritualists to carry the potential to alter both individual and collective moods or atmospheres. Samson explicitly declares this promise of pleasurable sound that is simultaneously an offer of spiritual shelter: "About to move into outer national selection, without further objection, giving us spiritual protection . . . right!"[33] This chapter's title, "Vibration," accordingly takes up this dual meaning as both "the motion in the particles of a sonorous body by which sound is produced" and an "atmosphere" or "intuitive signal."[34] Accordingly, the foundational conceit of the chapter as a whole might be condensed into a single statement: sound changes things (or, indeed, people). By attending to "vibration," I track the precise kind of changes sound might induce to arrive at another kind of account of why (Black) noise is so often taken as a sign of societal disease or collapse. If sound can substantively change people, objects, and environments, it may also have the capacity to disturb forms of acoustic power, including white supremacist regimes of sonic etiquette that demand quiet—sonic, political, sartorial, and more—as a condition of belonging in a neighborhood or a nation. Black sound, then, can engineer a sense of belonging that is not routed through appeals to sonic etiquette.

Fascinatingly, the chemical element that inherits the name of the messenger God, Mercury, is one known to be highly toxic to the human nervous system. In its naming, then, the sound system crew tethers its promise of transcendent, even divine, pleasures to the risk of exposure to harm. Mercury Sound, the "priests" of the party in McQueen's words, bear witness to and provide a forum for exploring and expressing (in both senses, as enunciation and as expulsion) the forms of slow violence that partygoers experience as Black Britons, the daily psychic terror of living with the routine threat of police and state violence and coping with being cast themselves as societal toxins responsible for the alleged degradation of British society. In ancient alchemy, mercury was lauded as a key catalyst in alchemists' aspirations to transmute base metals (such as copper) into "noble" metals (such as gold); so, too, the soundmen of Mercury Sound offer a space for partygoers to transmute their pain into power.

There are many moments of powerful soundscape curation and verbal and musical play in Mercury Sound's set. For my purposes, however, I draw attention to one sound for the ways the sound system crew uses it to confront and transmute the terror of antiblack state violence: the whine of a police siren. This is, of course, a mainstay of transnational Black sound system and deejay culture; to play a police siren in the sonic vernacular of the set is to indicate that the track that is about to play is hot, dangerous, subversive, and exciting. On numerous occasions over the course of the set, Mercury Sound deploys this sound effect. The first time we hear it, the crew uses it to transition between Errol Dunkley's slower love ballad "Darling Ooh" and the faster, more exuberant 1979 Sister Sledge hit "He's the Greatest Dancer," which prompts the partygoers' exuberant dancing. Seconds later, they use it to transition between Sister Sledge and Carl Douglas's "Kung Fu Fighting," a song so beloved to the partygoers that they cry out in excitement and break out into coordinated dances where they mime the movements of battle with one another. This joyful scene of play fighting—where partygoers express the strength of their comradery by pretending to strike and be struck by one another—is itself a powerful commentary on the party as a safe space not just to party but, indeed, to fight. The dangers of a police presence, then, which threatens to foreclose such joyful, cathartic play become aestheticized and incorporated as an important part of the party's pleasures.

The sirens play again just before Martha, our main character, meets her love interest, Franklyn; again when Jabba, the party's bouncer, confronts a mob of white men who harass Martha on the street outside of the party; and again just before Martha discovers and interrupts an attempted sexual assault. In one striking moment, the sirens play when an actual police cruiser quietly rides past the party while Jabba is arguing with Clifton, Martha's disgruntled cousin, and attempting to bar his entrance into the party. Mercury Sound uses the sirens routinely to transition between songs, to excite and please the partygoers and modulate the party's vibes; however, the sirens also signal actual danger within and outside the event. Again, sound here tethers together pleasure and danger, risk and reward. Toward the end of the party, Samson stands atop a chair with a raised fist and initiates a call-and-response with the partygoers: "Mercury Sound! Mercury Sound!" This eventually converts into "Jah! Rastafari!" and we see in this moment that the moniker "Mercury Sound," which the sound system crew has been calling out all night, has been an alias for a different kind of freedom cry all along.

The Bus

The story of Martha's night out might be said to be marked by a series of figures who are often stigmatized as frequent sources of racialized sonic anxiety. Let us begin with the first: "noisy (and often black) 'kids on buses.'"[35] Black youth in public spaces, on public transportation in particular, are routinely conjured as contentious figures, as disturbers of the peace. In many (though not all) cases, disturbing the peace *is* indeed the point. Noisemaking on public transportation should be understood within a longer history of contestations and reclamations of space, as a sonic-spatial rebuttal to the unspoken politics of public space that often stigmatize, marginalize, and isolate Black youths as hostiles, as problems waiting to happen. The determination that loud Black youth in public are a problem—at best nuisances and at worst threats—is a racial, gender, and sexual calculus.

When Martha and her friend Patty ascend onto the bus that will take them to the blues party, they immediately find themselves awash in the sounds of reggae. The source is a classic eighties double cassette boombox being carried and manned by a young Afro-Caribbean man who is surrounded by friends and by some spontaneous and enthusiastic observers of his sonic artistry. The moment the group catches sight of Martha and Patty, they begin cheering and wooting, calling out "Princess!" and "Daughter!" Martha and Patty blush and giggle in delighted embarrassment as they hustle to their seats. The young men then return their gazes to one another. They energetically cheer on the young man carrying the boombox, who dances with a cigarette clenched between his lips and a gleeful close-lipped smile. He is the true hero of the scene: the musicologist who has curated a celebratory sonic environment in an unexpected place, who has made the bus feel like a portal to an island home to which many of them cannot afford to return.

The young men on the bus conjure not only the trope of noisy (Black) kids on buses but also another racialized and gendered figure of sonic anxiety: the catcaller. Often envisioned as a working-class man of color, this figure is routinely narrated as one who terrorizes women with unwanted sexual advances and crude compliments, followed quickly by cutting insults and rebukes. This figure, much like the trope of noisy (Black) kids on buses, is rarely alone. Where both of these groups of figures are often conjured narratively and cinematically in ways that generate climates of anxiety, fear, and danger particularly (though not exclusively) for lone women travelers, in *Lovers Rock*, Martha and Patty meet their flirtatious advances—and the sounds emanating from the boombox—with delight rather than fear.

The bus scene restages the fraught relationship between Black Britons and public space in the 1970s and 80s, in a moment of heightened antiblack and anti-Asian public sentiment and political messaging, police brutality, and vigilante violence. In *Lovers Rock*, we see glimpses of this hostile environment when white teenagers look on menacingly as the party's sound engineers unload their equipment, or when Martha walks down the street at night only to be harassed by a group of white teenagers making monkey noises. The ambient danger of the era is thrown into sharper relief in the other films in McQueen's *Small Axe* anthology. For example, consider the opening montage of the first film in the series, titled *Mangrove*. This film—dramatizing the events that led to the 1970 Mangrove Nine trial—opens with Trinidadian-British community activist and restaurateur Frank Crichlow walking the streets of Notting Hill. In one scene, Crichlow walks alongside a construction site where young Black children play. The camera pans out to show a blue corrugated iron fence that features a message with a racial slur—"WOGS OUT"—spray painted ostentatiously in black.[36] A few frames later, he walks past another message, this time spray-painted in white: "POWELL FOR P.M." This message references Enoch Powell, the Conservative politician who delivered the infamous and inflammatory "Rivers of Blood" speech, and signals public support for his white replacement conspiracy views.[37]

Navigating public space was acutely dangerous for Black Britons in the 1970s and 80s in no small part because of the hostility of their ambient surroundings. Whether ostentatiously spray-painted slurs on walls, menacing looks and demeaning sounds from white passersby, or the unnerving cry of a police siren, public space was filled with a repertoire of sounds designed to terrorize Black Britons. This, too, is a function of the colonial sensorium: it is deployed to curate public space in ways that communicate the possibility and promise of harm, discrimination, and exclusion to people of color in multisensory, nonverbal registers, through sights and sounds. It is no surprise, then, that Martha and Patty—and their fellow Black bus riders—would delight in the ambient environment the young men on the bus create. It matters that the music is loud and suffuses the bus; it matters that their voices are bold, celebratory, and joyful. It matters even more that Martha and Patty are acknowledged, hailed not only as "princess" but also as "daughter." There is a bid for kinship in these words; they are hailed not as foreigners who do not belong in public space or in the nation but as family.

There is implied, too, a simultaneous bid for sexual connection. I would suggest that this transgressive twoness, kinship and sexual connection, is part of the "embarrassment" that Martha gleefully claims to feel at their greeting. These, her brothers—racially and politically, if not by blood—are like her engaged in a bold act of social and erotic transgression. They luxuriate in theatrical displays of sonic Black masculinity that are often seized upon to caricature them as national and civilizational threats: they are loud, brash, assertive, irreverent, openly sexually desirous, and hedonistic, each sporting cigarettes and beers in their hands. Martha and Patty dared to sneak out of their homes to seek the sensual pleasures of the night. They, too, will drink, smoke, dress alluringly, dance wildly and seductively, and make their own bids for romantic and sexual connection.

Martha glees in her embarrassment because she is staging a different relationship to shame; she is conspiratorially smiling at, and participating in, the very conduct that would readily be denounced as shameful in her Christian household. Shame, here, feels good; the pleasure of the transgression depends in some measure on the rigidity of the behavioral norms she is refusing. It feels good *because* it once hurt to abide by these norms—because it still does. Sound appears as pleasurable for the characters I examine in this chapter not because, as Bob Marley once famously declared, "When [music] hits you, you feel no pain." Instead, it is pleasurable because it enables pleasurable confrontations with pain. The music brings you back home, even as you reckon with the impossibility of going home (to the islands) or with the inconceivability of being at home in your house (in Martha's strict familial home). It is this "longing, non-fulfillment, and suspension," this confrontation with "a persistent sense of the insufficiency of existing modes of belonging" that constitutes, in Nadia Ellis's words, "diaspora culture at its most curious, eccentric, and I would argue, paradigmatic."[38] Martha does this repeatedly throughout the film; she uses the ambient sounds of her environment—of the soundtrack of lovers rock, the noises of passing trains, and the cacophonous setting of the blues party—to stage a different relationship to belonging and attachment, to her traumas and suspended longings.

The film offers us explicit evidence of Martha's complex trauma work in the frames that follow. While riding the bus, Martha spots from the window an elderly Black man in a gray suit walking down the street dragging a massive six- or seven-foot white cross behind him. (He has literally "taken up his cross."[39]) The joyful euphoria of escaping her home for the evening is momentarily disrupted; at the sight of him, the smile abruptly fades from her face. Though he never looks her way, she is transfixed in terror even as the bus pulls away. When he is finally out of sight, she hangs her head momentarily in shame. If the man's cross-carrying ritual represents self-denial and repentance, Martha's adventure this night is about the opposite: pleasure, self-indulgence, rebellion, and—as Martha cries out a few scenes prior—"Freedom!"[40]

There is much that is cryptic and haunting about this penitent figure. We never learn if Martha knows the penitent man or exactly what he represents to her, only that it is one of a few times in the film we will see our bold protagonist nearly paralyzed with dread. One straightforward reading of him is as a representative of her "God-fearing" father, a man who we later learn is infamous for his violent temper and for routinely, in Martha's cousin Clifton's words, "beat[ing] [Martha] and [her] mother half to death."[41] It would explain Martha's sudden dread at the sight of him; if she were to actually cross paths with her father on her way to this party, it would be a calamity. It also underscores the significance of the soundscape of the bus where Martha is greeted as "daughter" and celebrated rather than surveilled and condemned. Here on the bus, she finds an alternative paternal hailing: one that supports and celebrates her transgressive yearnings rather than surveilling and repressing them with the ever-present threat of violence.[42]

Moments after seeing the penitent man, Martha turns to Patty and they smile conspiratorially at one another, dispelling the pall of shame that threatened to derail Martha's night. She remembers that she is not alone in her adventure. Throughout this sequence, Martha confronts and restages her troubled relationship to familial connection. As her spectral "father" passes outside the bus, she is permitted to reflect momentarily on the trauma of familial abuse while surrounded and buoyed by a kind of chosen family. At the end of the film, when Martha is riding the bus back to her home, the penitent man with the cross appears again: he gets off the bus moments before Martha gets on. This time, however, she does not see him exit the bus: she is too busy passionately kissing her new love interest, Franklyn. As the penitent man begins to drag his life-sized cross behind him, Martha misses him entirely; instead, she sits, dreamy and satiated, with a smile curling at the corners of her lips as the bus pulls off. Martha, previously cowed by a mere glance at the penitent man, has been transformed by the pleasures of the night. Though he is still around, she does not notice him; the shadows that once made him seem fearsome and ghastly have now given way to daylight, revealing him to be just a man—a tall, gaunt figure, grunting with the hard labor of carrying his cross. In the pursuit of freedom and erotic autonomy, Martha finds a raison d'etre more powerful than fear. The bus provides Martha with a first crucial opportunity to reckon with the pain of her history of experiencing gender-based violence. It will not, however, be her last.

The Backyard

It matters that Martha's night begins in the backyard of her home. If, as Michael McMillan argues, the front room of the diasporic Caribbean home sought to register "the cultural capital of respectability, dignity and self-reserve where an etiquette of decorum, protocol, polite manners and proper behaviour are performed as rituals of the Victorian parlour," what, then, do we make of the backyard?[43] To own a single-family home with a backyard, especially as a Caribbean migrant family, was a mark of middle-class financial security and social respectability in an era marked by a sharp decline in council housing (or British public housing) and a gradual rise in rent prices.[44] Yet in the film, the backyard of Martha's home (as well as the backyard of the home where the party will take place) does not operate as a site of decorum, respectability, and protocol but one of transgression, illicit intimacy, and breaches of protocol. Indeed, that Martha descends perilously into the backyard, rather than walking out through the front door, is our first cue that she is already in breach of the protocols of racial, gender, sexual, and class respectability.

After Martha's furtive escape from her home, we move into a flashback that takes us to the place Martha is headed: another West Indian single-family home where a birthday blues party for a young Afro-Caribbean woman, Cynthia "Cee Cee" Marshall, will be held. Where Martha's home is cast in shadows, darkness, and silence, this home is full of light, joyous flirtation, playful quarreling, singing, dancing, and the labor of preparing for the party. Here, we witness the transformation of Cee Cee's ornate front room into a dance floor. In Cee Cee's home, the lines between the backyard and the front room are blurred; it is the sound system that precipitates this blurring.

Mercury Sound are the ones who engineer this transition: they work together to carefully carry first the plastic-covered sofa, and next a lush, ornate area rug covered in rich blue and earth-toned florals out of the front room.[45] They replace these items with their sound equipment, including stacks of speakers, a turntable, a microphone, and more. "In the dressing and maintenance of the front room," McMillan writes, "it was women who were traditionally judged on the basis of 'good grooming,' or rather for Caribbean migrant working mothers and wives 'gendered *racial* respectability' as a means of 'self-making' in the home to counter colonial and postcolonial representations of the black family as pathological."[46] In the restaging of the front room, then, we witness a symbolic reordering of a key site of gendered racial respectability into a site organized around a different set of sensual pleasures. The front room after its reorganization is spare, devoid of all furniture; the objects that frame the room now are speakers. The clearing of the room is not merely a practical matter of space but an acoustic matter. Less furniture in the room makes for better acoustics; it lessens the risk of sound dampening. This is a transition from visual plenitude—what McMillan calls the "kitsch" of West Indian front room material culture—to "sonic dominance."[47] If the West Indian front room is tasked with the work of representation, this transformed front room-turned-dancefloor is invested with the task of centering "embodied ways of knowing [. . .] where sound is a subject, a vehicle and a medium for the thinking process."[48]

Later in the film, during the evening's blues party, we see Cee Cee's backyard: the plastic-covered sofa has been transplanted outside, where the orderly symmetrical floral designs on the furniture rest alongside the chaotic overgrown greenery. That the carefully guarded plastic-covered furniture is outside in the backyard is a shock: the respectable rituals that typically surround the front room sofa—sitting, talking, and eating and drinking gingerly from china—are replaced by partygoers smoking blunts, pulling from bongs, drinking alcohol, eating from disposable paper plates, kissing sensually, and blowing cigarette smoke into their lovers' mouths. The backyard has been converted into a shadow front room: it is in the back of the house rather than the front; it exceeds rather than concedes to the spatial and acoustic limits of an indoor room; and it is a space that sanctions rather than prohibits transgressions of the mores of gendered racial respectability. Another reversal is how the interior of the house now constitutes something more akin to "public" gathering space, where the exterior backyard is where partygoers go to rest, to talk, to have a moment of privacy. It is the introduction of the sound system into the economy of the domestic space, then, that inverts the social rituals of the home. This is evidence of sound's power—particularly loud, dominating sound—to open new possibilities, to wrest the film's characters free from the suffocating, confining rituals of racial, gendered, and sexual respectability.

The space of freedom enabled by the blues party, however, is tenuous; it is subtly, persistently hounded by the threat of racial violence. (Recall the duo of white teenagers who stare disapprovingly as the sound crew guards the precious equipment van.) However, in *Lovers Rock*, their attempts to foil the party are ultimately dashed—the party's formidable bouncer, Jabba—a tall, broad Afro-Jamaican man with a sultry, gravelly bass, a Y-shaped scar beneath his left eye, and an imposing presence—puts an end their efforts to harass Martha when he confronts them outside the party. He stares in wordless warning, reversing the white mob's own strategies of silent intimidation. The white teenage mobs oppose the sonic surround provided by the party by weaponizing quiet: they stare threateningly. They later weaponize sound, too, voicing antiblack jeers. They are much quieter than the party itself and far more violent. The bouncer, like Martha, must be a student of the soundscape to do his job: he must be skilled in multiple registers of communication—verbal, gestural, and visual—to guard the partygoers and their space.

The New Cross Massacre

The exuberance and sense of possibility attached to the blues party in *Lovers Rock* is haunted by a historical reference: the New Cross Massacre of 1981.[49] There are a number of parallels between the two: *Lovers Rock* is set in London in 1980; the New Cross Massacre occurred in London in 1981. In *Lovers Rock*, the party at the center of the film is the seventeenth birthday party of a young Afro-Caribbean teenager named Cynthia Marshall or "Cee Cee"; the New Cross Massacre began as a house party celebrating the sixteenth birthday of Afro-Caribbean teenager Yvonne Ruddock. The New Cross Massacre began as a party of about sixty people; the party in *Lovers Rock* appears to be roughly the same size. Yvonne Ruddock's party, however, ends differently than Cee Cee's does; Ruddock's party is widely believed to have been firebombed, resulting in the deaths of fourteen teenagers, including Ruddock. No one was charged for the fire, despite investigators eventually conceding in 2004 (after over twenty years of claiming that it was the Black teenagers' allegedly unruly behavior that started the fire) that the fire was likely started deliberately and that it should be categorized as arson. "It is a widely held assumption in black communities," Kehinde Andrews writes, "that the fire was started by fascists, most likely using a petrol bomb."[50]

Though we widely understand the 1980s as a period of neoliberal backlash to the radical, transformative social and political gains of the 1960s and 1970s, a less-examined facet of this period is the role that calls for noise control played in surveilling and terrorizing Black communities in the United Kingdom and, indeed, globally. In this period, Caribbean house parties were frequently the targets of noise complaints; right-wing members of Parliament "call[ed] for such 'noisy' gatherings to be banned on the grounds of public safety, citing race relations as a reason the police's hands were tied."[51] Conservative member of Parliament Jill Knight was known, in particular, for her public statements "announc[ing] her displeasure at what were deemed to be noisy black house parties" and her push to ban them.[52] In February 1981, Knight made a motion in Parliament to recognize Black house parties as matters of urgent public concern, noting that although the "noise" of the music was troubling, it was the *people* who attended these parties that concerned her—in her words, "a seething mass of people, 99 percent of whom were the Rastafarian type, who can look a little frightening."[53] Knight relies on an antiblack common sense here; by presuming an audience that intuitively knows the *type* and the *look* she is referring to, she discursively produces a common sense in which "frightening" is the natural response to such "types." She produces her audience as sympathetic to her concerns by generating sensory consensus. She understands how this image of a "seething mass" contains all the notions of Black racial, gender, and sexual deviancy that would make descriptions of them as "frightening" and "terrifying" appear to be commonsense. She roundly avoids any explicit references to race, except to reassure her audience that she is *not* talking about race: "I have no doubt that anyone who complains as I am doing runs the risk of being called a racist. My contention has nothing to do with race. All persons living in this land have a right to equal blame or equal protection under the law. No one, whatever his colour, has a right to make life unbearable for his neighbors."[54]

There is much that is appalling in Knight's statements here, but perhaps most egregious was the timing of these remarks: Knight made this motion in Parliament less than one month after the New Cross Massacre. Without ever explicitly mentioning the New Cross Massacre, she frames the Black party as a public menace. By doing so, she both contributes to antiblack discourse that pinned the massacre on the alleged recklessness of the slain youths themselves and renders the victims of the massacre unsympathetic by crafting them as sensory Others, as those who do not belong to the sensory body politic. This event—a mass lynching of young Black teenagers—is reframed as a kind of racial self-sabotage through the deployment of sensory rationalism. More, Knight must disavow Black pleasure and joy to sustain her narrative. It is not enough that they are "frightening" to "residents" of the neighborhood (let us remember that Yvonne Ruddock was a resident of the neighborhood, too); it must also be the case that they "shout at each other," that they are allegedly terrors even to one another. She rhetorically frames Black house parties as sites of fomenting, "seething," self-destructive chaos, which threatens to bubble over at any moment and terrorize the residents of the neighborhood.

The Black Youth Movement (BYM), a group active in the 1970s and 1980s that advocated for Black youths who faced unjust treatment by the police, protested this targeted criminalization of Black parties and of Black sound in general. In an October 1981 statement on the New Cross Massacre, BYM stated,

> A hostile environment has built up against black peoples [*sic*] parties. The most recent demonstration of this has come from a Conservative MP, Jill Knight, MP for Edgbaston in Birmingham. She pointed out that West Indian parties are a nuisance and that they should be controlled.
>
> The police have also shown that they too are against black parties. Since black people have been in this country from the 50's, they have harassed our parties, clubs and youth clubs. There have been several closures of our clubs in London and outside of London.
>
> Over the Christmas holidays the police attempted to break up a West Indian party in Birmingham which ended in fighting between blacks and the police. One week later the National Front held a demonstration in Birmingham against black peoples [*sic*] parties.
>
> Our parties are also patrolled by council officials who attempt to control them with decibel meters—a noise reader.
>
> Sound systems and parties are part of black peoples [*sic*] culture and life style. It is the way in which we entertain ourselves.
>
> We have a right to hold parties and will continue to hold parties. For us to do this we must never forget this New Cross Massacre.[55]

Notice, in particular, how the BYM situates the use of the decibel meter as a key technology of racialized surveillance and harassment deployed within an antiblack environment generated through the coordinated efforts of members of Parliament, the police, and the National Front (a far right, fascist, white supremacist British political party that was active in this period).[56] They argue ardently for the central place of the sound system and the party as crucial Black institutions and for their fundamental right to use and enjoy them. More, they squarely name "entertainment" as vital to Black life—as a "right"—rather than merely making their case on the grounds of "culture." They do so, in my view, because they recognize that "culture" itself is highly contested and policed terrain, where distinctions between "high" and "low" art forms are negotiated. Often dismissed as frivolous, superfluous, or even anti-intellectual, (Black) entertainment is often regarded as a luxury that thwarts ostensibly more serious, nationally sanctioned social, economic, and moral values: industriousness, introspection, and efficiency. It is a radical rhetorical move to claim the party, entertainment, and indeed amplification as vital; in doing so, they refuse to constrain Black life only to the discursive terrain that was routinely invoked to stoke systemic antiblack sentiment. Black Britons were already routinely accused of being lazy, intellectually inferior, and morally substandard. The BYM sidesteps the trap of reactionary rebuttal by instead demanding that a wider, more robust range of values be acknowledged and respected.

Increasing concerns about noise, then, should be situated in the context of the 1970s and 1980s as decades that both "witnessed the definitive creation of black Britain, resulting in large part from the coming of age of the children of the Windrush generation of Caribbean migrants" and saw the flourishing of conservative and far-right fascist politics in the United Kingdom.[57] This neoconservative backlash was indeed a key feature of the global 1980s. This decade also saw the beginning of Ronald Reagan's presidential term in the United States in 1981, the escalation of the War on Drugs, the HIV/AIDS crisis, the U.S. military suppression of the Grenada Revolution in 1983, and several Caribbean nations' (including and especially Jamaica's) deepening spiral into dependency on predatory IMF / World Bank loans, among other crises. Despite these extraordinary threats to Black life and sovereignty, the "long 1980s," as Jafari Allen crucially reminds us, was also a moment of immense Black political ingenuity, seeing the rise of "autonomous organizations [which] arose to demand recognition and acknowledgment of the presence and contributions of lesbians/gay women and gay men within Black communities and within nation-states" whose members "cut their teeth in civil rights, Black power, peace, labor, antiapartheid, reproductive rights, and radical feminist movements" as well as "anticolonial liberation struggles [. . .] around the world."[58] It was also a moment of extraordinary creative and scholarly innovation, including the ongoing Black women's literary renaissance, the emergence of the "anthology" as "the major repository of Black political philosophy," and the field-building intellectual labor of Black feminist, Black queer, and Black British cultural studies scholars.[59]

Lovers Rock, however, tells a different story about the "frightening" Rastafarians who Knight invokes in her motion; here, the bouncer's presence is a vital guard against the very real threat of white supremacist violence. The exclusively Afro-Caribbean partygoers are able to enjoy the evening insulated from the incursions of the police or local fascists in large part due to his presence as enforcer and eyewitness. Against the backdrop of the New Cross Massacre, *Lovers Rock* might be read as a kind of alternate history—a speculative exercise in imagining how the party could have unfolded if antiblack violence had not foreclosed it. The film charts other possibilities for what freedoms are possible beyond the oppressive bind of antiblack racism and colonialism's legacies, rather than a commemorative episode that merely reorients us to the past. In McQueen's words, "It's never about the present, and it's never about the past; it's always about the future [. . .] it's all about [. . .] being somewhere else."[60]

Lovers, Eh?

When Martha meets the svelte, diplomatic, charming Franklyn, there is immediate chemistry. To make sense of their connection, Franklyn asks Martha a series of questions, trying (and failing) to place her. The camera zooms in on Martha's and Franklyn's faces as they chat, sitting in the backyard on the couch that was transplanted from the front room. Franklyn speaks in a deep, husky tenor and in easy, fluent Jamaican patois. Martha code switches, moving fluidly between standard British English and a coy Jamaican patois. His first questions to her are geographical: "Where your people dem come from?" After learning that her family is from Mile Gully, Jamaica—and after sharing that he is from Portmore—he concludes that Martha is a "country girl" (where he is a city boy). However, she immediately corrects his country girl designation, reminding him that she was born in London: "Not me. Born right here so."[61] The city versus country determination is, of course, not merely geographical: it is a social marker that is racialized and gendered. The country girl is often rhetorically and narratively conjured in Caribbean cultural production as a figure who is provincial and unsophisticated but ultimately "good," honest, and (sexually) inexperienced. The city boy represents the figure (and set of forces) against which she must be guarded: he is savvy, cosmopolitan, charismatic, and dangerous, likely to lead her astray, to encourage her to abandon her values, and to besmirch her (sexual) purity. By underscoring both that her family is from the "country" (Mile Gully) and that she was born and raised in the city (London), Martha refuses dichotomies of inexperienced versus savvy, (sexual) purity versus indecency, and good versus bad. She refuses to be marked in a way that might either make her an easy target for men on the prowl or prevent her from asserting her own sexual desires and will.

Franklyn's next set of questions to Martha is about her taste in music. He asks, "You a Rude Gyal or a Soul Head?" The question itself presupposes a binary distinction between Jamaican reggae (rude gyal) and U.S. American soul music (soul head). Martha refuses this distinction, too, and instead lists the artists she loves: Louisa Mark, Junior English, Gregory Isaacs, and Janet Kay. Franklyn hums in understanding, "Oh, seen, seen. *Lovers*. Eh?"[62] All of these artists—key figures in the genre of lovers rock—also transcend geographical boundaries, with significant personal and professional ties to both the Caribbean and London. That Martha names the artists rather than a specific genre itself serves as a kind of rhetorical refusal to deny them a place in either reggae or soul—and by extension, in Jamaica or the diaspora—or to consign them to a wholly different third genre that bears no relation to the former two. Seizing the opportunity to court her as a lovers rock soundtrack plays in the background, Franklyn asks Martha to come inside the house with him for a dance. She accepts.

Often "described and situated as a feminized version of reggae," lovers rock is a uniquely Black British musical genre that emerged on the London music scene in the 1970s.[63] With lyrics emphasizing the euphoric highs and lows of love, romance, and heartbreak—and often discursively cast as the frivolous "binary opposite" of roots reggae, which was regarded as "masculinised 'serious' reggae concerned with black oppositional politics"—lovers rock has historically been marginalized within the study of reggae music.[64] This marginalization has to do both with the feminization of the genre and, I would argue, with its emergence as a Black transnational genre. By bringing together the sounds of roots reggae and U.S. American soul music, and by taking off primarily on the Black British musical scene to become the soundtrack of the "blues parties" of the 70s and 80s, lovers rock was indelibly marked as a fusion genre that would, as a result, be dismissed by genre gatekeepers as mimetic and inauthentic, not "really" reggae (because it did not originate in Jamaica) and not "really" soul (because it did not originate in the United States).[65] Put simply, much of the dismissal of the genre is rooted in deeper concerns about "authentic" Blackness and in anxiety about how the transnational movement of Black people and cultural forms frustrates desires for purist accounts of "real" Blackness, and indeed, "real" Jamaicanness.

More, there was a fundamental concern with how reggae was gendered. "Lovers' rock was not only characterised as the softer, sensitive side of reggae," Lisa Amanda Palmer writes, "it was also seen as an obstacle on the path to righteousness. Lovers' rock was a musical interlude which allowed women to escape into the frivolity and utopian fantasies of romantic love."[66] An escape into the "frivolity" of romantic love, critics of the genre worried, bore the risk of disrupting the ostensibly more serious political work of decrying and opposing racism and colonialism's legacies. This, as Palmer elegantly argues, upholds a false gendered dichotomy between "erotic desire and political aspiration." Instead, proponents of the genre argue, lovers rock sought to explore and express how the racism, sexism, classism, and xenophobia that marked 1980s Caribbean life in Britain "were also interwoven into [. . .] loving and erotic relationships."[67]

Against claims that lovers rock was essentially frivolous, "lovey dovey" music for women, scholars and practitioners of lovers rock underscore that the genre in fact helped authorize Black youths—men and mascs in particular—to enhance their own emotional vocabularies. In Menelik Shabazz' 2011 documentary *The Story of Lover's Rock*, one interviewee recounted, "Sometimes as a young man, you might not have the right words to say to the young lady. So, you play the tune."[68] He underscores here how, for Black youths, lovers rock artists provided a model of articulation for a wide range of complex emotional and romantic situations, from how to express love and desire to indecision and ambivalence to issuing apologies for romantic and interpersonal transgressions. In the interviewee's words, lovers rock "always seemed to have the answers" to any kind of problem.[69] Another interviewee, the historical musicologist and former journalist Kwaku, remarks, "Even man dem, even the wickedest man with the biggest scar—murderer—when him hear lovers [rock], him ah look for gyal fi dance with too!"[70] Here, Kwaku stresses that in his view, what made lovers rock different from other variations of reggae was not that it was frivolous, feminine music but rather that it allowed space for all its listeners—even the toughest, most hardened men—to create moments of intimate, erotic connection. Lovers rock, then, offered not only a celebration of idioms of interpersonal desire, connection, fracture, and repair typically coded as feminine, but it also offered new ways to perform, and indeed to sound, Black masculinity.

It matters, then, that in an anthology series about the Windrush generation in Britain—about the impact of antiblack racism and xenophobia on Caribbean communities in the 1970s and 80s—that McQueen chose to include an ode to lovers rock. By doing so, McQueen not only squarely situates lovers rock within a continuum of Afro-Caribbean political and creative ingenuity under pressure (rather than dismissing it as frivolous and apolitical) but also centers "feminized" forms of Black cultural production as central to, rather than marginal to, the legacy of Black creative expression and struggles for political and erotic sovereignty.

Sis, Come Stand by Me

Martha's longing for freedom, release, and erotic connection is about more than mere teenage rebellion. We know that the sight of the penitent man likely triggered more than just an aversion to the punishing mores of her strict Christian household but intertwined memories of verbal and physical abuse. We learn this when Clifton, Martha's troubled cousin, arrives at the party. Martha is immediately alerted to Clifton's arrival because when he tries to enter, he is stopped forcefully by Jabba, the party's bouncer. Clifton is not barred from entry because he cannot pay the entry fee, because earlier in the film, we see Clifton breaking open the coin compartment of a public payphone to gather enough money to enter. Instead, he is likely being stopped because he is well-known among this community as a troublemaker. Despite Jabba's forceful refusal to let him enter, and Martha's pleas for him to stop antagonizing the bouncer, Clifton loudly, assertively demands to be allowed entry. Just as their conflict begins to escalate, a police cruiser on patrol in the neighborhood creeps quietly up the block. Spotting the cruiser, Jabba relents and pulls Clifton into the house, urging, "Come in!" and shuts the door behind him.

Though Jabba sees Clifton as a risky element and likely to get embroiled in a conflict that could interrupt or end the party, he knows he cannot risk arguing with Clifton in front of the police lest they use it as a premise for entering and shutting down the party. Jabba's may also be a calculus about Clifton's safety: he knows that if left to the streets of London, Clifton may come to grave or fatal harm at the hands of the police or the white mobs that linger outside the party. Perhaps noticing Clifton's failure to adequately register the dangers of the police and of the white mobs waiting on the streets, Jabba strategically seeks to register himself as the greater, more immediate threat to Clifton's safety. Grabbing Cliton by the front of his shirt and leaning only inches away from Clifton's face, he warns: "If I 'ear or see any stupidness happen in dis here dance [. . .] me and you. You hear what me say? Me and you."[71] Here, we see that Jabba's role as the force that wards off the forces of white supremacist violence—as the community protector—supersedes his suspicion of Clifton, a figure he knows is vulnerable to spectacular and fatal forms of violence because of his pugnaciousness, because he is in evident pain.

After entering the party, we learn the source of Clifton's grief: the recent death of his mother. More, he fumes at Martha because despite their close bond as children and his father's numerous interventions to forestall Martha's father's violence against his family, no one in Martha's family attended his mother's funeral or reached out to issue condolences to him or his family. Enraged, Clifton confronts Martha, publicly demanding an account from Martha about why she and her mother remain with her abusive father: "So, you tell me something Martha. How long your daddy beat up you and your mama half to death before the two ah you pick up and leave?"[72]

Clifton's words to Martha are so obviously cruel, insensitive, shaming, and violating that both Franklyn and Jabba rally, prepared to defend Martha. There is also sadness here: Clifton mourns the loss of his parents and of the extended family support structure he once enjoyed in Martha and her family. He, like Martha, is adrift, in search of an alternative kinship structure that can anchor him. This is why he is drawn to the sounds of the blues party, and he, too, will be transformed by the experience. Later in the party, Clifton will be welcomed onto the dancefloor and invited up to the mic to "toast," or to issue an improvised spoken performance, to the instrumental dub soundtrack of famed Jamaican artist and audio engineer King Tubby's "More Warning." In his performance, Clifton's bold words visibly move and enthrall the sound system crew because he verbalizes a deeply held collective sentiment: "Babylon! See you. Me nuh fear you. Jah! Me nah 'fraid. Nobody afraid!"[73] Again, it is fear that is being purged and transformed on the dancefloor. Clifton, too, stages a new relationship to fear and pain by confronting it, by declaring that he "sees" the forces that have harmed him but no longer "fears" them.

Clifton's bold confrontation with fear happens on the dance floor, but Martha's occurs in the backyard. Overwhelmed by Clifton's demand that she disclose "how long" she and her mother plan to stay with their abuser, Martha storms away, taking refuge in the backyard outside the party. Away from the sonic cover of the sound system's booming music, Martha begins to experience auditory flashbacks: she suddenly hears the sounds of her father's voice yelling furiously at her. Her memory of her father's voice grows louder in her mind, drowning out the sounds of the party's soundtrack issuing mutedly from inside the house. This audio memory, however, is soon corrupted by another foreign set of sounds that bleeds into it: the desperate sounds of a woman pleading to be released and the urgent whispers of her assailant trying to silence her.

Shocked out of her sad reverie by these unfamiliar sounds, Martha realizes that her past experiences with gendered violence are beginning to blur with a current crisis of sexual violence that is unfolding nearby. What she is hearing is not just the memory of her father's abusive speech but the voice of another abuser acting in the now. Alarmed, Martha begins searching the backyard for the sources of the voices; she circles to a nook concealed by a corrugated iron barrier and finds Cee Cee, the birthday girl, pinned to the ground by Bammy, one of the party's guests, ignoring her demands that he release her. As she struggles, Bammy whispers menacingly to Cee Cee, "I'm gonna christen you. . . . You never been christened before, you hear me?"[74] Witnessing his threat to "christen" Cee Cee—to introduce her to the world of patriarchal violence—Martha activates, tosses her lit cigarette at Bammy, and screams "Leave her, man!" Bammy retaliates powerfully: he yells at Martha, threatens her, pushes her, and grabs her by her neck.

Martha, however, is no longer paralyzed by the memory of her father's abuse. She uses this moment to act in defense of Cee Cee, perhaps also as an act in defense of her past self who was defenseless in the face of her father's abuse. She calls to Cee Cee, "Come stand by me, sis!" When Bammy attempts to restrain Cee Cee, Martha picks up a shard of broken glass and presses it to Bammy's neck in warning. He finally releases Cee Cee, who cries out, "Thank you!" to Martha as she runs back into the safety of the house party in terror. With Cee Cee free, Martha scowls at Bammy, and spits, "You wretch."

This is a notable turn of events in Martha and Cee Cee's relationship. Initially, Cee Cee's disdain for Martha is obvious: she questions who invited her, she ridicules the way Martha dances, and she makes a bold advance on Martha's love interest, Franklyn, and is disappointed when he refuses. Yet the first and only time Martha and Cee Cee speak directly to one another is when Martha rescues her from Bammy's attempted assault. The first time she hails Cee Cee, it is with a term of relational address: "sis." The first words Cee Cee ever speaks directly to Martha are "thank you." The young Cee Cee narrowly escapes her assailant only because Martha was there, willing to put her body on the line to interrupt an act of gendered violence.

When Cee Cee retreats to her room, she sits in wordless shock with her dear friend Grace, a quiet Black woman character who has been watching over Cee Cee all evening. It is Grace who dances excitedly with Cee Cee in her bedroom before the party; it is Grace who lovingly and carefully hot combs and styles Cee Cee's hair, it is Grace who affirms Cee Cee when she shows her friend her eye-catching scarlet red birthday dress, remarking, "You're gonna look so beautiful." It is also Grace who watches warily, knowingly throughout the night as Cee Cee both routinely rejects and gets rejected by her chosen suitors, before Bammy sets his sights on her. When Cee Cee retreats to her bedroom, still shaken from Bammy's assault, it is Grace who sits compassionately with her. Cee Cee, as if seeing Grace for the first time, leans into Grace for a kiss. Grace returns her kiss, before cupping her face and kissing her gently on her forehead. In the background as they kiss, a crucifix hangs on the wall in the background, peripherally.

The cinematographic staging and lighting details of both the assault scene and the scene of queer intimacy in Cee Cee's bedroom afterward are telling. The assault scene is shot in low-key lighting: it is full of deep shadows and cool hues, signifying mystery, uncertainty, gloom, and fear. When Martha discovers Bammy's attack on Cee Cee, the scene is captured through a high-angle shot. High-angle shots—which position the camera above the scene it is filming, such that the viewer "looks down" on the figures or objects in the scene—have the effect of making those figures or objects appear to be smaller. As such, high-angle shots often symbolically render those figures powerless, vulnerable, or at the mercy of forces greater than them. The shot is set at Martha's eye level; it is Martha, then, who "looks down" on Bammy; it is Martha who occupies the position of cinematographic power. Even after Martha interrupts the assault and Bammy stands to confront Martha—even though we can see that he is much taller than Martha—the camera angle remains at Martha's eye level. Though Bammy is the assailant, he is made to appear weak, vulnerable, and small.

Conversely, the bedroom scene is shot in high-key lighting: it is well-illuminated and awash in warm tones, devoid of shadows. This lighting style often accompanies scenes of clarity, sincerity, optimism, and openness; it is a lighting style that tends to flatter its subjects. Cee Cee's and Grace's kiss is captured through a low-angle shot, which has the opposite effect of high-angle shots; this angle tends to make its subjects appear larger and more powerful and positions the viewer as vulnerable. It is the first and only time we see Cee Cee shot from this angle. Cee Cee, though visibly shaken, has not been reduced by her violent encounter with Bammy. Instead, she looms large, empowered to express erotic desires that she has previously sublimated into friendship.

Part of the richness of this scene is in its ambiguity; it frustrates viewers' efforts to situate Cee Cee and Grace's relationship securely within dominant relational and sexual taxonomies. In the film, we rarely see Cee Cee in scenes without Grace; they dance together, get ready for the party together, and even retreat from the party together. How do we interpret the film's routine visual coupling of Cee Cee and Grace? How do we interpret the kiss on the lips, especially when coupled with the kiss on the forehead that follows? One way of understanding Cee Cee and Grace might be to interpret them as having a passionate friendship.

Discussing male passionate friendships, Black feminist cultural sociologist and hip-hop scholar Antonia Randolph explains, "Passionate friendships are just one of several identities that get overshadowed in conventional accounts of sexual identity, desire, and behavior. . . . They are emotional connections that get sexualized because of the way they scramble the assumed consonance between gender, romance, and sexual desire."[75] While, as Randolph notes, "close, openly affectionate friendships are consistent with heterosexual norms for women, but not men," the staging of these intimate kisses—kisses that remain in a gray space between romantic desire and friendship—challenge viewers to consider other possibilities for how we might describe their connection, moving beyond the conventions of heteronormative affectionate friendship between women.[76] Krystal Nandini Ghisyawan underscores the importance of the terms "friends" and "family" as vital frameworks for same-sex-desiring women in the Caribbean to "articulate their sense of belonging and the intimacy they experience in their relationships." These terms are vital because they center desires, experiences, bonds, and practices rather than "personhood" or "identity" (more common in Western, European, and American discourses about sexuality). More, they afford same-sex-desiring women a measure of erotic freedom precisely because "same-sex intercourse, marriage, and relationships, as well as various family forms, are subject to legal constraints that do not apply to friendships." Over the course of the film, Cee Cee and Grace never name what they are to each other; this is on purpose. The film disturbs easy sexual taxonomies, hierarchies, and assumptions about its characters, and indeed, about the implied "lovers" within the genre of lovers rock.[77]

This, too, is a prospect opened up through the scene of the blues party: those who gather in celebration are freed to redefine themselves on their own terms, or to eschew dominant categories altogether to explore other possibilities for relation. As Cee Cee and Grace's kiss unfolds upstairs, another scene of homoerotic sensuality unfolds downstairs: in a moment of embodied release, where the dancefloor is filled almost exclusively with men dancing exuberantly to lyricless dub and lapsing into the erratic, unrestrained movements of transcendent spiritual possession, they collapse onto the floor and into each other's arms, pull each other's clothes off, yelp, sing, and declare, "Power!" and, "I feel my soul!" Bammy, too, joins this crucial scene of release.[78]

It matters that McQueen stages scenes of Black queer erotic touch and connection at the climax of *Lovers Rock* and within the *Small Axe* anthology. Just as I signaled earlier in the chapter the importance of centering Black women in a film anthology documenting stories of West Indian ingenuity, resiliency, and thriving in the face of powerful anti-immigration policies and public sentiment, it is equally important that McQueen narrates queerness in the same frame. Writing on the postwar period in Britain, Nadia Ellis reminds us, "In the most prejudicial accounts of sexual and racial alarm, homosexuality and exponentially increased West Indian presence in Britain became indices of the nation's decline."[79] Though both queerness and immigration were routinely fixated upon as the roots of the nation's ills, they were often sourced to different groups. "Homosexual men," Ellis explains, "were figured largely as white, and troublesome migrants were figured mostly as black and brown."[80] This generated a kind of archival and rhetorical lacuna where Blackness and queerness were relegated to different problem-spaces, even as, Ellis elegantly points out, "the logic of homophobia and anti-migrant racism relies on strikingly similar language."[81] More, if queerness could be sourced to white men while immigration was embodied in Black men, Black queer women and femmes faced compounded erasure.

The kiss between Cee Cee and Grace, then, reveals that another story—one about Black queer erotic connection and power—has been unfolding concurrently all along. It is integral to the story of the vitality of the Black community in the face of the unyielding political and social backlash of the 1980s. Cee Cee emerges from the evening profoundly aware of the loving community of women that stands ready to mobilize to guard her against patriarchal violence. Our attention is drawn to something greater than the heterosexual romantic plots of waxing and waning desire being crooned about throughout the lyrics of the lovers rock soundtrack of the party. Cee Cee's bonds with other Afro-Caribbean women ultimately save her life. Consider again the narrative parallels between *Lovers Rock* and the New Cross Massacre and the film's function as a kind of speculative reimagining of that night, one in which the victims of the massacre had lived. McQueen imagines more than the labor of a watchful bouncer as vital to the survival of the partygoers but rather the often-erased labor of care, love, and defense that Black women perform for one another.

Conclusion: Bass

Describing the low-frequency vibration of bass tones as "a carrier frequency [. . .] for Africa's musical gifts to its diaspora," Julian Henriques reminds us that the use of powerful bass carries both auditory and socioeconomic significance.[82] The "bass" tones of the sound system reflect its emergence from "base culture." (As Henriques explains, "It comes from the street. . . . It is a subaltern popular form of expression.") More broadly, the "base" (in the Marxist sense, pointing to relations of production) as it shapes the hierarchical social, economic, and political dynamics of the body politic.[83] The affecting power of bass is also a creative preoccupation for McQueen himself. In a 2024 exhibition entitled *Bass*, McQueen staged an installation composed solely of light and sound, namely "60 ceiling-mounted lightboxes emanating a shifting spectrum of visible light and three stacks of speakers transmitting bass sounds from different points in the gallery."[84] To create a surround of bass tones, McQueen employed an ensemble of Black diasporic bass musicians (including Grammy award-winning singer-songwriter and bassist Meshell Ndegeocello and influential composer and bassist Marcus Miller) to "record a musical improvisation that collectively responded to the changing light, resonance of the space, and one another, with McQueen as conductor."[85] Siddhartha Mitter, in his review of the exhibition, noted that it "prompted (in this viewer) memories of the ecstatic party scene in 'Lovers Rock.'"[86] McQueen responded by citing Stuart Hall's work on "the cathartic necessity of Black music and parties." He remarked, "Without those shebeens, those blues parties, there'd have been a psychosis. . . . We needed these things. . . . [T]he bass, the sweat, took on a religious dimension. In those spaces, things became experimental. There's a necessity to venture and transcend."[87]

I am drawn to McQueen's insistence on the visceral experience of feeling and moving to the bass as a form of embodied experimentation and transcendence. Rather than thinking of the party and its attendant sonic artistry and intensity as merely a means of escaping (the threatening and confining pressures of one's home, job, or society at large), I am interested in understanding how these sonic-haptic experiences actually make it possible for partygoers to restage their relationships with themselves and others, to experiment with forms of intimacy, community, and "self-regard" that are deemed taboo.[88] Fascinatingly, Mitter reported, "Presented with this connection to the film [*Lovers Rock*], McQueen, who is not keen on trite observations, partly swatted it away."[89] I wonder if McQueen "swatted away" Mitter's attempt to draw a link between *Lovers Rock* and *Bass* in part because he bristles against any attempt to define the exhibition, which embraces abstraction and features "no set historical or political cues," as being about any one historical conjuncture, any fixed set of experiences.[90] McQueen clarifies that though *Bass* is rooted in Black history and creativity, "I'm not trying to underline all that. . . . It's about exploration and experimentation, and where we can go from here."[91] McQueen's investment, then, is in forging new frontiers of creativity and innovation, not (or not only) in historical memory. I embrace the link between *Bass* and *Lovers Rock* because they both evidence McQueen's investment in exploring the uses of sonic intensity as a route to experimentation, transcendency, and freedom. McQueen writes about the exhibit that it "[puts] the public in a situation where everyone becomes acutely sensitive to themselves, to their body, and respiration."[92] I embrace McQueen's conviction that sonic intensity can bring one back to oneself, to one's embodiment and aliveness ("respiration"), especially because it is so often condemned as that which makes it impossible to think (in complex or nuanced ways), to create, or to be at peace with oneself. Bass notes are also frequently tethered in cinematic scores to tension, threat, aggression, foreboding, dread, doom, and the sublime. By scoring novelty, exploration, experimentation, and transcendency to the sounds of an ensemble of bassists, McQueen challenges these deeply entrenched sonic-psychic associations. Bass becomes an invitation to look within rather than to brace ourselves against peril without.

In *Lovers Rock*, the party is essential because it is a site of creative imagination and speculation, that which makes it possible to begin to realize the kind of self and community one wants. Martha arrives at the party as a guilty fugitive from her home but will leave with a powerful and joyous sense of her own freedom and autonomy. The end of the film is a mirror image of the beginning: Martha furtively returns to her bedroom now alight with gentle rays of sunshine, climbing in through the window she left ajar the night before. In her bedroom, a crucifix hangs above her bed, facing the very window through which she escaped. This artifact—often endowed with the power to ward off evil—might initially be read as a symbol of surveillance: it watches Martha as she sneaks back into her room after a night of revelry. On the other hand, we might interpret the crucifix here instead as a symbol of transformation: just as the crucifix signifies Christ's confrontation with and transcendence over death, Martha, too, has ventured into the night, confronted her demons, and returned a different person. The Martha that returns is optimistic, rather than haunted—whimsical, bold, and mischievous, rather than frightened.

Martha gingerly removes her coat and shoes and slips into her bed. Seconds later, we hear footsteps climbing a staircase, drawing nearer to her room. Then, a heavy knock on the door: "Get up, get up! Time fi church, time fi church!" At this announcement, Martha smiles conspiratorially to herself. We never see her family or her daytime persona: we do not know how Martha comports herself under the strict scrutiny of her parents. We cannot say for sure what long-term transformations her evening excursion have brought into effect. What we do know is that the call to attend church now brings a smile to her lips. The dread and shame Martha once felt upon encountering Christian rituals and symbolism—such as her response to the sight of the penitent man earlier in the film—has transmuted into joy, relief, and possibility. Her relationship to this ritual is ameliorated precisely because she has attended the party, not in spite of it. The secular nighttime Black party is so often rhetorically cited as the inverse of sacred daytime Black worship spaces and rituals. Yet as McQueen underscores, the blues party itself takes on a "religious dimension" and becomes a vital vehicle of self-realization for the film's characters.

Lovers Rock, then, might be said to ultimately be a film about radical transformations and about the importance of the skillful curation of sonic environments to enable these scenes of transformation. Yet the film is lauded as a tantalizing outlier in the *Small Axe* anthology in part because its political "message" appears to be less overt, more subtle somehow. In what follows, I query the ways that Black artists are often lauded for restraint and subtlety in the realm of artistry but conversely lauded for bold, overt, declaration in the realm of politics. This, too, I suggest is a kind of sonic bind that constrains Black people, artists, and scholars. Next, and finally, we proceed to the realm of "ultrasound" and "subtlety."

4

Ultrasound, or Subtlety

There is a little-examined essay in the prolific, stunning oeuvre of Jamaican poet, novelist, and essayist Kei Miller. It is vulnerable and ambivalent, vacillating between assuredness and uncertainty. It is an essay where Miller reveals that he doubts the terms of his own success in British literary circles. He admits this is in part because of the way he has noticed his poetic voice is registered: his work, he notes, is often described by critics with words like "subtle, quiet, restrained, elegant."[1] Miller writes, "These are words which I suggest act as a sort of dog whistle criticism. The majority of people might not hear what is happening beneath such accolades, not even those who genuinely meant to compliment me, but to some extent I am being praised for the extent to which I am black, but not too black—the ways in which I have pitched blackness at an appropriate volume."[2]

We may find clues to what Miller means by "dog whistle criticism," the backhanded praise for "pitching blackness at an appropriate volume," by attending to the sonics of his performance. One of Miller's most striking performances is that of the poem "Place Name: Oracabessa." The poem's origin story is fascinating: in 2014, the Royal Collection Trust—a charity devoted in part to "caring for the Royal Collection," the aggregated art collection of the British monarchy over the past five centuries—mounted an exhibition simply entitled *Gold*.[3] Envisioned as an exploration of the "distinctive qualities that make this rare and precious metal an enduring expression of the highest status, both earthly and divine," the exhibition was comprised of fifty gold items drawn from the Royal Collection, items that originated, unsurprisingly, from other parts of the world such as Ecuador and India.[4] As a part of the exhibition, the

Royal Collection Trust commissioned Miller to pen a new poem and premier it at a live reading event in February 2015. Miller humorously recounted the exhibition during a reading several years later at the 2018 Key West Literary Seminar, remarking: "The Queen took out all her gold in Buckingham Palace once, and they invited a poet to write a poem about this display of gold. I don't know why they asked me; that's rather stupid, right? I mean, they know what they're gonna get."[5]

Miller's poem "Place Name: Oracabessa" meditates on the naming of Oracabessa, a town in St. Mary Parish on the northern coast of Jamaica. Noting the prominence of "gold" in the naming of the town itself (from the Spanish *ora cabeza* or "golden head") and in the naming of several luxury estates in the town—including Ian Fleming's "Goldeneye" estate where he penned the James Bond series, the U.S. politician Ruth Bryan Owen's "Golden Clouds" estate, and the "Golden Cove" resort villas—Miller ponders this obsession with the precious metal in a place where "not an ounce of metal" was found. Instead, Miller declares the only "gold" was "light glistening off the bay, and bananas, and perhaps ackee, and such language as could summon wind to capsize Columbus's ships—and if that's not gold, then what is?"[6]

The sound of Miller's voice as he performs the poem at the Key West Literary Seminar is pensive, gentle, perhaps even mournful, and punctuated by moments of subdued yet pointed urgency. He moves between the affective performance of an academic inquiry ("Oracabessa—origins disputed but most likely leave over from the Spanish. Oracabeza, Cabeza de Ora, Golden Head") and that of a sharp indictment ("In those days the Italian tried to name the island Santa Maria, as if not knowing it already had a name, in another language, a language whose speakers would soon die"). Miller does not punctuate the horror of the historical facts—such as the mentions of Native genocide or the deadly Spanish colonial fervor for gold—with marked shifts in volume or tone; indeed, the matter-of-factness Miller performs at the citation of these facts makes them even starker, even more damning. Instead, he punctuates the driving, nimble pace of the poem with a few moments where he slows down and pauses, where he stresses words by slowing to luxuriate in their enunciation. The pause—allowing a moment of silence for his words to linger with the audience—and the enunciative stress are his vehicles of punctuation. He pauses meaningfully, for example, midway through the poem when he says, "Could someone please go back in time and tell Columbus, in Taino there is no word for gold." I dwell on the sonic particulars of Miller's performance here as a way of fleshing out Miller's quip with what he names "dog whistle" criticisms—those that laud the subtlety, restraint, and indeed *quiet* of his performance. These accolades contain, Miller suggests, an unspoken juxtaposition with the abstract conception of Blackness as loud rather than "quiet," confrontational rather than "restrained," explicit rather than "subtle," crude rather than "elegant." He is praised for containing all the excesses that Blackness is said to represent. Perhaps he is praised for these qualities expressly because of the historical horrors that lurk in the backdrop of the poem. Yet for this reader and listener, Miller's use of the pause (especially on the tail end of a breathlessly recited cluster of lines), of enunciative stresses, and of matter-of-factness are just as powerful, just as loaded with meaning—just as laced with condemnation of the genocidal European colonial enterprise—as if he had yelled them.

I am captivated by the sonic metaphor of the dog whistle here, by the metaphorical turn to ultrasound (and infrasound), or those registers of sound that vibrate at frequencies beyond the limits of human hearing. At these frequencies, sound is still audible to other beings, such as dogs, even as they are inaudible to humans. In these realms, sound can still act on the body, causing anything from nausea to death, despite its inaudibility.[7] This, then, is an apt metaphor for Miller for criticism that appears laudatory but that does something else under the cover of praise: it furtively condemns modes of poetic expression that eschew subtlety by rewarding those that are appropriately quiet. It erodes his sense of belonging in literary circles even as it lauds him as a paragon of the craft. More, it works this way even in the hands of those who sincerely mean to compliment him. In other words, it operates as a poetic common sense; it appears obvious to this circle of critics that subtlety, restraint, elegance, and quiet are artistic virtues. It is possible that Miller registers disturbance at the way he is being embraced by these critics not only because of the implied conflict between the presumed sonics of Blackness and the sonic qualities attached to poetic virtuosity but also because much of his art contains political speech. Across his poetry and prose, Miller centers explicit and pointed condemnations of the colonial project in the Americas, of antiblackness and colorism both in the Caribbean and globally, of the brutal state repression of Rastafarians in Jamaica, and of the subtle and overt racism and xenophobia of the elite literati in Britain, among other things. Here, sensory rationalism takes on another life as a logic that governs not just the soundscape but also shapes values of artistic expression and political speech.

In another interview, Miller expounds on the anxiety that he is being rewarded for "pitch[ing] blackness at an appropriate volume." He explains:

> I think I have been pretty successful as a poet and a novelist. And to what extent does that mean I was able to conform? You know, I'm very aware of my place in the British landscape—being the first writer of color to win the Forward Prize, things like that—but very wary of people taking that on as a marker of Black progress, perhaps? Because I'm aware that my voice that is educated, that doesn't come from Britain, that makes a sound that is of a particular class, of a particular education. It doesn't threaten Britain really. . . . And so though there is this gesture and a tokenism of allowing Black voices,

> you're not always allowing the voices you should be listening to and you should be hearing. And so I think a lot about that these days—owning the fact of my own education, but always trying to turn the volume up slightly. Trying to make the British ear adjust itself to be able to hear another kind of resonance.[8]

Here, Miller links the material phenomenon of antiblack sonic policing, the policing and management of "the volume in which words are pitched," to the lauding of subtlety as a poetic value. Subtlety is lauded in part because it is read as an extension of sonic etiquettes around quiet as an elite aesthetic. Subtlety most commonly denotes "a discreet or diplomatic manner or approach" and also "tact, sensitivity to the feelings of others." However, it also gestures toward "abstruseness of language, a subject" and its "complexity" and "intricacy" or "involving distinctions that are fine or delicate, especially to such an extent as to be difficult to analyse or describe."[9] To be subtle, then, is to be inconspicuous, to avoid explicit, direct declarations, to resist being easily understood, and to address matters in a way that avoids causing offense.[10] If Blackness has historically been troped as loud, confrontational, "publicly assertive," resistive, and demonstrative, then the "compliment" of subtlety when issued to a Black poet is necessarily entangled in this rhetorical web of associations.[11] Much like Black artists and writers being praised for being "eloquent" or "intelligent," these words take on their character as so-called compliments because of their departure from all the undesirable qualities Blackness is supposed to represent.

There are political stakes attached to these artistic virtues. Miller names them when he expresses a wariness that his success will be taken as a "marker of Black progress," especially because he is aware that his voice is "of a particular class, of a particular education" that is not "threatening" to Britain. He is being listened to and embraced (in a way) by the British literati. Yet he is concerned that their listening is actually a way to conceal the systemic barring of other voices, "voices [they] should be listening to and [they] should be hearing," under the appearance of having listened. Sara Ahmed's vital concept of the "non-performativity" of antiracism, which she elaborated almost two decades ago, names the conundrum Miller is describing. In Ahmed's words, "non-performativity" explains "when naming something does not bring something into effect or (more strongly) when something is named in order not to bring something into effect. When yes does not bring something into effect, that yes conceals this not bringing under the appearance of having brought."[12]

Yet Miller underscores that embracing "volume" as a Black poet, both as literal loudness and as a kind of bold, explicit declarative quality, also comes at a cost. In his essay "In Praise of the Fat Black Woman and Volume," Miller tells the story of an instance in 2014 where he coheadlined an event in Johannesburg with queer Jamaican poet, writer, and activist Staceyann Chin, who is often billed as a spoken word and performance poet. Chin, Miller remarks, is one of his greatest poetic inspirations and influences. After seeing her perform for the first time at the Calabash International Literary Festival—where Chin performed with "raw energy" despite her nervousness about performing as an out lesbian in Jamaica—Miller's poetry was "profoundly and forever changed" by the "dizzying decibels of [Chin's] own volume." Chin is known for the boldness of her artistic voice, for her dauntless poetic condemnations of antiblackness, patriarchy, homophobia, and empire. Her "volume" is not merely a metaphorical reference to the boldness of her address but also a literal descriptor of the sonics of her performance. Very often, she is projecting powerfully—even yelling—and gesticulating sharply and expansively when she performs. The might of her performances is punctuated even more by the abruptness with which they conclude; as soon as she finishes her performances, she speedily gathers her belongings and exits the stage. She does not linger even briefly with the often uproarious applause of her audience. Chin's poetry, like Miller's, is also known for its audacious political speech, for unyielding condemnations of patriarchy, homophobia, colonialism, and U.S. empire.

Take, for instance, Chin's performance of the poem "Homophobia" at WNYC's eleventh annual Dr. Martin Luther King Jr. celebration at the Apollo Theater in 2017.[13] Chin opens her performance boldly, loudly, and explosively, declaring, "'Being queer has no bearing on race,' my white publicist says. 'True love is never affected by color.' I curb the flashes of me crashing across the table to knock his blonde skin from Manhattan to Montego Bay to bear witness to the bloody beatings of brown boys accused of the homosexual crime of buggery." It is not just the volume of her performance but the use of her body: she crosses her arms in sharp disapproval before widening her stance and throwing open her arms, a visualization of the distance between Manhattan and Montego Bay between which she fantasizes about knocking her publicist. She continues, "Amidst the newfangled fads and fallacies—the New Age claims that sexual and racial freedom has finally come for all—these underinformed, self-congratulating, pseudo-intellectual utterances reflect how apolitical the Left has become." Chin's poem decries what she regards as a squeamishness among young activists to acknowledge the ongoing salience of intersecting structures of oppression in favor of what she calls a "pretense of unity." Chin expresses outrage at, as Cathy Cohen once warned against, "the limits of a lesbian and gay political agenda based on a civil rights strategy, where assimilation into, and replication of, dominant institutions are the goals."[14] Instead, both Cohen and Chin call for "a Left framework [which] makes central the interdependency among multiple systems of domination" rather than following "those individuals who consistently activate only one characteristic of their identity, or a single perspective of consciousness, to organize their politics, rejecting any recognition of the multiple and intersecting systems of power that largely dictate our life chances."[15]

Perhaps most notably, Chin performs all the things Miller is praised for not being: she performs in ways that are loud, confrontational, explosive, and even vulgar. In "Homophobia," she admits, "even in friendly conversation, I have to reign in that bell hooksian urge to kill motherf-ckers who say stupid shit to me *all day*. All day, bitter branches of things I cannot say out loud sprout *deviant* from my neck. *F-ck you*, you f-cking racist, sexist turd!" Her bold, sharp gestures, her yells, and her use of obscenities elicit peals of applause, cheers, and laughter from the audience. Even so, the audience does not escape her criticism. She remarks pointedly, "While we all stand here well-dressed and rejoicing, *well-dressed and mourning what we have lost* [referencing the election of Donald Trump in 2016], in India, in China, in South America, a small child cuts the cloth to construct your new shirt, your new shoe, the old imperialism upheld by the misuse of impoverished lives."

The delighted fervor of Chin's audience, who are enraptured even as they are being indicted by her, is ambiguous. One interpretation might read their cheering as an indication that they share her political commitments. Another might read them as delighting in her audacity as a Black queer woman engaging in poetic and political speech in a moment when reactionary right-wing politics are flourishing, when systematic attacks on Black political speech are taking root. Yet another, more complex interpretation of Chin's audience, especially in moments when they are being indicted for their complicity or their ignorance, might read them as experiencing what Jennifer Nash and Samantha Pinto once described as a libidinal economy of "racial bondage," where performances like Chin's can deliver for audiences "pleasurable experiences of racial masochism."[16] Describing the curious forms of pleasure that white women can take in consuming Black feminist texts that espouse "models of correction, discipline, and ownership"[17]—particularly those that call out white women's duplicity, hypocrisy, and treachery—Nash and Pinto explain,

> Indeed, white women's consumption of texts that point out their duplicitous tears are seen as proof of white women's commitment to Black feminism, to reforming their white selves and those of "their people" as yet another form of necessary and gendered care work, to being different kinds of feminists. A kind of erotics undergirds this relationship where Black women act as racial dominatrixes who inflict a kind of racial wounding on white women, reminding them again and again of their bad politics—and how their "job" is to take it, to confess it, to revel in their abjection and abdication of intellectual power. This performance of contemporary feminist politics as a racial bondage constitutes an understudied site of pleasurable performance for Black women and the flip side of pleasurable experiences of racial masochism for white women.[18]

In other words, it is possible that Chin's audience cheers because they agree with her. It is equally and simultaneously possible that they cheer because they take pleasure in the experience of being boldly confronted and dressed down by a Black woman. By "taking it" and "reveling in it," they can experience a kind of moral redemption. In this instance, the loud, bold, confrontational qualities of Chin's performance are crucial to audiences who seek the sensory, erotic, and moral pleasures of bathing in the cleansing fire of her outrage. While Miller fears being embraced by the British literary establishment in ways that silence other important Black poetic voices and prematurely mark Black progress, I submit that Chin's audiences may also embrace her in ways that minimize the efficacy of her bold articulations.

In contrast to the poetic descriptors that Miller notes critics have used to describe him, Chin has been described by critics and reviewers with words like "brave," "forthright," "irresistible," "seductive," "unflinching," and brimming with "raw, sexual, revolutionary poetic power."[19] Once, a critic went so far as to describe Chin's poetry as "jet fuel from the hot center of the body" and as "unmitigated life-force."[20] Where Miller's poetry is described as subtle, restrained, and elegant, Chin is often described as "raw" and affecting to her audiences. Walter Mosley celebrated the much-awaited publication of Chin's poetry in print, noting, "Now all of us who have been lucky enough to have seen her on stage, heard her from the ramparts, can be joined at last by readers in the quiet spaces to properly celebrate this remarkable voice and watch her take her place in American letters."[21] According to Mosley, Chin, who was well-known for her affecting performances, was marginalized in the "quiet" world of American letters. She was marginalized in that world precisely because her poetic voice was regarded as too loud, too noisy, and as lacking in subtlety. Noisiness, as Amber Jamilla Musser elegantly elaborates, indexes the ways "difference is met with nonrecognition, disorientation, and perhaps overwhelm. Noise, then, allows us to sense how questions of recognition, legibility, and comfort underlie reception."[22] Questions of sonic intensity here are less about volume per se and more about "the fabric of social relation."[23]

Miller, too, comes to the same conclusion as Mosley after reflecting on his and Chin's shared Johannesburg performance. Though he was once awestruck by Chin, he feels more ambivalent about the Johannesburg reading; he notices the effect that sustained poetic tone policing has had on Chin's poetry. On the massive stage reserved for their performances—a stage, Miller remarks, "you would imagine for a rock concert rather than a poetry reading"—his own reading does not go "particularly well."[24] The audience does not rally to attention when he begins reading; they continue chatting in their individual circles as he reads. "It seems I had become the kind of poet whose volume does not demand immediate attention," Miller reflects. "I had become a poet without flailing hands because those hands needed to hold onto the books that I was reading from."[25] Though he is lauded for his subtlety on the page, he worries that as a result, he struggles to command the attention of a live audience. Yet when Chin arrives on stage, the crowd is immediately enthralled; she is able to "hold the crowd in the swell of her energy." Miller finds it remarkable that she is able to do so even though she is primarily reading from her memoir, yet "her prose was pitched at the same volume with which she used to read poems."[26]

By the end of her performance, Chin does read a few poems—haikus—but Miller is disappointed by them, finding them "lazy, didactic," and "lack[ing] images." Though he worries that he is "judging [Chin's] poetry through the same aesthetic lens that [he] has tried to challenge" in the essay, he nevertheless insists that Chin had "given up" after feeling "the brunt of rejection from the poetry gatekeepers for so long." Her poetry now "no longer made even the smallest attempt to please them." Miller reflects, "It was as if she had accepted that she would never publish a collection, that she was more of an activist than she was an author." Puzzling over the sense of loss he feels when he hears Chin's poetry, he questions himself: "Remember—this was a night in which my own poetry has failed to spark anything in that crowd while Staceyann drew them all towards her and ignited a kind of fire. Why should I feel any loss, any sadness, any emotion textured with any sort of pity? Who was I to pity her?"[27] Miller, like Mosley, notes that the "volume" and "pitch" of Chin's poetic voice marked her as an activist (presumed to be loud) rather than a poet (presumed to be subtle and quiet), exiled her from the halls of American letters. Yet Miller, who has been embraced in international literary circles, insists that Chin's voice "echoes inside [his] own—textures the edges of it." He remarks poignantly, "I want to challenge that old and unrelenting aesthetic that has tried (whether knowingly or not) to set limits on the volume at which good poetry can be pitched."

I find Miller's reflections remarkable not merely because he makes explicit the ways quiet and subtlety signal a racialized form of aesthetic and sonic policing that attaches itself to art as well as quotidian utterances, practices, and performances. I am drawn to them because he, too—even as someone who has garnered recognition in elite literary circles that value quiet and subtlety—feels constrained, policed, and limited by the demands imposed on his poetic voice. He is not sure what it means that Chin's popularity exiles her from literary circles while his popularity fails to command the attention of his live audience in Johannesburg. Both artists are stuck, anxious, and unsure of their audiences, as well as of the terms on which they are being listened to and of the cost of being listened to. These Afro-Caribbean poets' relationships to audience, poetic voice, subtlety, volume, and popularity are fraught here. I began this book by tracing colonial preoccupations with governing resonance, or the capacity of sound (and therefore bodies, cultural forms, and sexual practices) to carry and move freely. In this final chapter, I attend to the governance of the realm of subtlety and the ways Caribbean writers both subversively embrace and transgress demands for poetic and political subtlety and expressivity.

On Sound and Political Capacity

A core concern that animates my inquiry in this chapter is artistic and political erasure. I trace how, and to what effect, our vocabulary for describing desirable artistic and political qualities tethers itself to ideas about sensory perception and sonic intensity. In contexts where, for example, the hallmarks of artistic achievement are discussed through recourse to ideas of elegance, restraint, subtlety, quiet, and perceptiveness, while the quintessential marks of empowered political subjectivity are boldness, outspokenness, loudness, insistence, and even qualities of the pedagogical and moralistic, artistic and political labors may be discursively placed in an artificial dichotomy, such that, as Miller notes, one can be made to feel "more of an activist than [. . .] an author." Audre Lorde wrote against this false dichotomy, declaring, "It has become fashionable to separate the spiritual (psychic and emotional) from the political, to see them as contradictory or antithetical. 'What do you mean, a poetic revolutionary, a meditating gunrunner?'"[28] More specifically, then, I am interested in how Afro-Caribbean artists' joint poetic and political labors are frustrated, managed, and muted when they are interpreted through the dominant lenses of artistic and political common sense. I am intrigued by the ways writers use their work to disturb these forms of sonic common sense. In earlier chapters, I wrote about sounds—about the cluster of associations that tend to get attached to sonic phenomena and their material consequences. In this chapter, I turn my attention instead to narratives and rhetorics that rely heavily on a sonic repertoire of metaphors to convey and normalize ideas about artistic value and political subjectivity.

It is worth meditating more on how sonic common sense can govern the ways we think not just about artistic values but also about political speech, capacity, and subjectivity. Consider, for example, the colloquialisms "speaking out" and "being silenced" as expressions that index notions of political capacity, whether empowerment or repression. Here, the voice and the ear are invoked as the metaphors of choice for describing both positive political capacity and a liberal inclusionist impulse to "listen." Speaking gets represented as the primary (even sole) route through which the disempowered are encouraged to reclaim social and political power (discursively and representationally, if not materially), but the capacity to listen gets represented as the gauge through which the privileged and empowered can be deemed morally redeemable or not.

Yet Black feminist scholars like Shoniqua Roach have questioned the political limits of discursive strategies of "breaking silence" as a means of redressing unjust material conditions. Roach writes:

> Black feminists use publicity as a governing frame for both injury and its redress, generating cultures of exposure and confession and obscuring the extent to which publicity continues to be predicated on whiteness as property right and blackness as fungible. . . . I contend that black feminist critics have mistaken the map for the territory [Wynter] when we have called for moves to publicity that, on some level, presume that visibility in and of itself is sufficient to address and redress the symbolic position of black femininity as always already a condition of "unrepressed injury" (Hartman 80). This condition of "unrepressed injury" cannot and will not be addressed by breaking (sexual) silence, confessing our stories in public, or staking claim to pleasure in the public sphere. This is not a denial of the importance of such acts, but rather a challenge to the implicit presumption, and sometimes explicit assertion, that breaking the silence is the logical conclusion, end goal, and answer to the historical and ongoing discursive and material violence that was foundational to the very constitution of black female subjectivity.[29]

By questioning the common sense that both "visibility" and "breaking the silence" are the expressions par excellence of a liberatory Black feminist politics, Roach reveals that our turn to a multisensory vocabulary (visibility, breaking the silence) to describe political capacity is not an accident of language. Such sensory metaphors often index an investment in being perceived, detected, sensed by or within (often) a white public sphere. In other words, when we aim to "make our voices heard," what is left unsaid is the *who* that is doing the hearing (implied to be a white public who is either hostile to the articulations of the marginalized or is indeed intently "listening and learning") and what precisely we hope will happen as a natural consequence of being heard.

Jennifer Stoever has elucidated how, in the U.S. context, both listening and breaking silence have historically operated as "sonic privilege[s] of whiteness." Noting the space accorded to descriptors of vocal timbre and listening affects in antebellum slave ads, Stoever writes that "slaveholding whites imagined power flowing directly through acts of disciplined listening." Rather than invoking breaking silence solely in the context of a Black discursive tradition of "speaking truth to power," Stoever elucidates another racial-sonic history in which the power to initiate (or foreclose) conversation was imagined as a key privilege of whiteness. Black affects of docile listening and speech were thus emphasized as desirable qualities in enslaved people, and expectations of docile Black affect continue to govern standards of engagement in (white) public spheres. This history is integral to the ways sonic-political expressions like "speaking out" discursively represent a (white) sonic public sphere as a key site of justice. Yet we must ask: for whom are Black histories and perspectives "silent"? How might the privileging of this lexicon for political speech and capacity serve to discursively narrow the field of meaningful political action to the reform of (already hostile or resistant) antiblack institutions and sensibilities?

I am curious about the kinds of political fantasies, aspirations, and fears that subtend these sonic vocabularies. In both of the aforementioned examples, the figures of both the willful "speaker" and the (un)willing "listener" are conjured in a conflictual drama in which the sounds—as metaphorical proxies for the needs and interests—of the marginalized either triumphantly break through into privileged zones or are held at bay. Here, sound comes to represent a specific set of political fantasies, in which being perceived, sensed, understood, heard, and seen by those who wield structural privilege not only automatically produces a freer and more just future but also represents the apex and endpoint of racial justice struggles. Sensation, in other words, becomes a way to index the extent to which we are fully known by those who do not wish to know us. Or, perhaps, sensory metaphors index a striving toward an acknowledgment of presence that is not about being "fully known" but simply about counteracting denial, erasure, or sanitization. In either case, the value of being attended to, understood, acknowledged, watched, listened to, and felt within the zone of the powerful, privileged, and unwilling is presumed in ways that exceed the specificities of any one particular political context. It operates instead as a political common sense. However, as the history of antiblack surveillance has taught us, being seen and listened to can at times frustrate or foreclose liberatory possibilities rather than open them.

I am interested in how sensory metaphors for political capacity and commitment can subvert the substance of political demands by substituting perception for material concessions. Perhaps such turns of phrase emerged in part from the conviction that oppression cannot stand when subjected to the light of scrutiny; I, too, believe that the project of naming—as it is connected to a longer history of Black struggle against the naturalization of white supremacist world orders—is essential and invaluable. Yet what I trace here, and what the Afro-Caribbean writers and artists I examine in this chapter compellingly elaborate, are the limits, the dangers, and the chaotic potential that opens up when they are embraced, lauded, and listened to by various audiences.

This raises questions about the liberatory possibilities of recognition within and incorporation into particular public spheres. Feminist sound studies offers valuable insight into this. As Roshanak Kheshti writes, "Feminist sound studies reveals that there has always been a sonic under commons and gendered outside, which has at times become absorbed as the business model or epistemic center."[30] Elsewhere, Kheshti frames the conundrum as such: "On the one hand the critical theorist *cannot not* point out the logical flaws inherent in hegemonic discourse. On the other hand, doing so makes the very disposition/perspective/identity vulnerable to systemic appropriation. . . . [H]ow can one shake a common sense without objectifying and fetishizing abject, subaltern or secondary modes of perception?"[31] How do we situate Black scholarly and creative production within this schema? What might we learn from closer attention to work that explores the possibilities of speech, analysis, creative production, and more outside of the expository frameworks that seek to make Black people and cultural production accessible to "wider publics," that recruit the (un)willing listener?

Roger Reeves, in his brilliant essay, also approaches the question of the limits of the public sphere as a question of corporate appropriations of Black political speech. "I do, however, want to think about how the compulsion to talk, to articulate our rage, our ire, our feelings might actually participate in the transformation of our feelings, our protest into capital," Reeves reflects. "In other words, telling the world how we feel on Facebook, Instagram, and Twitter does not free us from the labor or the yoke of our dispossession but sinks us further in it, sinking us into labor, into capital, our discontent mined for data points to sell to the highest bidder. And, maybe, we get a blue check mark for the work of putting our Black pain to work."[32]

Against Publicity

Black feminist and queer scholars have long put pressure on dichotomies of silence (read as private) versus sound (read as public) as opposing poles of empowerment, where public assertions and declarations become the ultimate marker of redress, inclusion, or resistance. As Shoniqua Roach stresses, "If black femininity is the ground upon which the white public as such has been constructed and recognized, then the appearance of black female subjectivity in public (and/or private) is always already a violent enterprise."[33] Put differently, a concession of space or a kind of recognition in a white public sphere—that is itself constituted through "binary oppositions such as blackness and whiteness, masculinity and femininity, publicity and privacy"—cannot redress the very violence that it relies on to stabilize its own taxonomies and hierarchies.[34] Public declarations and representations matter enormously, and yet, their liberatory possibilities are limited.

Public recognition often backfires. Instead of producing meaningful structural changes, it can produce performances of acknowledgment that can produce political stasis. Criticizing discourses of heterosexual "tolerance," Sarah Schulman problematizes the ways that dominant groups' mere acknowledgment of the existence of minorities gets enshrined in media, art, and public discourse as a mark of the humaneness and moral capaciousness of privileged groups rather than the fruit of the long-term collective efforts of marginalized people. Schulman writes: "Today we face a 'tolerance' defined by the diminishment of the minority and the heroization of the majority, a 'tolerance' that simply acknowledges that the minority exists and that claims that acknowledgment as an act of generosity. The fact that this minor recognition is the result of the suffering and insistence of millions of gay and lesbian people over centuries is completely erased."[35] Ahmed, commenting on Schulman's crucial insights, writes, "When recognition is understood as a gift from the straight world, our collective labor and struggle are forgotten."[36]

Relatedly, Black feminist and queer historians have questioned the common sense that breaking discursive or archival silences necessarily represents a transformative intervention against racial, gendered, and sexual orders. As Kwame Holmes explains: "The impossibility of privacy for those 'running' in Washington's black gay circles offers insight into a potential source of queer black ambivalence toward political mobilization. In the face of the federal government's massive accumulation of authority to investigate and expose, in light of queer black Washingtonians' historically compromised access to sexual privacy, the liberatory power of 'coming out' may have emerged as anticlimactic, a continuation of the sexual order rather than an intervention against it."[37]

Kevin Quashie has called for attention to Black interiority, reclaiming "quiet" as "a metaphor for the full range of one's inner life," moving against the ways Blackness is understood "only through a social public lens, as if there were no inner life."[38] Distinguishing quiet from silence, stillness, or an otherwise apolitical realm, Quashie reaches for a more nuanced sonic political vocabulary beyond the dichotomy of public-expressive-empowered versus private-silenced-disempowered. He reminds us through his work that our sonic metaphors accrue meaning by being embedded in a broad cluster of associations. The common sense that "speaking out" is a consummate expression of positive political capacity rests on the assumption that the public sphere is where politics happen, or happen meaningfully. It presumes a public discursive realm in which battles for scarce rhetorical and ideological space become the engines through which political subjectivities are constituted and dissolved. More, as Quashie points out, Black people are routinely constructed as public political subjects, both as an extension of histories of dehumanizing, antiblack rhetoric and image-making *and* through Black artists' efforts to contest dehumanizing images and representations of Black people in the public sphere. Quashie writes: "As an identity, blackness is always supposed to tell us something about race or racism, or about America, or violence and struggle and triumph or poverty and hopefulness. The determination to see blackness only through a social public lens, as if there were no inner life, is racist—it comes from the language of racial superiority and is a practice intended to dehumanize black people. But it has also been adopted by black culture, especially in terms of nationalism, but also more generally: it creeps into the consciousness of the black subject, especially the artist, as the imperative to represent."[39] In this schema, struggles to either reify or contest antiblack imagery—haunted by the ever-present specter of a white gaze—constrain the possibilities for the kinds of conversations, insights, and creative and intellectual visions Black writers and artists can generate as a condition of entering into the public sphere. The burden of representation weighs heavily and unrelentingly.

Black scholars of ability have also questioned the ableism inherent in such declarations of political desire that revolve around "speaking out" and "making one's voice heard." As Derefe Chevannes pointedly asks in his writing on Black and deaf communities and political expression, "If one's communication cannot be recognized as speech, can one be a political subject or is one reduced to an object of other people's decision-making and action?"[40] Citing Lewis Gordon's analysis of the Greek and Egyptian etymological roots of the work "idiot"—the Greek *idiotes* signaling "a private person" and the Egyptian root *idi* meaning "deaf"—Chevannes writes: "Therefore, to be anti-/apolitical or deliberately to avoid partaking in the construction of public life was to be an idiot, which was akin to someone who did not hear, to be deaf."[41] Language bears the traces of the ableist roots of the construction of the public sphere as the key locus of meaningful political engagement. More, the fetishization of audist modes of political engagement carries assumptions about personhood. If speaking out and hearing others out are the liberal emblems of full civic participation and functional political personhood, those who do not speak and hear in conventional audist modes are consigned to the realm of the repressed, of "silence." As Chevannes writes, "Those who 'hear' become the standard form of what it is to be somebody. Absent this, deaf political speech becomes an impossibility with the consequence that *only* the hearing speak."[42] Other idioms of political expression *and* other publics in which those articulations take place are erased, assumed ineffective.

Despite these challenges, sonic metaphors remain the discourse par excellence of political possibility and constraint, even as they are routinely appropriated by right-wing reactionary groups, institutions, and political actors (through, for example, a fervency around "free speech") to insist upon their "democratic" right to retrench racial, gender, sexual, and class hierarchies. In the liberal imagination, every voice matters, all ideologies can exist unproblematically alongside one another, and we must make room for all sorts. This fantasy, though framed as a nondefensive, all-embracing ideology, actually encodes a reactionary terror of upheaval, a concern that a more just world will require a profound unsettling of supremacist hierarchies. In other words, the true desire conveyed through liberal visions of "all-inclusiveness" is not that we can all live happily together but rather a deferral of transformation through the performance of a paralyzing inclusiveness, where the doomed search for a world in which all ideologies can coexist unproblematically together drains our collective energy for change.

My broad concern is with examining the limits of sound as a useful vocabulary for describing political and artistic values, desires, aspirations, and constraints. More, I seek to catalog what we might learn from work—particularly the creative work of Afro-Caribbean artists—that maintains a stance of cautiousness toward the public sphere as a site of transformative possibility. Caribbean writers insistently call attention to how colonial power leveraged itself both through acoustic force and explicit declaration, as well as quiet coercions that were sedimented beyond speech—a taken for grantedness, a going without saying. I am curious, then, about what an attention to other registers of sound, and of political speech, can generate for our methodological approaches to the study of Black life and for our understandings of political possibility and desire. To this end, I turn to the work of the Tobagonian-Canadian poet and essayist M. NourbeSe Philip.

A Profound Distrust

Once, M. NourbeSe Philip, the Tobagonian-Canadian poet, lawyer, essayist, and literary giant, was invited "as a last-minute replacement" to a poetry performance where famed Jamaican dub poet Linton Kwesi Johnson was headlining.[43] She does not name names: we never find out what the event was, who organized it, or where and when exactly it was. We never discover who she was called in to replace, only that it was a "Cuban poet who had not been able to obtain a visa to enter the United States."[44] What we do know is that the headliner of the event, the famed Jamaican dub poet Johnson, is a poet she "greatly admires." She recounts that when she arrives at the venue "with very few minutes to spare and somewhat out of breath," Johnson notices her breathlessness and offers to perform first to allow her time to prepare her selections of poetry. This is a small but meaningful gesture of care and community: he notices that she needs a moment to catch her breath, and he creates that moment for her. As Johnson takes the stage, Philip observes how enthusiastically the audience responds to his engaging performance: he "works with a band; it is rhythmic, imbued with rhyme and carries an in-your-face political message."[45] She becomes anxious and is now reticent about how the audience will receive her work. She notes that her own work is "page bound and far more in the modernist tradition which abandoned rhyme and rhythm, if not metre, a long time ago."[46] In the end, she decides to read poems that she hopes the audience will respond more enthusiastically to. She writes, "I found myself reading my more *politically obvious* poems—earlier works by and large—and avoided those poems that challenged me as reader and them as audience."[47] It is, she recalls, "one of the most difficult readings I have ever done."[48]

The reading is difficult because she anticipates that she—and her poetry—will be marked as difficult. Yet the nonnarrative form of Philip's poetry—and what Samantha Pinto describes as Philip's "commitment to opaque play"—are essential features of her work.[49] "Philip names," Pinto explains, "rather than the postcolonial 'condition,' our unease with the communal failure of our fields to fully articulate and name such a condition in totality."[50] Philip's art, then, fundamentally revolves around "imagining impossible worlds beyond narration." The "difficulty" of her work—the absence of a "politically obvious" narrative or charge—is steeped in a desire to explore the place of—and demand a place *for*—uncertainty, the unknowable, the unsettled, doubt, and subtlety in the ways we think about African diasporic life, history, and aesthetics. Although this artistic commitment often marks her as "difficult," it is sometimes confused for an antipathy toward audience, as a desire to "restrict" her audience.[51] However, Pinto points out that Philip's purpose is to build community rather than restrict it: "Her [Philip's] purpose is to think about how form, particularly difficult, book-length refusals of linear clarity in poetry and poetic prose, produces 'readerly' texts, or ones that create a certain community and experience of how to read, interpret, and organize that which lacks the clarity of normative syntax, chronology, and narrative."[52]

The mental calculus Philip must do to connect with her audience during her performance tells us something about the conditions of receptivity in particular public spheres and about the gendered dynamics of Black political speech. What constitutes an artistic challenge, and whose challenges are embraced and engaged? What exactly does the audience hear when they hear Johnson's poetry? To what can we attribute their pleasure in his performance? What does Philip fear the audience will not hear—or more precisely, will not hear with enthusiasm, pleasure, or interest—because of her chosen genre of poetic expression, because of its refusal of an overt or expository political message?

I am compelled by Philip's conundrum here and intrigued by the subtlety of her account, as fascinating for what it reveals as it is for what it does not disclose. This moment of uncertainty, anxiety, and perhaps even insecurity is a different kind of account of Philip than what we often get in the public sphere. Known for speaking out boldly against the persistent operations of racism, sexism, and xenophobia in the so-called multicultural space of Canada, Philip has dealt with hostile audiences many times before. Described by Paul Barrett as a "model of a critic and public intellectual" and a master of the art of "poetic disturbances" (and again, "disturbance" appears as a key feature of the art and aesthetic of Caribbean literary experiments with sound), Philip's career as a seasoned activist and public intellectual has many times come at the cost of her "disappearance" as a writer on the Canadian literary scene.[53]

One instance Philip has recounted in her work is her participation in the September 1989 demonstration outside the fifty-fourth PEN Congress in

Toronto. Philip, along with several other writers, artists, and activists, gathered to engage in a leafletting campaign outside of Roy Thomson Hall in an effort to call the delegates' attention to "the fact that there was and is a very real problem with racism in writing and publishing here in Canada which, in many instances, serves to silence African, Asian, and First Nation writers."[54] One stark example of this fact, which the leafletters highlighted, was that "most of the writers and moderators comprising the Canadian delegation were white."[55] Philip clarifies that their aim was not "to change PEN Canada or PEN International" but underscored that "the ethnic and racial composition of the Canadian contingent [was] a startling yet predictable example of the official face of racism in the arts in Canada."[56] At the end of a long day of leafletting, Philip approached the then incoming president of PEN Canada, June Callwood, to offer her a leaflet. Callwood infamously responded "swiftly" and "viciously," telling Philip to "f-ck off" and repeating the same words to her fellow leafletters. "The irony is that," Philip reflects, "as president of PEN Canada, Callwood is head of an organization whose members are sworn to uphold freedom of speech, particularly for writers, the world over."[57] The media, Philip notes, largely "censored" the demonstration outside of the PEN Congress by refusing to report on it, though some outlets published indifferent or vitriolic condemnations of the protest as an uninformed exercise in "witch-hunting." The Canadian literary scene's history of erasure of the work of nonwhite writers, in addition to Philip's history of activism on the Canadian literary scene to redress these issues, has resulted in a persistent erasure of her artistic labors. "While many of her contemporaries have taken up comfortable positions as creative-writing instructors or editors in publishing houses," Barrett writes, "Philip has yet to find prominent footing in the larger CanLit scene. Outside the country, she has been given the Casas de las Américas prize and a Guggenheim Fellowship among other international honours, but she has never received any major national literary award at home. Her 2008 collection, *Zong!* [. . .] was mostly ignored by Canadian critics despite being praised around the world."[58] Here again we see a version of the conundrum Miller described earlier when reflecting on Chin's career and work: Philip—marked as a loud, outspoken protestor of racist, sexist, and xenophobic erasure within the Canadian literary establishment—is herself exiled, denied recognition within literary circles in Canada. Yet Philip's poetry and prose have simultaneously been marked as difficult and dense and, at times, as eschewing "politically obvious" messages for more complex political and artistic meditations.

Much of Philip's oeuvre and preferred styles of performance center around preserving space for what cannot be easily articulated, generating expressive modes that evade and frustrate processes of definitional, expository, or narrative description and interpretation. In an interview in the *Toronto Review of Books*, Philip remarked on the importance of posing "challenges [to] a

Western norm that establishes that it is possible to talk about anything and everything," a norm rooted in "practices of empire and colonialism that everything can and should be made subject to the Western gaze." Likening artists and poets to "keepers of secrets," she advocates for a methodological approach that unsettles dominant historical narratives: "It is in the unravelling and untelling (which is different from not telling) of the silence that we can begin to approach a new awareness, while continuing to honour that larger Silence, that the noise of knowledge attempts to drown out."

Philip indicates that there is another register of political speech in her work, one that does not take the stage. For Black diasporic people, the importance of not allowing certain utterances or provocations to reach the explicit register of public speech has been an essential mechanism of knowledge transmission, coalition-building, and survival. However, beyond strategies of countersurveillance, I want to think about the ways that the efficacy of other registers of political utterance rely on their capacity to evade the public sphere—not just because they may be resisted and suppressed if heard but because they may be *embraced* in ways (and from locations) that can produce political inertia.

Examining registers of political speech in art and scholarship cuts to the heart of questions about who is seen or heard as a political actor along lines of race, gender, class, and sexuality; dominant understandings of how, why, and in/from which locations meaningful political speech occurs; and what the societal roles of art and scholarship are. I am interested in what careful, sustained attention to political speech in Philip's oeuvre—what constitutes and prompts it, its modes of address, its relationship to the public sphere, and when and how it diverges from readers' or characters' expected effects of such speech—might elicit for our own approaches to the study and practice of Black writing, art, and political expression. What conundrums, contradictions, and challenges arise, particularly for scholars, when we attempt to examine and learn from the registers of infrasonic speech that interest women artists like Philip? I pay special attention to Philip's oeuvre for the ways she deftly navigates the figure of the (un)willing listener. Often marked as a "complex" and esoteric artist who writes in ways that are inaccessible to her audiences, Philip often conjures the presence of the (un)willing listener in her writing.[59]

Unbearable Routines

There is a little-examined short story titled "Stop Frame" in Philip's prolific oeuvre. This 1993 award-winning work is, simply put, a bizarre and haunting tale. The majority of the story's action takes place in 1958 in a fictional postwar Caribbean village called Bethlehem. The young adolescent narrator, Miranda, never discloses exactly where she is in the Caribbean, merely that she is "on a hot, dry island. Somewhere. In the Caribbean."[60] The people of the village of Bethlehem are plagued by a harrowing problem: routinely, they hear an incessant chorus of screams issuing from the local dentist's office. The screams, Miranda discloses, are the screams of her neighbors: "Everybody," she notes, "scream[s] like this at least once" when they go to visit the dentist's office for routine care.[61] The screams are so common that they have become a routine and unsurprising feature of the village's soundscape, of life in Bethlehem.

The dentist—a white German man named Dr. Ratzinger (but who the protagonist mischievously calls Dr. Ratfinger)—is something of a mystery. What Miranda knows about him, she learns through eavesdropping, rumor, and fragments of information that her parents sparingly offer. Her mother recounts that Dr. Ratzinger arrived during World War II, a former Nazi who fled to the Caribbean amidst the collapse of the so-called Third Reich. His arrival is sudden and unexplained; Miranda's mother recounts that she simply woke up one day and Dr. Ratzinger was there, "brip brap, just like that" installed in the "biggest [house] in the town of Bethlehem."[62] He quickly establishes a dental practice that operates out of his house, and it is then that "the screams of friends and neighbors" become a routine feature of life in Bethlehem for the village's longtime residents.[63] Though Miranda never articulates her suspicion aloud, she divulges to the reader later in the story that she believes Ratzinger has come with the intention of "carrying out experiments on the people of Bethlehem."[64]

Perhaps more unsettling than the speculation about the dentist's experiments is that despite how loud his victims' cries are, there is a profound silence surrounding his activities. No one in the village, except the young Miranda and her friends, talks explicitly about the screams or about his suspected experiments. In fact, many of the people of Bethlehem still routinely go to see him for dental care. Some people of the village, such as the character Nurse Pamela, even work for him; she restrains patients while Dr. Ratzinger performs his procedures, and she is rumored to be sleeping with him. The story never explains or dwells on why the people of the village do not speak out or openly, unambiguously, and publicly denounce the dentist's experiments. It is simply never put up for consideration; it has no place in the story's drama. What Miranda does tell us, in a passing comment, is that the word around Bethlehem is that Dr. Ratzinger meets "with 'important collar-and-tie' big shots" and occasionally "send[s] people to the mad house."[65] This, Miranda notes, "frightening us even more than the pain sometimes."[66] Perhaps then, public declaration and confrontation are dangerous in Bethlehem because Dr. Ratzinger has the power and connections to institutionalize those who accuse him of abuse.

The fact that the premise itself sounds unbelievable—that a Nazi dentist could take up residency in a Caribbean village for well over a decade after the war's end and conduct experiments on Caribbean people—speaks to the ways the Caribbean is obscured as a region that participated in and was acutely impacted by World War II. As Miranda notes, her unnamed "tiny Caribbean Island" home seems "far away from events like 'the final solution,' panzer divisions, and the Desert Fox." Despite this supposed geographical and temporal distance from World War II, Miranda experiences an acute proximity to the war through sound. Though her mother declares dismissively that the war has long been over, Miranda insists that "when nighttime falling, I hearing the bombs dropping on London over the wireless."

Philip, too, underscores how impactful World War II was in the development of her own political and social consciousness growing up in Tobago and how deeply she and her Afro-Caribbean peers identified with the struggle against Hitler. "We understood," Philip writes, "what the fight against Hitler meant, and many Black men joined up and fought overseas on behalf of the Allied powers to prevent the culmination of an obscene racist ideology that had fingered everyone who wasn't 'white.' As a matter of course, many of us have taken the Jewish experience in World War II into our lives as I did as a teenager."[67] As Sarah Phillips Casteel rightly point out, "Holocaust history is not fundamentally divorced from the postslavery landscape of the Caribbean. . . . [T]he influx of Jewish refugees from the Nazis coincided with an inverse movement of Caribbean soldiers into the European theater of war—among them Frantz Fanon, who fought in the Free French Army."[68] For Afro-Caribbean writers like M. NourbeSe Philip, Derek Walcott, Michelle Cliff, Paul Gilroy, Caryl Philips, and others, Casteel argues, the Holocaust served as "a site of surrogate memory for Caribbean/diaspora writers who came of age during the war or in the decades immediately following" in part because they "came of age in a postwar moment in which the Holocaust had become an accepted topic of discussion but slavery had not yet been afforded the same recognition."[69] The presence of Dr. Ratzinger in Bethlehem, then, symbolizes not only the Caribbean reach of World War II but also the excruciating persistence of the antiblack logics and legacies of plantation slavery.

In "Stop Frame," as the bombings of London are being rebroadcast and commemorated across colonial radio broadcast programs, Miranda mistakes the broadcast for coverage of a current crisis. For her mother, the war took place in another place and time; for Miranda, the war is ongoing here and now. Both are true, in some sense: the war did formally end in 1945, and the agents and exercises of Nazi racial violence are still active and present in Bethlehem. The presence of Dr. Ratzinger in the village and the routine screams of his Caribbean patients, then, is evidence of the ways the horrifying violence, messy outflows, and repercussions of the war persisted in places that were not regarded as the primary theaters of war.

The people of Bethlehem have eschewed the kind of triumphant public declaration or demand that readers might expect as the highest enactment of political capacity. The story, instead, emphasizes a range of other quotidian, "ultrasonic" zones of political action and consciousness-raising. Rumor, "pappyshow" (ridicule), and prank instead become critical sites of political action; their efficacy is enhanced because they can take cover under humor and secrecy, because they do not require the authorization of truth-value or historicity, and because they depend on ambiguity and unintelligibility. They do not require substantiation; in fact, they resist it. This is a zone where "truth" can be untethered from facticity.

There is a robust Caribbean literary studies bibliography on the potency of gossip as a subversive social force that can be strategically deployed to undermine figures and forces of structural oppression. Carol Bailey underscores that gossip—often considered to be a feminized genre of speech—is regarded by many as a "negative communication genre" whose impact is "thought to be destructive or at best frivolous."[70] Bailey writes, "Since women are generally believed to have a stronger predilection to gossip, it is not surprising that the association between women and gossip presents another opportunity for essentializing women and censoring their behavior."[71] Denunciations of gossip as a disordering social force, then, often also function as a form of sonic, racial, gendered, sexual, and class surveillance and policing. Caribbean writers and artists challenge the stigmatization of gossip and instead reclaim it as a "subversive genre" that may operate "as a means of affirming one's social position" and of troubling one's own investments in hierarchical social systems.[72] More, gossip can function as a disturbing, disordering force in Caribbean literature, as Raphael Dalleo elaborates, because it appears "as a sort of counterpublic where those excluded from the dominant public sphere pass along knowledge."[73]

On the surface, the people of Bethlehem appear resigned to Dr. Ratzinger's unethical practices out of necessity; after all, he is the only dentist in town. As Miranda reasons, "Bad teeth not caring about politics."[74] Even so, Ratzinger, and those affiliated with him, remain the butt of a relentless stream of lewd rumors about sexual liaisons and practices, ridicule of their social etiquettes (or lack thereof) and "high mind" aspirations, pranks, and the thinly veiled disdain of the people of the village. The people of Bethlehem do routinely seek Ratzinger's services; however, the constant circulation of rumor and ridicule prevents him—and those associated with him—from gaining esteem in the eyes of the people, and particularly, in young Miranda's view. By the time Dr. Ratzinger's audibly inhumane medical practices catch the ears of Miranda and her friends, they are already primed—through the village's low hum of disapproval, as a result of the formation of an effective counterpublic where knowledge is being shared—to be suspicious of him and to contest his practices.

For example, sexual rumor becomes the primary vehicle through which we (and Miranda herself) learn that Dr. Ratzinger is a Nazi. While eavesdropping on a debate between her parents about whether Dr. Ratzinger is sleeping with

Nurse Pamela, Miranda's father declares assuredly, "I telling you de man is a Nazi, and if he is a Nazi, dere is no way he doing it with her."[75] The discussion of his Nazism is itself submerged within another, seemingly trivial, debate about rumored sexual liaisons in the village. The question of whether Dr. Ratzinger is sleeping with Nurse Pamela becomes a way to debate about the possibility (or probability) that Dr. Ratzinger is a Nazi. It becomes a way to debate about whether antiblack contempt and intimacy or desire can coexist. Ultimately, Miranda's mother dryly concludes that "a standing prick knows no mercy," that anyone might become the subject of masculine desire.[76]

In another scene, Miranda overhears the colorist character, Mrs. Standall, demanding that Nurse Pamela allow her to see Dr. Ratzinger without an appointment. She presents her ancestry as an authorizing credential, boasting to Nurse Pamela, who is dark-skinned, that her own ancestry can be traced "right back to a white sailor who settled on the island a long time ago."[77] It is on the presumed grounds of her and Dr. Ratzinger's shared whiteness that she claims access to Ratzinger's services. Having overheard this exchange, Miranda rushes home and relates the story to her mother. Her mother retorts that Mrs. Standall's ancestral tale is nothing to be proud of because "anybody with an ounce of sense" knows that "sailors [have] syphilis and gonorrhea and [. . .] the morals of a dog in heat."[78] It is telling here what kinds of ideas find their home in the zone of public declaration and which live elsewhere. Named appropriately for her penchant for grandstanding and her naked belief that she is "plenty cuts above everybody else in the village," Mrs. Standall's turn to the zone of public declaration is an attempt to reinforce a white supremacist, colorist social hierarchy.[79] The young Miranda knows, however, to turn to the ultrasonic register of her private conversations with her mother for a counter-reading, one in which Mrs. Standall's near-whiteness signals a history of violence rather than one of prestige. Miranda's mother remarks that the only thing Mrs. Standall's skin means is that there is a "crook, robber, or rapist in [her] family."[80] In Bethlehem, the quiet modes of articulation that evade the dominant public acoustic sphere subtly and effectively undermine through the formation of what Dalleo refers to as an anticolonial "counterpublic."[81]

Miranda also relies heavily on imagination and humor as modes of critique. For example, she imagines herself as being part of the war effort and recounts feeling "important" when the people of the village refer to her and her friends as "the war babies."[82] Many of her efforts are comical: she and her friends imagine "farting out loud" as an affront to Hitler (for whom Dr. Ratzinger operates as a proxy), yelling "Take dat, Hitler, take dat!" each time one of them does it, and "laughing out big and loud and hard like we already big women."[83] Much of Miranda's "war effort" revolves around eschewals of the mores of social and sonic etiquette expected of young Caribbean girls and women: she is loud, brash, mischievous, and vengeful. She rebuffs Dr. Ratzinger by refusing feminine propriety and by refusing to adopt the kind of political naïveté that is expected of children.

Miranda and her friends also invent obeah rituals in the hopes of bringing Dr. Ratzinger misfortune, steal produce from his garden, and play pranks on him and his nursing staff. In one instance, they break into Dr. Ratzinger's office and car and rub the seats down with "cow-itch grass"; they watch gleefully as Dr. Ratzinger begins uncontrollably scratching himself. Miranda's mischief eventually becomes a sore spot for Dr. Ratzinger: after Miranda and her friends begin routinely stripping his mango trees of their fruit while he is away, he gets "angry" and demands to know who is committing what he calls "predial larceny" (theft of agricultural produce).[84] It is notable that he turns immediately to the language of the law; he is aware that if this feud were being waged in a certain kind of public legal discursive register, his race, gender, class, and national markers would have granted him an overwhelming advantage. However, Miranda and her friends have learned—in part from observing how the adults around them deftly navigate the presence of the dentist—how to evade the dangers of public declaration by speaking and acting in another register.

Though Ratzinger demands to know who has been stealing from him, he never gets the answer he seeks. Just as he has foreclosed the possibility and efficacy of public declaration for the people of Bethlehem, his public demand goes unanswered. In fact, Miranda's prank has an unexpected financial benefit to the fruit vendors of the village: because all his fruit is gone, he goes to the fruit market more often. The market women immediately recognize this as a valuable business opportunity and quickly "double their price" the moment they see him coming. None of the people of Bethlehem know with certainty that Miranda is the one responsible for these pranks (though her mother suspects her); nevertheless, we still glimpse a broad, interconnected web of quotidian practices of resistance that manage to collaborate without explicitly coordinating, that emerge from an understanding that public declaration may not deliver up the just futures they desire. Unable to force Dr. Ratzinger to leave, Miranda resolves to make his life in the village unlivable.

When Miranda herself develops a toothache and her mother brings her into Dr. Ratzinger's office to be examined, she bites down on his hand so hard that he refuses to provide dental care for her again, despite her mother's repeated pleas. When Miranda's mother asks her why she bit him, she responds, "I remembering how he making people scream, Ma, so I biting him, Ma—hard, hard. . . . And is Dr. Ratfinger turn: is he who screaming and yelling at me."[85] In this moment of inversion, Miranda meets Dr. Ratzinger's attempt to embed himself in Bethlehem by initiating him into the village's sonic landscape of audible and routine pain. This is Miranda's revenge: Miranda inflicts pain in response to the pain he inflicts on others. She steals from him as he has stolen from the village, and she furtively uses the local terrain and flora against him in ways that make it impossible for him to hold her accountable, just as the people of the village struggle to hold him accountable.

In "Stop Frame," the question of what does—and what does not—achieve explicit verbal articulation in the village of Bethlehem becomes essential to understanding the terrain of political speech and action in the story. I write with attention to scales of articulation: there are weighty, horrifying truths that are mentioned only casually, in passing, without pausing to dwell on their gravity, and there are salacious yet banal truths that are openly and hotly debated. There are other matters that linger quietly in the background of the story that never find explicit articulation. More, there are shocking details that emerge into the terrain of the narrative without explanation or resolution.

"Stop Frame" contains an explicit and obvious political problem and a very clear antagonist, whose centrality to the story is reinforced by the fact that the problem is persistently and hauntingly loud. The problem of the story is serious, and it is obvious; the reader can, it seems, instantly identify protagonist and antagonist and can easily name the histories that are being allegorized in this story (i.e., the confluences between colonial violence and Nazi racial violence). Yet by the end of the story, we learn that what has been (literally) loudest and most obvious in the story has displaced and obscured another set of more complex and opaque problems. When this quiet, submerged set of problems emerges in a private conversation between Miranda and her mother, it complicates how we understand the meaning of the story's central problem; it challenges the triumphalism of Miranda's war of attrition against Dr. Ratzinger.

The Silent Cry

In a startling scene at the very end of "Stop Frame"—in 1988, thirty years in the future—a now adult Miranda reflects on the horror of Dr. Ratzinger's presence in, and eventual departure from, Bethlehem. As she reminisces, she is suddenly bombarded by an old, repressed memory: she recalls in fragments a moment when she was a child when her mother pretends to drink poison and stages her own suicide. She recounts the memory using the filmic imagery of stop frame animation: in a series of mnemonic "stills," she recalls her mother lying on the floor screaming that she is drinking poison and killing herself. The language of the scream recurs over and over, but it is something she "sees" in her memory, rather than *hears*, as she did the screams of the people of Bethlehem.[86] This sudden, quiet memory is so disturbing to Miranda that she seeks out her now aged mother looking for answers, to ask why she did it. "So Ma," the adult Miranda asks her elderly mother, "is why you doing it? You know, Ma—pretending you killing yourself?"[87]

It is notable that her mother "stages" her suicide rather than attempts it in earnest: this is a demand for recognition, for acknowledgment. But from whom? There is no sign that anyone other than the young Miranda witnesses this scene. How and why, then, might Miranda's mother have wanted Miranda to attend to her pain? A story that begins with the anguished screams of Dr. Ratzinger's tortured patients ends with a different kind of cry: the screams of Miranda's mother grappling with an unexplained pain, a moment of (perhaps) psychic crisis. Miranda's mother's cries complicate our understanding of what and where the "problem" is; if Ratzinger turned our eyes toward the confluences between the horrors of colonialism and the horrors of the Holocaust, Miranda's mother's cries turn us elsewhere—to Black women's pain, to the home, to intramural conflict.

For the majority of the story, our readerly attention has been directed toward Miranda's triumphant campaign against Dr. Ratzinger. In this moment, though, we are forced to consider the possibility that Miranda's campaign against Dr. Ratzinger may have been for her a proxy for another, more complex kind of crisis and conflict. We also confront the unreliability of Miranda's witness: she is capable of repressing, of forgetting, and of omitting. The details she has put before us as readers (and the ones she has prioritized in her own memory) are not the details that can help us to understand this moment of profound alienation from her mother.

When Miranda asks her now aged mother about this disturbing memory, insistent on understanding why she did it, her mother refuses to address Miranda's questions and instead repeatedly defers to the crimes of Dr. Ratzinger, expressing outrage that the dentist refused to see Miranda again after she bit him so many years ago. Miranda, however, persists in her demand for an explanation. In response, her mother simply—eerily—smiles and says to her, "A memory is just like a rotten tooth—if it hurting too bad, you must be taking it out. . . . [Y]ou wait for the visiting dentist."[88] She enjoins Miranda to repress the memory, to learn to live with it. By encouraging Miranda to wait for the "visiting dentist" to "take it out," she seems to recommend that Miranda repress her pain and confusion, to simply omit them from her catalogue of memories. She suggests that not all questions can be answered and that not all efforts to assign meaning and significance to the chaos of life will hold. In Miranda's memory, her mother's act attempts to disrupt the primacy of the struggle against Dr. Ratzinger; it appears as a bid for recognition. Yet decades later, her mother seems to have divested from Miranda's belated recognition; she has learned to live with the unrecognizability of her pain even to her loved ones.

It is notable that Miranda's mother recommends that she wait for the visiting dentist to resolve her painful and confusing memories. As we know from the story, the visiting dentist—an outsider to the community—whose role was to resolve pain, in fact, exacerbated and prolonged that pain. Indeed, Dr. Ratzinger relies on the persistent and interminable pain of the villagers of Bethlehem to carve out a secure livelihood in Bethlehem. When the villagers request from Ratzinger a recognition of and healing response to their pain, he makes a business of recognizing and responding to their pain, but his response is exploitative, not healing; it exacerbates rather than remedies. Ratzinger, then, may operate as an allegory for the dangers of vesting our political hopes for redress and repair in the benevolence of (or even in a demand for recognition from) a privileged public whose group interests rely on our subordination. Conversely, we might read Miranda's mother's invocation of the visiting dentist as an allegory for irresolvable trauma. Miranda's mother's directive to "forget," to extract, and to repress is unsatisfying because it suggests that some questions cannot be answered, and some pain cannot be healed.

Yet we must grapple with the fact that it is the campaign against Dr. Ratzinger, the fervor around expelling him from the village, that drowns out the noises of Miranda's mother's pain. Miranda recalls this shocking expression of crisis only decades later when she is an adult. Dr. Ratzinger is a spectacular character; he—as a white former Nazi experimenting on the residents of a Caribbean village—represents the politically obvious object of our critique. Miranda's mother, however, calls our attention to other kinds of sites of political struggle—intramural sites—which can require different kinds of strategies of articulation. We begin in the open soundscape of Bethlehem with the villagers' screams, and we end in the kitchen with a Black woman's cries. For the story to be "about" Ratzinger, Miranda's mother was recruited as the fountain of counterdiscourse, as the site Miranda goes to fuel her resistance to Ratzinger's claimed space in the village. Her mother's cries are a radical break from a kind of political serviceability; she cries out because she needs to be cared for rather than to care for.

Miranda's mother not only withholds from her daughter an explanation of a confusing and traumatic memory but withholds from the reader any neat explanation of how this subplot squares with the drama of the Nazi dentist that has occupied our readerly attention so far. This scene represents a profound disruption to the narrative economy of the story: it is as much a problem for literary critics as it is for Miranda. As literary critics, who are often charged with interpreting texts for readers, a character who resists such decoding produces a conundrum for a form of literary analysis that depends on its ability to render texts and characters legible. What do we make of the fact that Miranda's mother appears to be no longer invested in even intramural recognition?

By the end of the story, Miranda has produced herself as the (un)willing listener. Even as she prides herself on being a character who hears the cries of her people and responds in kind, she realizes that she is guilty of unhearing the cries of her mother. We might read this as Philip's way of asking what kinds of pain and violence tend to draw the bulk of our readerly and scholarly attention and which kinds tend to go unnoticed? More, how do we think of political capacity when sonic acts of declaration are either unavailable or ineffective? Though her refusal to offer up an explanation to Miranda is profoundly disturbing (and perhaps emotionally abusive), Miranda's mother demonstrates how withholding encourages a process-oriented (rather than "corrective") approach to trauma that questions the common sense that declaration (or recognition) can correct or dissolve harm. Miranda's mother demonstrates a model of "living with"—a model she has developed out of conditions of invisibility and inaudibility—rather than one of dissolution or resolution.

Coda

A Quiet Place

The book has thus far inquired into a range of ways quiet has been produced, on one hand, as an object of desire, a rights object, a tool of racial surveillance, an elite aesthetic and entitlement, an artistic and political value, and a horizon of civilizational possibility. By following the operations of sensory rationalism as a discursive strategy—a set of commonsense logics applied to the sensorium that justify quotidian forms of racial, gender, sexual, and class surveillance, displacement, and violence—I work to defamiliarize "quiet," to disturb the near-ubiquity of its signification as a universal good. Rather than pronouncing quiet to be inherently sinister or valuable, I am instead interested in the effect that the production of quiet as an elite entitlement has on people, neighborhoods, countries, and entire regions. In a sense, then, this work is again not about sound alone but about the ways that moralized discourses about good, right, and appropriate sounds can harbor other kinds of phobic ideologies. I am tracking an indirect, everyday, common-sense mechanism by which Black diasporic people's claims to belonging, autonomy, space, and expressive freedom are routinely undermined. The artists I trace in the book rely on multimodal art forms: film, music, literature and poetry in print and on stage, missives, op-eds, and more to make felt what regimes of sonic surveillance do to Afro-Caribbean communities and how these communities turn to sound and as a placemaking strategy under conditions of economic and political pressure, alienation, and dispossession.

Central to the work of this project is elaborating the link between the politics of sound in the world as we hear it and live it and the politics of sound as it is narrated on the page. Stories about people, places, and practices can condition how we experience them in the realm of the senses, yet the senses are a realm we tend to produce as experiential rather than narratological. More, narratives can be felt as noisy or disturbing because of their content, their style, and their mode of address rather than their sonic intensity. Text is thus an important archive for documenting sound's full reach and range of meaning even beyond the lived multimodal experience of sound as vibration. Finally, novels, short fiction, and poetry specifically are essential textual-sonic archives that offer insight into the lived experience of sonic surveillance, pleasures, and pressures. Studies of what Carter Mathes calls "Black literary sound,"—in which writers engage not merely in sonic documentation but also imagination, "the literary creation and manipulation of sound"—enable us to expand the archive of sound multimodally.

Finally, this book represents an experiment in exploring the ties between the study of the sensorium and the study of common sense as a mode of everyday thinking. If sensory rationalism achieves its potency precisely through its evasion of analysis, through its turn to commonsense notions of sensory norms and etiquettes, then we benefit from inquiries into the sensory, felt life of commonsense thought. This entails inquiring into the sensory codes that cue us to the fact that we are in alignment with, or in breach of, a given common-sense logic. If common sense's efficacy is grounded precisely in the fact that it, as Stuart Hall and Alan O'Shea put it, "requires no sophisticated argument," "does not depend on deep thought or wide reading," "works intuitively, without forethought or reflection," and "[gives] the illusion of arising directly from experience," then more precise attention to the ways the sensorium is recruited into the intuitive operations of common sense might allow us to further disturb the smooth, seamless operations and implementations of these logics. Like quiet, what other sensory experiences are said to represent the hallmarks of wellness or sound judgment and decision-making, and which appear as the harbingers of individual, communal, national, or societal collapse?

Quiet, though often invoked in its capacity to promote well-being, also has an active life in our cultural imagination as a kind of nightmare—as an unsettling, disturbing, and even horrifying sensory experience. Even as sonic surveillance allows elites to exclude, there are certain acute pains, doubts, even horrors that can attend the ideal of inclusion, of being embraced, welcomed into the neighborhood, an institution, or even acknowledged as a master of one's craft. In the works of some Afro-Caribbean women writers, quiet can appear as emblematic of the nightmare of total social isolation, of disconnection from affirming community, from the self, and from a sense of place. Though quiet might afford privacy, it can also engender paranoia, erode physical and psychic well-being, and be haunted by the very figures characters either fear or long for. In closing, I want to attend momentarily to the appearance in Afro-Caribbean cultural production of quiet as nightmare, as a harbinger of the dawning of a dystopic world. I underscore the ways quiet appears as an idiom of loss rather than a symbol of luxury, rejuvenation, peace, or enlightenment in order to better understand how the Caribbean writers and artists I study illuminate the bleak underside—the costs—of good-life fantasies staged in and through the Caribbean region and its people.

In the closing chapter of the Jamaican writer and essayist Nicole Dennis-Benn's 2016 *Here Comes the Sun*, the novel's queer Afro-Jamaican protagonist, Margot, has achieved her lifelong dream. She wakes up in a beachfront villa—"*her* villa," the novel clarifies—in a "king-sized canopy bed with its dark wood frame and its white netting."[1] The scene is one of luxury: she has a black Range Rover parked in her driveway; her floors are fashioned with marble tiles; arched French doors mark the transition points between rooms; she sports a silk robe; and she is waited on by Desrine, her "house girl." The luxury is a shock to the reader who has followed Margot's journey from the beginning of the novel, where she scrambled to make ends meet as a front-desk clerk by day and, by night, a sex worker—and later, a madam—at the fictional Palm Star Resort in Montego Bay.

When we first meet Margot, she is living in a shack in the rural town of River Bank; she is supporting her mother Delores, who works as a market woman selling wares to tourists, and her teenage sister Thandi, who attends the prestigious Saint Emmanuel High School and is preparing diligently, anxiously for the CXCs (or Caribbean Examinations Council exams). It is a struggle to keep the lights on, literally: because their home is not "legally wired," they must siphon electricity by "stealing it from a nearby light pole."[2] Their evening activities—Thandi's studying and Delores's cooking—often happen by the light of a small kerosene lamp. Though Margot's relationship with her family is fraught and tense, she boasts that she has no dreams of her own; rather, she lives to see her younger sister excel in school and go on to achieve professional success in a respectable but lucrative vocation. She is prepared to go to any lengths, to incur any cost—financial, social, or ethical—to make this happen. Yet we learn early on that Margot does in fact have a disavowed dream of her own: she dreams of owning her own home and living openly in domestic bliss with her lover, Verdene, "seeing [Verdene's] slippers parked next to hers on a welcome mat."[3] Both Margot and Delores sublimate their own dreams of financial stability and autonomy—of a better life and all that might entail—into a fervor for Thandi's individual scholastic and professional success. They each fantasize that through Thandi, in Delores's words, "someday all her sacrifices will be paid back. Tenfold."[4]

We see the payoff of Margot's sacrifices at the end of the novel. She owns a beautiful custom-built home and lives a life filled with material markers of luxury and privilege. She no longer waves down taxis to make her way to and from work; she now clicks down the sidewalk with "her Italian leather pumps" and "her Chanel handbag, the Range Rover keys dangling from her manicured fingers."[5] But Margot's sacrifices have included her relationships with all those who formed the fabric of her old life: Delores, Thandi, and perhaps most importantly, Verdene. Margot has bargained her entire community in River Bank for her new life: in exchange for serving as a key engineer of a scheme to raze River Bank, push the community's residents out of their homes, and help the Palm Star Resort seize the land for their expansion, she has been granted her new, luxury home in the wealthy expat neighborhood of Lagoons. Margot's profound grief expresses itself, in part, through a set of complaints about sensory irritation. Her beautiful home—absent the people she loves—is simply too quiet. She tries to break this vexing quiet by hiring domestic workers who she hopes will offer her a regular sense of human connection, people who will "populate her property" and whose presence will "[keep] her afloat."[6] When Desrine and Cudjoe, the workers she has hired to maintain her home, arrive each morning, Margot is maddened to find that the quiet of her home intensifies rather than abates. Margot explains:

> Whenever they are there, the house is still quiet—too quiet: the lull of the ocean, the intermittent billowing of curtains by the breeze. In River Bank she was used to hearing the crowing of roosters. But here, in Lagoons, when she wakes up, there is silence, as though the day has held its breath. Desrine and Cudjoe speak in whispers to each other or make no sound at all after their initial, "Howdy, Miss Margot." It's this frozen formality that sparks an occasional burst of fire inside Margot's chest that makes her snap at them for no reason. . . . This, she hopes, would force them into a conversation, or even a protest. But that never happens. They simply nod in agreement and apologize profusely.[7]

Rather than being delighted, Margot is disturbed by the sounds of the Caribbean beachfront villa that she has so longed for: the "lull of the ocean" and "intermittent billowing of curtains by the breeze" do not soothe her. Instead of signaling a blissful escape from the grind of daily life—from her fraught relationship with her mother, to the indignities of working for her exploitative and inept boss Alphonso, to living in mortal fear of homophobic violence—these sounds pronounce in her a sense of alienation, lifelessness, and stasis, a "frozen formality" and the feeling that "the day has held its breath." The sonic experience of quiet—in combination with the haptics of the brush of silk against her skin and the cooling breeze of her overhead fan, and the visual of the "clean, clear white" paint she has chosen for her walls—fails to deliver its promise of peace, rejuvenation, well-being, and arrival. Earlier in the novel, Margot reveled in being with Verdene "in the pleasant silence of the [bed]room, contained within its four walls."[8] Now, in the bedroom of her beachfront villa, she has become anguished, miserable, and desperate for human connection.

The surprise of the novel's ending, while jarring in its contrast with the earlier events and setting of the novel, does pick up on a throughline in the book: Margot is a character around whom others whisper, tiptoe, and hold their tongue. "All her life," the novel's narrator remarks, "her presence has brought about pauses and silences louder than the white-hot sun and screaming crickets at the height of dusk."[9] Margot, it appears, has always been sensorially potent; she bears a strange and powerful presence. Her arrival elicits pauses and silences that are "louder"—more noticeable and halting—than the glare and heat of the sun and the atmospheric "screaming" of crickets. When Margot arrives at work, her fellow employees cease their joyful chatter, and "the hush returns" to the grounds.[10] The narrator adds that in Margot's presence, "the laughter drains like the last bit of water from a bottle."[11] Margot is, throughout the novel, haunted by the dread that she is being watched, listened to, talked about, and surveilled by others. "It's strange," the narrator notes, "how people always sense her. Before she approaches them, they look up and over their shoulders."[12]

The novel captures here the sensory-affective life of gender and sexual surveillance; Margot is anxious because she *is* indeed being surveilled by her mother, her neighbors, and her coworkers. She has been marked as suspicious because she is unpartnered and has no children. Her coworkers muse among themselves about why this is—some suspect she sleeps with married men (including her boss), others speculate that she is "selfish" and "mean" and has therefore been struck "barren."[13] Margot shields herself from the most socially damning speculation of all—that she is queer—by refusing to debunk or address presumptions of other forms of stigmatized sexual and social behavior. Though unaware of her love for Verdene, Margot's neighbors nevertheless mark her as "queer" in the sense of the term as "a signifier of sexual and gender nonnormativity, a break in the line of gender."[14] The hush that falls over her coworkers when she arrives—and the whispers that trail her when she leaves—represents another quotidian use of quiet as a strategy of social surveillance and as a sensory ritual for imposing and making felt social stigma. These whispers of gossip and speculation threaten Margot with exposure expressly by concealing what they "know." It is the fact that Margot does not know what, or how much, they know that haunts her. Gossip, here, operates as what Isis Semaj-Hall calls a "misnamed moral policing," a tool used "to deny desire, control social deviance and maintain dominant order."[15] The end of the novel—staged in Margot's beautiful, quiet villa—is tragic precisely because Margot has survived these forms of dogged sexual and social surveillance and isolation only to be met with them again, and even more profoundly. It is tragic because she learns only after it is too late that her new life cannot make good on the promise she invested it with. Quiet, for Margot, is a haunting; it is a specter she cannot shake.

In this book, I approach in various ways the paradoxical ways that the Caribbean is produced sonically as a quiet paradise—and therefore a site of elite relaxation, rejuvenation, and self-realization—even as Afro-Caribbean people and cultural production have been repeatedly and historically cast as fundamentally noisy, disruptive, and unable to display the requisite sonic etiquettes on which belonging (local, national, and civilization) is subtly and overtly conditioned. By calling attention to this conundrum, I have endeavored to disturb and make strange sensory rationalism, or forms of sensory common sense, that continue to cast the region, its people, and its resources as serviceable to the whims of Global North travelers, investors, and interests. More fundamentally, I probe the production of quiet as a regulatory norm regularly imposed on minoritized people. My hope is that in disrupting the fantasies of universality and cohesion proffered by sensory rationalism, we might clear space to better imagine a world that more radically embraces difference.

Acknowledgments

Thich Nhat Hanh once wrote, "To write a book, we must write with our whole life, not just during the moments we are sitting at our desk." Though I can only offer a partial and incomplete list of the people whose companionship and support made this book possible, I am overwhelmed with gratitude for the mighty and beautiful community that surrounded and supported me on the journey to this book's completion. To those I list and those I don't, thank you for keeping me and this book in tender and loving company, for making up the "whole life" within which this book was written.

This book has a prehistory. Before it was even a germ of an idea in my mind, I found fellow travelers and trusted guides and mentors who taught me it was possible to think and write as a life project. To Salamishah Tillet, Herman Beavers, Tsitsi Ella Jaji, Tanji Gilliam, and Deborah Thomas, thank you for being my first models of scholarship. Dr. Beavers, thank you for walking me to the Kelly Writers House as a freshman and believing in my ability to write. Salamishah, thank you for tolerating my insistence on taking every class you taught; you pulled me aside after one class and encouraged me to trust my voice, and your words fortified me in a delicate time in my intellectual development. Deborah, thank you for always taking a moment to connect, to share your professional wisdom, and for the gift of your incredible body of work; you are a model of brilliance and grace. Tanji, thank you for being a fierce intellectual and creative and for giving me a powerful morsel of grad school advice that changed my life. Tsitsi, yours was the first Caribbean literature seminar I'd ever taken. It was where I encountered Derek Walcott's *Omeros*, Kamau Brathwaite's *The Arrivants*, and most importantly, M. NourbeSe Philip's *Zong!* for the first time, and I have never looked back. Years later, your own poetry moved me to tears in the same way the works of the Caribbean literary giants you introduced me to did. Thank you for agreeing to mentor me as a curious and scattered undergraduate; what a profound privilege to call you a colleague and dear friend.

I would not be here if not for the pipeline programs that took it as their mission to invest in minoritized students and help us create pathways to realize our professional ambitions. I attended the now defunct Robert F. Kennedy Incentive Program—an advanced, experimental middle school for minority and low-income students—and through them, I connected with and enrolled in the Oliver Scholars program, another program dedicated to preparing minority and low-income students for high school. In high school, I participated in the Diversity Awareness Initiative for Students (DAIS). DAIS meetings brought together minority students across New York City for exciting, thoughtful discussions about systemic injustice; it was the first place I began asking the questions I now explore for a living. In college, I was a Mellon Mays undergraduate fellow and a McNair fellow; both programs were vital and indispensable to my journey into academia.

In a past life, I sang with some of the most gifted vocalists I've ever known. My years in The Inspiration were where I first trained my love of sound, of music, of the beauty of the Black voice. To Jodine Gordon, Jonathan Howard, Gabrielle Banks, Kristan Sock, Jared Watson, Janée Moses, Israel Durham, Malcolm Spaulding, Donnie Johnson, Danielle Noel, Morgan Rogers, Samantha Thomas, Nina Blalock, Sara Hassan, Wes Spiro, Gaby Esensten, Rich Cesar, Thando Ally, Marcel Rosa-Salas, Janay Sylvester, Nnesochi Ajukwu, Sean Mendez-Catlin, and Jordan Lowe: we made beautiful music together. ('89! I sing!) Jodine, you are my dream interlocutor! I am so impressed and awed by how you savor language, love and pursue art, and study the world around you with such precision, novelty, and boldness. Thank you for being one of my favorite people to bounce new ideas off of, to talk about the arts with, and to reenergize my creativity with. You are, as Toni Morrison once wrote, a true "friend of my mind."

In graduate school, I was trained by the best mentors I could ask for, including Colin Dayan, Hortense Spillers, Ifeoma Nwankwo, Kathryn Schwartz, and Peter James Hudson. Colin, you are a master of the craft; if ever my writing achieves clarity, depth, ambition, and poetic vision, it is because I watched and learned from you. Dr. Spillers, I studied and practiced with you the art of reading deeply and writing boldly as an act of intellectual love; enjoying your profound wisdom and easy laughter has been one of the great joys of my life. Ifeoma, your lifelong dedication to and heart for community-building and your deep-rooted Caribbeanist ethos shaped me; thank you for your always open door. Kathryn, I live in constant awe of your genius and generosity; from you, I learned curiosity as an art and discipline. Thank you to you and the wonderful Katie Crawford for your mentorship, friendship, and for the best homemade brownies I've ever had! Peter, I have no sufficient words for the profundity of your impact on my life and my intellectual journey. Thank you and the inimitable Jemima Pierre for being formative models and dear friends; thank you for inviting me over for meals, for remembering my birthday, for workshopping my writing, and for encouraging and emboldening me in my moments of deepest doubt. To everyone: thank you for training me with rigor and grace, for your loving challenges, and for your unwavering support well beyond grad school. A major thank you to my fellow travelers in graduate school: Nikki Spigner, Donika Kelly, Destiny Birdsong, Kathleen DeGuzman, Faith Barter, Lucy Mensah, Rosalee Averin, Joseph Jordan, Mariann VanDevere, Annette Joseph-Gabriel, Roxane Pajoul, Nadejda Webb, and many others. What incredible journeys we've had! Thank you for the hours you spent writing with me, talking through ideas, reading my writing, commenting on my job materials, and more. I cannot wait to continue to toast together on our journeys!

I was a postdoctoral fellow at the Carter G. Woodson Institute's Postdoctoral Fellowship at the University of Virginia, and it was perhaps the most intellectually formative experience of my early career. I am grateful for Deborah McDowell's visionary and unflagging stewardship of the institute and for her brilliance and unwavering investment in the intellectual development of the institute's fellows; thank you for being at every one of our weekly writing workshops and for the generous and insightful feedback you offered us all. Thank you to Debbie Best for your administrative labor, kindness, and humor—you made the institute feel like a home away from home! Thank you to my fellow cohort-mates for being some of the most rigorous, joyous, and brilliant people I've ever met. Julius Fleming Jr., Dionne Bailey, Tiffany Barber, Tony Perry, Lindsey Beutin, Ebony Jones, Ashleigh Greene-Wade, Chinwe Oriji, Seth Palmer, Xavier Pickett, Corey Hunter, and Ashley Rockenbach: you are my dream colleagues! A special thank you to Tsitsi Jaji and Kaiama Glover for so generously serving as interlocutors during my workshop sessions at the Woodson: your comments inspired me deeply and changed the direction of my work for the better. Finally, a heartfelt thank you to the Caribbean studies working group at UVA for being an enlivening intellectual community; I so looked forward to our meetings! To Njelle Hamilton, Marlene Daut, and Kaiama Glover—it was a cosmic gift to connect with all of you while I was at UVA!

It was a joy and privilege to participate in Duke's Summer Institute on Tenure and Professional Advancement. I benefited enormously from the professional relationships I formed there, and this program sparked in me many moments of divine purpose and joy that we can do the work we do in community. I extend a special and heartfelt thanks to Andreá Williams, whose mentorship and guidance modeled for me the kind of scholar and mentor I want to be. Thank you for being solution-oriented, fiercely brilliant, compassionate, and kind; thank you for keeping in touch and extending a supporting hand to me long after the two-year term of the program ended. Your keen clarity of vision for your career—and your encouragement and support with developing my own—fortified and changed me.

My writing groups and partners have been as vital as oxygen to me on my intellectual journey. Faith Barter: you've logged more writing hours with me than anyone else! I am continually amazed at your capacious imagination, expansive reading practice, elegant writing, and incredible sense of humor. Thank you for your calm lucidity and encouragement through many panic texts and phone calls; I know in theory that people's instincts aren't perfect, but your razor-sharp, nearly precognitive insights convince me that some people can see the future. To Randi Gill-Sadler: you are a visionary thinker, a gifted and principled writer, and a wonderful friend; thank you for writing with me for countless hours, for always inquiring lovingly after my well-being, and for being a model of what literary scholarship should be. I am deeply grateful to the Black World Writing Group—Peter James Hudson, Jemima Pierre, Charisse Burden-Stelly, Lucy Mensah, Sobukwe Odinga, Destin Jenkins, and Keston Perry—for sustaining a life-giving writing community during the alienation of the pandemic. I am in awe to have witnessed and been a part of the meeting of such brilliant minds in one place! To Shoniqua Roach (my Taurus twin) and V Varun Chaudhry (my Cap moon twin), my dear and lovely friends! Writing with you both powers me endlessly. Meeting you both felt like a reunion with kindred spirits whom I've known for many lifetimes. To Nikki Spigner, Justin Mann, Tracy Vaughn-Manley, and Miriam Petty: may everyone be so lucky to write with people they adore as much as I do you all! You all are fierce intellectuals, generous readers, master level chefs, and dear, dear friends. Nikki, I could write about you in every section of my acknowledgments—it is a reflection of the fact that, for me, you transcend neat categories of colleague, mentor, friend, and family. You are simply all of these and more.

I am so grateful to my home department, the Department of African, African American, and Diaspora Studies at UNC Chapel Hill, for creating an incredible and supportive intellectual environment for me. A special thank you to my dear departmental colleagues: Maya Berry, Kia Caldwell, Brandi Brimmer, Shakirah Hudani, Eunice Sahle, Claude Clegg, LeRhonda Manigault-Bryant, Nadia Mosquera-Muriel, Lydia Boyd, Charlene Regester, and many more. I am so grateful for the unyielding support of a wonderful community of Black women scholars at UNC through the shifting tides of the campus and global climate: Tanya Shields, Sharon Holland, Rebekah Rutledge-Taylor, Meta DuEwa Jones, Antonia Randolph, Danielle Purifoy, Candice Merritt, and Lyneise Williams—you are the dream team! Tanya, you have miraculously read nearly every draft of everything I've written since I've been at UNC; thank you for always making the time. May everyone be graced with mentors as generous, brilliant, and conscientious as you are. I've also had the joy of working with so many brilliant, inspiring undergraduate and graduate students over the years who renew my joy and passion for what I do every semester. To Keiara Price, Sam Nicol, Elizabeth Stafford, Aradella Wood, Tyler Layne, Didier Exantus, Jess Blumenthal, Simone McFarlane, Dalia Marquez, Patrice McGloin, Noah Clapacs, Blaine Purcell, Alasia Jenkins, Julia Clark, Kayla McManus-Viana, Imani Williams, Zenith Jarrett, Samantha Davis, and so many more than I can name here, I rest easy knowing the future is in your brilliant, capable, and fearless hands. A special thank-you to Didier Exantus, a magnificent visual artist who first introduced me to the breathtaking artwork of Firelei Báez, which now graces the cover of this book. I cannot express enough gratitude to Firelei and her team. Firelei, when I heard you describe your work in an interview as "anchored in the senses," I felt an immediate intellectual and artistic resonance; thank you for the gracious permission to feature your art on the cover of the book. For me, your work has been a revelation. My sincere gratitude to the team at Hauser and Wirth Los Angeles, especially Tiffany Wang, for so patiently answering all of my many emails and phone calls and for facilitating my connection with Firelei's team.

I was a beneficiary of several fellowships and grants that made this work possible. A special thanks to the Institute for the Arts and Humanities at UNC where I was a faculty fellow. I extend my heartfelt gratitude to my wonderful cohort for your thoughtful comments on my work and your generosity and friendship during the uncertainties of the pandemic: Rebekah Rutledge-Taylor, Jocelyn Chua, Michael Figueroa, Torin Monahan, Vicki Rovine, John Sweet, Susan Pennybacker, Maggie Fritz-Morkin, and Aleksandra Prica. A major thank you also to Tim Marr for your steady guiding hand as our faculty coordinator. Finally, thank you to Philip Hollingsworth for your intellectual and administrative labor; what a joy and privilege it was to talk to you on the IAH podcast about my work! I also extend my gratitude to the American Association of University Women for awarding me an American Fellowship, which provided financial support and teaching leave during the most important stage of the book's completion. I could not have completed my archival research without the support of the Junior Faculty Development Award and an Arts and Humanities Research Grant from UNC.

I was able to hold a book manuscript workshop with several of the scholars I most admire during the earlier stages of the book's development. Those conversations inspired and propelled me at a critical stage of my book's development. Thank you to my wonderful interlocutors, including Fatih Smith, Nadia Ellis, Njelle Hamilton, Meta DuEwa Jones, Tanya Shields, and Lydia Boyd. The time, love, and care you all invested in reading my work—and in braving our marathon workshop day—brings tears to my eyes. I still return to your comments to ground me when I feel unmoored. To Tanya Shields, Kia Caldwell, and Lydia Boyd: thank you for taking me under your wing as your mentee! Your empathetic and pragmatic guidance kept me on task and ushered me steadily through moments of extraordinary political and campus turmoil. A special thanks to Jen Nash and Kevin Quashie, who so generously read and commented on my work and have helped me begin to map a pathway through the second project. What a privilege to be in community with you! Jen, what a wonderful gift to have you in the Triangle; I always leave our coffees with such beautiful kernels of wisdom and optimism. Kevin, thank you for encouraging me to trust my mind; your words that day are etched in my heart (and my notebook!). I am deeply grateful to Cathy Hannabach and Rachel Fudge at Ideas on Fire for fantastic developmental editorial support at the middle stages of the project's development and for your indexing labor. Your support for this book means the world!

The journey through academia is not for the faint of heart. I owe an unpayable debt to two incredible women who encouraged and supported me during my lowest lows and in the seasons of profound upheaval in my life: Rachel Silvers and Ariel Harris. Rachel, you saved my life; that is not an exaggeration. Thank you for teaching me how to heal through writing, and for attending and encouraging the closing of one chapter of my life and the beginning of another, beautiful one. Ariel, thank you for your incisive, compassionate wisdom, and for helping me develop the courage to be seen, known, and loved. I also thank Mary McKinney for your marvelous writing coaching, and for reminding me that "every book is the death of a perfect idea"; thank you for helping me to overcome my fear of messy drafts, and for supporting me as I rebuilt my intellectual confidence.

Importantly, this book was ushered to print with enormous care and sensitivity by the editorial team at Rutgers University Press. Thank you to Kimberly Guinta, Elizabeth Graber, and Emma-li Downer for your enthusiasm about the book and your warm responsiveness. I also extend enormous gratitude to the series editors of the Critical Caribbean Studies series. To Yolanda Martínez-San Miguel, Carter Mathes, and Kathleen López: thank you for your careful read of the book and thoughtful, incisive commentary on its framing ideas. Without a doubt, this book is sharper and stronger because of your generous commentary, your leadership of the series, and your brilliant, field-defining scholarship that blazed the path forward for my own long ago. What a gift to join the singular intellectual space you all have curated!

I have a wonderful community of friends and supporters who have been cheering me on long before academia was even a twinkle in my eye. To Briana and Jennielle: with you both, it was love at first sight! We were instant, lifelong friends from the moment we met; I believe in soulmates because of you. To Mona, my oldest friend: there is nothing like a phone call with you on a Sunday morning! Talking to you about anything and everything is one of life's great joys for me. I cannot adequately capture here the depth and breadth of inspiration, joy, laughter, and dreaming we've shared over the years. All I can say is—in Nao's words—"If perfect's out there, it's you." May we sit on the front porch and sip tea together when we're old and gray.

To my second parents, Aunty Thecla and Uncle Leslie—my favorite times of year are the times we all get to spend together! Thank you for seeing me through every major life milestone and for always having a warm meal and a soft place to land ready for me. Leila, Ethan, and Ryder—I never smile so big and laugh so hard as when I'm with you! Thank you for inspiring me and filling my cup in all of our small moments; whether we're doing a puzzle together, baking cookies, playing Uno, or going on a family adventure, watching you all grow up so beautifully has been one of the great and profound joys of my life. To my godparents, Aunty Delia and Uncle Junior—what stunning, brilliant forces of nature you both are! Watching you both blaze your own trails through academia reassured me that anything is possible. Thank you for your ever-extended hands.

Throughout the writing of this book, I gained a beautiful new family. To Miss Pennie, Mr. Henry, Paulette and Dwayne, Alicia, Melissa and Charles, and Aaron and Aiden: thank you for embracing me as your own from the day we met. Your profound love of life, your deep respect for others, your delight in each other, and the firm and steadfast ways you honor, cultivate, and share your own gifts have transformed my sense of what's possible in the world and what's possible within myself. Thank you for the deep belly laughs I have when we're together, for expertly creating moments for us to build beautiful memories together, and for finding me at just the right time.

To my parents: Dad, my earliest memories of euphoric joy were of being awash in the sounds of your booming music, in the basement, in the living room, in the car. One of my favorite childhood pictures is one of me clinging to your back as you walked me through the pool. What a fitting image for the way I feel about you: you have carried me with such profound strength and assurance. Mom, my closest friend: our phone calls still last a minimum of two hours, and I wouldn't have it any other way! I am so awed by your profound strength. Your shared love for and pride in Saint Lucia changed me at an early age; the poster of Derek Walcott and your reminder that the region's only Nobel Laureate came from our small island lit my path on the journey to becoming a writer and scholar. I am so proud to be Lucian! Because of both of you, I have a spirit of fearlessness, fierceness, and willfulness in me that won't budge. To my brother, Nat, thank you for being a much-needed boost of energy, hype, and boldness—you've so many times broken the spells of doubt that have gripped me on my journey. Thank you for being the fiery sun that you are!

And finally, to Kevin: to me, you are a miracle—all the virtuosity, power, artistry, and tenderness of you. I love you indulgently. Let's build a world together.

Notes

Introduction

The chapter subtitle references Kei Miller's, "In Praise of the Fat Black Woman and Volume," *PN Review* 44, no. 5 (2018), https://www.pnreview.co.uk/cgi-bin/scribe?item_id=10209.

1 Kevin Quashie, *The Sovereignty of Quiet: Beyond Resistance in Black Culture* (Rutgers University Press, 2012), 6.

2 See, for example, Jennifer Lynn Stoever, *The Sonic Color Line: Race and the Cultural Politics of Listening* (New York University Press, 2016); Daphne Brooks, *Liner Notes for the Revolution: The Intellectual Life of Black Feminist Sound* (Harvard University Press, 2021); Mark M. Smith, *How Race Is Made: Slavery, Segregation, and the Senses* (University of North Carolina Press, 2008); Roshanak Kheshti, *Modernity's Ear: Listening to Race and Gender in World Music* (New York University Press, 2015); Ronald Radano and Philip V. Bohlman, *Music and the Racial Imagination* (University of Chicago Press, 2000).

3 Steve Goodman writes with depth and lyricism about the capacity of sound to modulate "collective moods or affects" and to generate what he calls an "ecology of fear" in which "sound contributes to an immersive atmosphere or ambience of fear and dread—where sound helps produce a *bad vibe*" (emphasis in original). Goodman opens with the example of the Israeli air force using "sound bombs" in the Gaza Strip in 2005. He queries: "What is the aim of such attacks on civilian populations, and what new modes of power do such not-so-new methods exemplify? . . . The objective was to weaken the morale of a civilian population by creating a climate of fear through a threat that was preferably nonlethal yet possibly as unsettling as an actual attack. Fear induced purely by sound effects, or at least in the undecidability between an actual or sonic attack, is a virtualized fear. The threat becomes autonomous from the need to back it up. And yet, the sonically induced fear is no less real. The same dread of an unwanted, possible future is activated, perhaps all the more powerful for its spectral presence. Despite the rhetoric, such deployments do not necessarily attempt to deter enemy action, to ward off an undesirable future, but are as likely to prove provocative, to increase

the likelihood of conflict, to precipitate that future." Steve Goodman, *Sonic Warfare: Sound, Affect, and the Ecology of Fear* (MIT Press, 2010), xiii–xiv.

4 Miller, "In Praise of."

5 Here, I draw on Stuart Hall and Alan O'Shea's definition of "common-sense." See Stuart Hall and Alan O'Shea, "Common-Sense Neoliberalism," *Soundings* 55, no. 55 (2013): 9–25.

6 As Sharon Holland argues, "*Everyday* racism defines race, interprets it, and decrees what the personal and institutional work of race will be." See Sharon Patricia Holland, *The Erotic Life of Racism* (Duke University Press, 2014), 3, emphasis in original.

7 Pumla Dineo Gqola, *Female Fear Factory: Unravelling Patriarchy's Cultures of Violence* (Cassava Republic Press, 2022), xvii.

8 Gqola, *Female Fear Factory*, xvii.

9 There is a long history of transnational Black feminist scholars theorizing the everyday: from the Combahee River Collective's emphasis on developing a framework for analyzing Black women's "day to day existence" to Sharon Holland's work on "everyday racism."

10 Gqola, *Female Fear Factory*, xiii.

11 Gqola, *Female Fear Factory*, xiii.

12 It is important to note that the notion of the Caribbean as a site of desire, relaxation, and rejuvenation is a decidedly late nineteenth and twentieth-century construction. In earlier eras, the Caribbean was notorious for being a site of disease, malaise, death, and extraordinary sensory discomfort. Krista Thompson writes that in the late nineteenth century, "the West Indies were widely stigmatized as breeding grounds for potentially fatal tropical diseases. Yellow fever, malaria, and cholera had claimed the lives of many white civilians and soldiers who ventured to the islands, ensuring what historian Philip Curtin describes as 'death by migration.'" The historian Annike Raapke writes that the Caribbean was often narrated by European colonial figures as a site of "pain" and "sensory irritation," traced to a wide range of phenomena including the disorienting sounds of the environment, the troubling sight of enslaved people, anxieties about the effects that "tropical food might have on European bodies," and the deleterious effects of the heat on European bodies and minds. See Krista Thompson, *An Eye for the Tropics: Tourism, Photography, and Framing the Caribbean Picturesque* (Duke University Press, 2007), 4. Also see Annike Rappke, "The Pain of Senses Escaping: Eighteenth-Century Europeans and the Sensory Challenges of the Caribbean," in *Empire of the Senses: Sensory Practices of Colonialism in Early America*, ed. Daniela Hacke and Paul Musselwhite (Brill Press, 2017), 117–118.

13 For example, see Ian Gregory Strachan, *Paradise and Plantation: Tourism and Culture in the Anglophone Caribbean* (University of Virginia Press, 2003); Mimi Sheller, *Consuming the Caribbean: From Arawaks to Zombies* (Routledge, 2003); and Angelique Nixon, *Resisting Paradise: Tourism, Diaspora, and Sexuality in Caribbean Culture* (University Press of Mississippi, 2015).

14 Thompson, *Eye for the Tropics*, 6.

15 Susan Harewood, "Listening for Noise: Seeking Disturbing Sounds in Tourist Spaces," in *Sounds of Vacation: Political Economies of Caribbean Tourism*, ed. Jocelyne Guilbault and Timothy Rommen (Duke University Press, 2019), 108.

16 Harewood, "Listening for Noise."

17 Thompson, *Eye for the Tropics*, 11, 7.

18 Thompson, *Eye for the Tropics*, 11.
19 Thompson, *Eye for the Tropics*, 11.
20 Carolyn Cooper, *Noises in the Blood: Orality, Gender, and the "Vulgar" Body of Jamaican Popular Culture* (Duke University Press, 1995), 4.
21 Edwin C. Hill, *Black Soundscapes White Stages: The Meaning of Francophone Sound in the Black Atlantic* (Johns Hopkins University Press, 2013), 3, emphasis in original.
22 See, for example, Cooper, *Noises in the Blood*; Belinda Edmondson, *Creole Noise: Early Caribbean Dialect Literature and Performance* (Oxford University Press, 2022); Martin Munro, *Different Drummers: Rhythm and Race in the Americas* (University of California Press, 2010); Martin Munro, *Listening to the Caribbean: Sounds of Slavery, Revolt, and Race* (Liverpool University Press, 2022); Alejandra Bronfman, *Isles of Noise: Sonic Media in the Caribbean* (University of North Carolina Press, 2016); Hill, *Black Soundscapes, White Stages*; Jocelyne Guilbault and Timothy Rommen, eds., *Sounds of Vacation: Political Economies of Caribbean Tourism* (Duke University Press, 2019).
23 For example, see Colin Grant, "Jamaica: The Loudest Island on the Planet?," BBC News, September 27, 2012, https://www.bbc.com/news/world-latin-america-19636160.
24 V. S. Naipaul, *The Middle Passage: The Caribbean Revisited* (Vintage Books, 1962), 50.
25 An important exception to the representational frame of Caribbean-as-paradise is Haiti. Jemima Pierre, invoking Michel-Rolph Trouillot's work, underscores that "the forms of exceptionalism through which Haiti is read are similar to the forms of exceptionalism through which Africa is rendered. We are tasked to see the context that structures and upholds that slot, to destroy both the context and the slot, and to create new structures and narratives of emancipation." Pierre also stresses that it is important to move away from "the common strategy of enumerating the negative representations of Haiti (what Trouillot would call the 'internal tropes of the savage slot'), and the forms of anti-Blackness they represent, to analyzing the *structure* and *force* of white supremacy. . . . It demands not only an examination of the micropolitics of what is happening *to* Haiti, but also an interrogation of why Haiti is necessary for the continued fortification of global white supremacy and the contemporary political-economic regimes of neoliberalism." See Jemima Pierre, "Haiti and the 'Savage Slot,'" *Journal of Haitian Studies* 19, no. 2 (2013): 114, emphasis in original. Also see Michel-Rolph Trouillot, "The Odd and the Ordinary: Haiti, the Caribbean, and the World," in *Trouillot Remixed: The Michel-Rolph Trouillot Reader*, ed. Yarimar Bonilla, Greg Beckett, and Mayanthi L. Fernando (Duke University Press, 2021), 85–96.
26 See Thompson, *Eye for the Tropics*; and Sheller, *Consuming the Caribbean*.
27 See Hill, *Black Soundscapes, White Stages*, 2.
28 Hill, *Black Soundscapes, White Stages*, 3.
29 In one infamous example of an animal noise complaint, German ambassador to Jamaica Volker Schlegel wrote an open letter in 2007 to his neighbors in Jack's Hill complaining that he and his wife "have not been able to get a normal night's sleep because of the high level of noise." He noted that motorcycles and "reckless DJs and microphones from the Barbican region" were part of the noise problem, but his main qualm was with "the permanently barking dogs" in the neighborhood. In his letter, he cited the Noise Abatement Act (which prohibits noise

between 10 A.M. and 6 P.M.) and accordingly asked his neighbors to "take the necessary measures that the dogs on your premises are not barking between 10:00 P.M. and 6:00 A.M." The ambassador expressed confusion at the neighborhood dogs' ostensible lack of sonic etiquette, noting, "I have a German Shepherd and he does not bark unless somebody comes to the door." Schlegel's complaint was generally dismissed and even ridiculed by Schlegel's neighbors who reportedly found the complaint "funny," to Schlegel's chagrin. Ultimately, Schlegel threatened to call the police if his neighbors could not control their dogs' barking and subsequently threatened to leave the island if the police "are too busy fighting crime to do something about it." See "Dogs' Incessant Barking Irritates Ambassador," *Jamaica Observer*, February 13, 2007, https://www.jamaicaobserver.com/2007/02/13/dogs-incessant-barking-irritates-ambassador/, and Keril Wright, "No Barking . . . Please," *Jamaica Observer*, February 14, 2007, https://www.jamaicaobserver.com/2007/02/14/no-barking-please/.

30 Jennifer Morgan, "'Some Could Suckle over Their Shoulder': Male Travelers, Female Bodies, and the Gendering of Racial Ideology," in *Laboring Women: Reproduction and Gender in New World Slavery* (University of Pennsylvania Press, 2011), 15–16.

31 For example, Morgan writes, "Vespucci's familiarity with icons of difference led him to expect American women whose hanging breasts, along with their efficient labors, would mark their difference; thus, he registers surprise that women's bodies and breasts were neither 'wimpeled' nor 'hanginge.'" Morgan, "'Some Could Suckle,'" 17–18.

32 Nathaniel Parker Willis, *Health Trip to the Tropics* (C. Scribner, 1853), 63. Nathaniel Parker Willis's wife, Cornelia Grinnell Willis, employed Harriet Jacobs as nanny and seamstress in New York and purchased Jacobs to deter her previous enslavers' longstanding efforts to pursue her North and force her back into slavery. It was at the Willis's home, Idlewild, that she composed her famous *Incidents in the Life of a Slave Girl*.

33 Willis, *Health Trip*, 62, emphasis in original.

34 Willis, *Health Trip*, 62–63.

35 Willis, *Health Trip*, 63.

36 Willis, *Health Trip*, 63.

37 Fred Moten, *In the Break: The Aesthetics of the Black Radical Tradition* (University of Minnesota Press, 2003).

38 Marisa Fuentes, *Dispossessed Lives: Enslaved Women, Violence, and the Archive* (University of Pennsylvania Press, 2016), 142.

39 Willis, *Health Trip*, 7.

40 Fuentes, *Dispossessed Lives*, 143. Also see Saidiya Hartman, "Venus in Two Acts," *Small Axe* 12, no. 2 (2012): 3.

41 Ronald Radano, *Lying Up a Nation: Race and Black Music* (University of Chicago Press, 2003), 92.

42 Radano, *Lying Up a Nation*, 92.

43 Jenny Sharpe, *Immaterial Archives: An African Diaspora Poetics of Loss* (Northwestern University Press, 2020), 4, 20.

44 Joan Anim-Addo, "Gendering Creolisation: Creolizing Affect," *Feminist Review* 104 (2013): 18.

45 Sharpe, *Immaterial Archives*, 56. Also see Tina Post's stunning analysis of "deadpan aesthetics" as yet another example on the spectrum of "black modes of

reserve" that are dense with meaning even as they may appear on the surface to be inexpressive or repressed. See Tina Post, *Deadpan: The Aesthetics of Black Inexpression* (New York University Press, 2022), 22.

46 Harry A. Franck, *Roaming Through the West Indies* (Century Co., 1920), 49.

47 Franck, *Roaming Through*, 49.

48 Franck, *Roaming Through*, 47.

49 Franck, *Roaming Through*, 115.

50 Franck, *Roaming Through*, 151.

51 Franck, *Roaming Through*, 152.

52 Franck, *Roaming Through*, 152.

53 Archie Bell, *The Spell of the Caribbean Islands* (L. C. Page, 1926), 164.

54 Harry La Tourette Foster, *The Caribbean Cruise* (Dodd, Mead, 1935), 111.

55 Susan de Forest Day, *The Cruise of the Scythian in the West Indies* (F. Tennyson Neely, 1899), 239.

56 Richard Henry Dana, *To Cuba and Back: A Vacation Voyage* (Ticknor and Fields, 1859), 47.

57 Julian Henriques, *Sonic Bodies: Reggae Sound Systems, Performance Techniques, and Ways of Knowing* (Continuum, 2011), xvii.

58 Jennifer Nash elegantly unpacks this in her analysis of Black feminist self-help genres. She writes, "Of course, this idea that body care is self-care, that body work is self work, that the body and the self are actually synonymous, has become central to a popular Black feminist form that has championed care, rest, hydration, and quiet not just as forms of bodily attention but as practices of 'self-care.' . . . How might we think—beyond banishment—of the ways that the interior is a site filled with complex, sometimes undermining logics about self, appearance, weight, desirability, that Black feminists themselves have thought with and through? What might it mean to launch Black feminist politics from the starting point that there is no *returning* to an unproblematic relationship with the body because to have a body is often to feel conflicted?" See Jennifer C. Nash, "Black Feminist Self-Help: Or Notes on the Genres of Contemporary Black Feminist Political Life," *Signs: Journal of Women in Culture and Society* 49, no. 3 (2024): 565–566, emphasis in original.

59 Lauren Berlant, *Cruel Optimism* (Duke University Press, 2011), 2.

60 See Goodman, *Sonic Warfare*, xiii–xiv.

61 Goodman, however, issues a valuable critique of the "typical limits to a politicized discussion of the sonic," which tend to either "cash out pragmatically, on the one hand, in the moralized, reactionary policing of the polluted soundscape, or, on the other, its supposed enhancement by all manner of cacophony." Goodman's book explicitly "refuses both of these options." I see Goodman's critique here as, in part, about the study of sound as a set of "arbitrary fetishizations"—in other words, the tendency to study sound as metaphor rather than material phenomenon with a "physicality," a history, and a "vibrational force." Though my study dwells with the social and political meanings that get attached to Caribbean sound, I, too, am invested in the historical and political contexts in which sounds take on meaning. I am also interested in the physicality of sound, though perhaps against the grain of Goodman's emphasis on the uses of sound to induce terror: I attend more often to the declared pleasures that Caribbean people and artists tend to take in sounds that are otherwise cast as exhausting, harmful, and otherwise incompatible with a peaceful, serene, and therefore "good" life.

62 Henriques, *Sonic Bodies*, xvii.
63 I am grateful to Faith Smith for her valuable comments on an earlier draft of this manuscript and for offering me the language of "claiming the world anyway" in spite of surveillance and hyper-policing.
64 George Lamming, *Sovereignty of the Imagination: Conversations III* (House of Nehesi, 2009).
65 Aliyyah Abdur-Rahman, "The Black Ecstatic," *GLQ: A Journal of Lesbian and Gay Studies* 24, no. 2–3 (2018): 343–365.
66 Mecca Jamilah Sullivan, "Pedagogies of the 'Irresistible': Imaginative Elsewheres of Black Feminist Learning," *Journal of Feminist Scholarship* 20 (2022): 1–18. Sullivan also includes in this piece an elegant discussion of what she describes as "blackgirl sensorium and interiority" as a vital critical lens for navigating antiblack demands for "presentability," "the impossible burden of representation, and the pain of hypervisible 'wrongness.'"
67 Sara Ahmed, *Living a Feminist Life* (Duke University Press, 2017), 21.
68 Harewood, "Listening for Noise," 109.
69 Petal Samuel, "Black Gravity, or a Hidden History of Empire," *Differences* 35, no. 2 (2024): 139.
70 June Jordan, "Report from the Bahamas, 1982," *Meridians* 3, no. 2 (2003): 8.
71 Jordan, "Report from the Bahamas," 6.
72 As Thompson discusses in her work on "tropicalization": "This region [the Caribbean] receives the greatest intensity of direct sunlight on the planet. Tropicalization then appropriately draws attention to light in the geography of the Caribbean and, by extension, vision and visual representation in the imaginative geography of the islands." See Thompson, *Eye for the Tropics*, 6.
73 *Oxford English Dictionary*, s.v. "colorful (*adj.*)," accessed June 17, 2025, https://www.oed.com/dictionary/colourful_adj?tab=meaning_and_use#8932166; *New Oxford American Dictionary*, s.v. "colorful (*adj.*)," accessed June 17, 2025, https://www-oxfordreference-com.libproxy.lib.unc.edu/display/10.1093/acref/9780195392883.001.0001/m_en_us1234553?rskey=BIKPLO&result=1.
74 Jordan, "Report from the Bahamas," 7.
75 Jordan, "Report from the Bahamas," 7.
76 Another Caribbean feminist writer famous for prompting inquiries into the possibilities and perils of sensation is Audre Lorde. Lorde remarks, in the opening frames of Dagmar Schultz's *Audre Lorde: The Berlin Years 1984–1992*, "Poetry is the most subversive use of language that there is because it attempts to bring about change by altering people's feelings." Lorde is perhaps the most famous Black feminist theorist of feeling as a "resource"—as a source of "power which rises from our deepest and nonrational knowledge." For this reason, Lorde has been read by many Black feminist scholars as a theorist of the sensorium. See Dagmar Schultz, dir., *Audre Lorde: The Berlin Years 1984–1992* (Third World Newsreel, 2012); and Lorde, "Uses of the Erotic: The Erotic as Power," in *Sister Outsider: Essays and Speeches* (Crossing Press, 1984), 53.
77 Patricia Hill Collins, "Mammies, Matriarchs, and Other Controlling Images," in *Black Feminist Thought: Knowledge, Consciousness, and the Politics of Empowerment*, 2nd ed. (Routledge, 2000), 69.
78 Jennifer Stoever, *The Sonic Color Line: Race and the Cultural Politics of Listening* (New York University Press, 2016), 4.
79 Quashie, *Sovereignty of Quiet*, 3.

80 A key feature of the Sapphire trope, "loudness" appears as one among a long string of pejorative descriptors of Black femininity that is "nagging, assertive," "brash, independent, hostile," masculine and "emasculating," invulnerable and unempathetic. See Melissa Harris-Perry, *Sister Citizen: Shame, Stereotypes, and Black Women in America* (Yale University Press, 2011), 88.

81 Meina Yates-Richard, "'What is Your Mother's Name?': Maternal Disavowal and the Reverberating Aesthetic of Black Women's Pain in Black Nationalist Literature," *American Literature* 88, no. 3 (2016): 478.

82 Stoever, *Sonic Color Line*, 2; Mendi Obadike, "Low Fidelity: Stereotyped Blackness in the Field of Sound" (PhD diss., Duke University, 2005), 21, ProQuest (3179330).

83 Farah Jasmine Griffin, "When Malindy Sings: A Meditation of Black Women's Vocality," in *Uptown Conversation: The New Jazz Studies Reader*, ed. Robert O'Meally, Brent Hayes Edwards, and Farah Jasmine Griffin (Columbia University Press, 2004), 104.

84 Brooks, *Liner Notes*, 4.

85 Belinda Edmondson, *Making Men: Gender, Literary Authority, and Women's Writing in Caribbean Narrative* (Duke University Press, 1999), 8, emphasis in original.

86 Maryse Condé, "Order, Disorder, Freedom, and the West Indian Writer," *Yale French Studies* 97 (2000): 158.

87 Edmondson, *Making Men*, 159.

88 For more, see Obadike's insightful elaboration of "mythic blackness," which distinguishes Blackness as cultural, visual, or historical phenomenon, from those invocations of Blackness which reference a set of "mythical qualities"—and a set of ideas about fundamental difference—which "function mostly to provide a contrast to whiteness." See Obadike, "Low Fidelity," 14.

89 Jennifer Nash, "Pleasurable Blackness," in *The Palgrave Handbook of Sexuality Education*, ed. Luisa Allen and Mary Lou Rasmussen (Palgrave Macmillan London, 2017), 262.

90 Makeda Silvera, "Man Royals and Sodomites: Some Thoughts on the Invisibility of Afro Caribbean Lesbians," *Feminist Studies* 18, no. 3 (1992): 526.

91 Silvera, "Man Royals and Sodomites," 529.

92 Kaiama Glover, *A Regarded Self: Caribbean Womanhood and the Ethics of Disorderly Being* (Duke University Press, 2021), 1.

93 I am indebted to Aliyyah Abdur-Rahman, "Black Ecstatic," Christina Sharpe's *In the Wake: On Blackness and Being* (Duke University Press, 2016); and Kevin Quashie's *Black Aliveness, or A Poetics of Being* (Duke University Press, 2021) for their calls for us to attend to the ways marginalized communities create livable worlds in the "ruinous now," rather than suspending such possibilities indefinitely into the future.

94 For example, Krista Thompson's *Shine*, which moves between the United States, Jamaica, and the Bahamas, uses both "circum-Caribbean" and "African diasporic" to describe the scope of her work. Giselle Liza Anatol, in her work *The Things That Fly in the Night*, similarly uses "circum-Caribbean" and "African diaspora" in concert. See Krista Thompson, *Shine: The Visual Economy of Light in the African Diasporic Aesthetic Practice* (Duke University Press, 2015); and Giselle Liza Anatol, *The Things That Fly in the Night: Female Vampires in Literature of the Circum-Caribbean and African Diaspora* (Rutgers University Press, 2015).

95 Thompson, *Shine*, 3.
96 Thompson, *Shine*, 3.
97 Rosamond King, *Island Bodies: Transgressive Sexualities in the Caribbean Region* (University Press of Florida, 2014), 3–4.
98 Kei Miller, "The Broken (II): V," in *There Is an Anger That Moves* (Carcanet Press, 2007), 49.
99 Kaiama Glover, Erna Brodber, and Nicole Dennis-Benn, "Critical Caribbean Feminisms: Erna Brodber and Nicole Dennis-Benn," reading, New York, NY, October 9, 2018, posted November 28, 2018, by Barnard Center for Research on Women, YouTube, 1 hr., 23 min., 20 sec., https://www.youtube.com/watch?v=DqWJ3WemXL8&t=2297s, 1:01:10–1:01:58.
100 Petal Samuel and Erna Brodber, "Put Your Bucket Down," *SX Salon* 19 (2015), http://smallaxe.net/sxsalon/interviews/put-your-bucket-down.
101 PennSound, "Introduction" and "Opening Remarks," Segue Series Reading at the Bowery Poetry Club, February 17, 2007, https://writing.upenn.edu/pennsound/x/Philip.php.
102 Rinaldo Walcott, "'Inner Plantation': Caribbean Studies, Black Studies, and a Black Theory of Freedom," *Small Axe* 25, no. 3 (2021): 116–117.
103 Obadike, *Low Fidelity*, iv.
104 Obadike, *Low Fidelity*, iv.
105 Peter James Hudson, *Bankers and Empire: How Wall Street Colonized the Caribbean* (University of Chicago Press, 2017), 12.
106 Ashon Crawley, *Blackpentecostal Breath: The Aesthetics of Possibility* (Fordham University Press, 2016).

Chapter 1 Resonance

1 David V. Trotman, "Spectacle and the Colonial Imagination: Performances of White Power in Trinidad," *Caribbean Quarterly* 68, no. 4 (2002): 490, 496.
2 See M. NourbeSe Philip, "Fugues, Fragments and Fissures—A Work in Progress," *Anthurium* 3, no. 2 (2005): 6; M. NourbeSe Philip, "Dragon Come Down, Dove Gorn Up: The Poetics of Silence and the Unvoiced," in *A Genealogy of Resistance: And Other Essays* (Mercury Press, 1997), 178; Jamaica Kincaid, *Lucy* (Farrar, Straus and Giroux, 2002), 135; Andrea Levy, "This Is My England," *Guardian*, February 18, 2000, https://www.theguardian.com/books/2000/feb/19/society1; and Stella Dadzie, "The Complicated Resistance Efforts of Enslaved Women in the West Indies," Literary Hub, October 20, 2020, https://lithub.com/the-complicated-resistance-efforts-of-enslaved-women-in-the-west-indies/. The protagonist of Kincaid's *Lucy* refuses to sing the song in choir practice, noting, "I was not a Briton and [. . .] until not too long ago I would have been a slave."
3 Michelle Cliff, "Caliban's Daughter: The Tempest and the Teapot," *Frontiers: A Journal of Women Studies* 12, no. 2 (1991): 36.
4 Cliff, "Caliban's Daughter," 37. The debate about the symbolic violence wrought through the act of collectively singing colonial anthems resurfaced some sixty years later around the organizing of the 2020 Henry Wood Promenade Concerts (or the "Proms"), an annual classical music summer concert series in London. Controversy arose around the last night of the Proms, the second half of which is typically reserved for performances and singalongs of British patriotic anthems, including the aforementioned "Rule, Britannia." Following a summer of protests

against antiblack police violence, the BBC opted instead to air an instrumental version of the song, citing anxiety about the song's "perceived association with colonialism and slavery." Prime Minister Boris Johnson condemned the decision, complaining, "I think it's time we stopped our cringing embarrassment about our history, about our traditions, and about our culture, and we stopped this general fight of self-recrimination and wetness." Stephen Bell, a musical director, defiantly organized a crowd of hundreds of people to sing "Rule, Britannia," lyrics and all. "I've never set up a Facebook group so fast because that was driven by emotion," he declared. "No, don't take our words away from us." Johnson and Bell both deploy the very same colonial rhetorical strategy that we see in the archives, invoking an embattled white British collective whose history, traditions, culture, and words are under attack. Others, such as Black studies professor Kehinde Andrews, were stunned by the ardor of the backlash: "If dropping racist propaganda from taxpayer-funded TV is controversial, then there is no hope for the serious work that needs to be done to address racism." Andrews also noted in an appearance on Good Morning Britain that his school had removed "Rule, Britannia!" from the hymn sheet twenty years ago "because they realized it was totally inappropriate and offensive" and that the real shame was that the nation as a whole was only beginning to have this conversation in 2020. See Jim Waterson, "Proms Row: Johnson Calls for End to 'Cringing Embarrassment' over UK History," *Guardian*, August 25, 2020, https://www.theguardian.com/music/2020/aug/25/boris-johnson-scolds-bbc-over-suggestion-proms-would-drop-rule-britannia; Frank Langfitt, "A Row Erupts in Britain over 'Rule, Britannia!' at the Proms," NPR, September 11, 2020, https://www.npr.org/2020/09/11/912045003/a-row-erupts-in-britain-over-rule-britannia-at-the-proms; Kehinde Andrews (@kehinde_andrews), "If dropping racist propaganda from taxpayer funded TV is 'controversial' then there is no hope for the serious work that needs to be done to address racism," Twitter (now X), August 24, 2020, https://x.com/kehinde_andrews/status/1297795554399981568; see also "Is the Song 'Rule Britannia!' Racist? | Good Morning Britain," posted August 24, 2020, by Good Morning Britain, YouTube, 8 min., 31 sec., https://youtu.be/4lYwwNrUmcc?si=Ua-M2B4nRB065waw.

5 Cliff, "Caliban's Daughter," 36.

6 Cliff, "Caliban's Daughter," 36.

7 Cliff, "Caliban's Daughter," 36.

8 *Oxford English Dictionary*, s.v. "resonate (*v.*)," accessed July 18, 2025, https://www.oed.com/dictionary/resonate_v?tab=meaning_and_use#25658265.

9 *Oxford English Dictionary*.

10 Emily Lordi, *Black Resonance: Iconic Women Singers and African American Literature* (Rutgers University Press, 2013), 6.

11 "Most Disgraceful!," *Daily Gleaner*, March 8, 1934.

12 "Most Disgraceful!"

13 See, for example, the 1828 Slave Law of Jamaica, which contained provisions targeting Black sound: "And be it further enacted, by the authority aforesaid, That if any master, owner, guardian, possessor, or attorney, overseer, or book-keeper, of any plantation or settlement, shall hereafter suffer any strange slaves to assemble together and beat their drums, or blow their horns or shells, upon any plantation, pen, or settlement, or in any yard or place under his, her, or their care or management, or shall not endeavour to disperse or prevent the same, by immediately

giving notice thereof to the next magistrate or commissioned officer, that a proper force may be sent to disperse said slaves." *Slave Law of Jamaica: With Proceedings and Documents Relative Thereto* (James Ridgway, 1828), 19.

14 "Most Disgraceful!"

15 "Most Disgraceful!"

16 Cliff, in an interview with Meryl Schwartz, described herself as belonging to a transnational community of "political novelists" including writers like Angela Carter, Arturo Islas, Luisa Valenzuela, Nawal El Saadawi, and Ama Ata Aidoo. "The community there wasn't limited to Caribbean or African or Latin American or whatever," Cliff remarked, "it was a community of political novelists. And I see myself much more in that category. We're writing out of different origins, perhaps, but we have a lot of the same interests." When Schwartz asked Cliff if her "concept of affiliation" was "based on political allegiance rather than origins," Cliff offered an important correction: "Political enthusiasms." It mattered deeply to Cliff that her chosen relationship to place and politics revolve not around ideas of loyalty or devotion (nationalism's privileged register) but rather around eager curiosity, intensity of feeling, and enjoyment. See Meryl F. Schwartz, "An Interview with Michelle Cliff," *Contemporary Literature* 34, no. 4 (1993): 597–598.

17 Michelle Cliff, "Notes on Speechlessness," *Sinister Wisdom: A Journal of Words and Pictures for the Lesbian Imagination in All Women* 5 (1978): 7.

18 Cliff, "Notes on Speechlessness," 7.

19 Opal Palmer Adisa, "Journey into Speech—A Writer Between Two Worlds: An Interview with Michelle Cliff," *African American Review* 28, no. 2 (1994): 273.

20 Schwartz, "Interview with Michelle Cliff," 603.

21 Cliff, "Notes on Speechlessness," 8–9.

22 Cliff, "Notes on Speechlessness," 6, 9.

23 Adisa, "Journey into Speech," 274.

24 Allen underscores that "the anthology—not the academic journal, single-authored academic or trade book, or press-mediated reader—became the major repository of Black political philosophy of the long 1980s. In this anthological tradition the editor is not a single author or even necessarily the most important. She is, rather, a sort of arbiter, consensus builder, keen observer, and laborer—as well as shaper of discourse. . . . In the anthological tradition a collection purposefully makes a multivocal statement of the political and aesthetic commitments of a group of artists and/or scholars engaged in what they—or at least the editor—believe is a collective (that is, not necessarily 'unified' but rather harmonious) project." See Jafari Allen, *There's a Disco Ball Between Us: A Theory of Black Gay Life* (Duke University Press, 2022), 9.

25 It should be noted though that Cliff's inclusion in these anthologies was occasionally controversial. In the introduction to *Her True-True Name*, the editors Pamela Mordecai and Betty Wilson remark about Cliff: "The only one of the recently published Caribbean writers who does not affirm at least aspects of being in the Caribbean place is Michelle Cliff, who along with [Jean] Rhys could be regarded more in the alienated tradition of a 'francophone' than an anglophone consciousness. Personal history perhaps provides important clues: like Rhys, who also felt isolated, Cliff is 'white'—or as light-skinned as makes, to the larger world, little difference. Also like Rhys, she went to the kind of school—quite comprehensively described in *No Telephone to Heaven*—which promoted the values of the metropole. Like Rhys, she left her island early and never really came home. One of the

prices she has paid is a compromised authenticity in some aspects of her rendering of the creole." More, the editors, draw links between Michelle Cliff and Mayotte Capécia—whose work they note was "harshly condemned by Fanon"—because of both writers' attention to themes of alienation. They assert that a key feature of the work of anglophone Caribbean women writers of the 1980s is that "There is no ritual pursuing of pseudo-feminist agendas; rather there is sufficient detachment to allow for women to make their novels male (Velma Pollard, for example), not through any mimetic impulse but deliberately, a part of the creative statement." And finally, they claim that women writers of the period, while acknowledging Caribbean "society's pretensions, foibles, failings, and fragmentations," still nevertheless "[affirm] the island place, its language, and its right to work out its salvation in fear and trembling." Cliff, then, while included in this anthology, is cast as inauthentic due to her color, her education, the fact of her migration to the United States, her deep investment in feminist artistic and political movements, and her rendering of themes of alienation from the region. (I would add that, though left unmentioned in the anthology, Cliff's queerness, too, likely rendered her an outsider in the eyes of her peers.) Cliff responded to these comments, which she called a "nasty swipe" and "just plain bitchy," in an 1993 interview with Meryl Schwartz, noting, "Most African-American people know somebody in their family who looks like me. There's a very wide spectrum of racial types. I think in Jamaica how one is perceived is not based just on skin color, but on property and privilege, and if people see somebody like me, they assume my alliance is with the colonizer. That is the usual assumption. So that they could make that kind of remark, even having read *No Telephone to Heaven*. They could still seem to assume that my alliance would be with the colonizer." See Pam Mordecai and Betty Wilson, "Introduction," in *Her True-True Name: An Anthology of Women's Writing from the Caribbean*, ed. Pamela Mordecai and Betty Wilson (Heinemann International, 1989), xvii–xviii. Also see Schwartz, "Interview with Michelle Cliff," 607–608. For the other anthologies listed above, see: Carole Boyce Davies and Elaine Savory Fido, eds., *Out of the Kumbla: Caribbean Women and Literature* (Africa World Press, 1990); Evelyn O'Callaghan, *Woman Version: Theoretical Approaches to West Indian Fiction by Women* (St. Martin's Press, 1993); Myriam J. A. Chancy, *Searching for Safe Spaces: Afro-Caribbean Women Writers in Exile* (Temple University Press, 1997); Belinda Edmondson, *Making Men: Gender, Literary Authority, and Women's Writing in Caribbean Narrative* (Duke University Press, 1999).

26 See Barbara Smith, ed., *Home Girls: A Black Feminist Anthology* (Rutgers University Press, 2000); Gloria Anzaldúa, *Making Face, Making Soul/Haciendo Caras: Creative and Critical Perspectives by Feminists of Color* (Aunt Lute Books, 1990).

27 Schwartz, "Interview with Michelle Cliff," 597.

28 Michelle Cliff, "Love in the Third World," in *The Land of Look Behind: Prose and Poetry* (Firebrand Books, 1985), 103.

29 Cliff, "Love in the Third World," 103.

30 Matthew Chin's analysis of the formation of the Gay Freedom Movement (GFM) in Jamaica has been vital for challenging "the contemporary positioning of Jamaica in terms of homophobic essentialism" and the erasure of Jamaica from "transnational histories of activism around same-sex desire." "It is curious," Chin astutely points out, "that groups like Amnesty International now call for an end to

Jamaican homophobia, when a historical perspective reveals that the same organization contacted GFM decades earlier seeking advice as to whether it should seriously consider persecution on the basis of sexual orientation an issue worth its attention." See Matthew Chin, "Tracing 'Gay Liberation' Through Postindependence Jamaica," *Public Culture* 31, no. 2 (2019): 323, 334–335.

31 Of the ways quests for Caribbean authenticity have historically been gendered, Edmondson writes, "The impulse to return to 'real' Caribbean culture can be linked to a larger thematic of 're-masculinization,' if you will, of the Caribbean space, that occurs in Caribbean narrative. If, as we have seen, the marking of the Caribbean through ownership and 'taming' of the land was identified in European discourse as a specifically masculine enterprise that in turn defined European masculinity, then the institution of a specifically Caribbean agency which could 'mark' the land was also conceived of, explicitly and implicitly, as a competing 'masculine' enterprise." See Edmondson, *Making Men*, 60.

32 I am deeply indebted to Faith Smith for the language of "claiming the world anyway" and thank her for her generous and encouraging engagements with my work in its draft stages.

33 Kara Keeling, *The Witch's Flight: The Cinematic, the Black Femme, and the Image of Common Sense* (Duke University Press, 2007), 21–22.

34 "A Check Needed," *Daily Gleaner*, February 28, 1934.

35 "Hell Begins Again," *Jamaica Gleaner*, March 21, 1934.

36 As Hilary Beckles writes, "The many slave revolts and plots in [the British West Indies] between 1638 and 1838 could be conceived of as the '200 Years' War'—one protracted struggle launched by Africans and their Afro-West Indian progeny against slave owners. Such endemic anti-slavery activity represented, furthermore, the most immediately striking characteristic of the West Indian world." See Hilary Beckles, "Caribbean Anti-Slavery: The Self-Liberation Ethos of Enslaved Blacks," *Journal of Caribbean History* 22, no. 1 (1988): 1.

37 Jamaica Kincaid, *A Small Place* (Farrar, Straus and Giroux, 1988), 32.

38 Henry Bleby, *The Reign of Terror: A Narrative of the Facts Concerning Ex-Governor Eyre, George William Gordon, and the Jamaica Atrocities* (W. Nichols, 1868).

39 Priyamvada Gopal explains the disparity in Eyre's account of the rebellion and what historical records actually show: "Within three days the outbreak had been completely suppressed, the troops apparently meeting with little resistance. Martial law was nevertheless declared in the whole county of Surrey. . . . Over the next several days, as troops rampaged through the eastern portion of the island, hundreds of actual and presumed rebels were summarily shot, while others were executed after cursory military trials. Additionally, over 600 men and women, many of whom had nothing to do with the uprising, were subjected to brutal floggings, and some thousand dwellings were burned to the ground in what would later be described by a Royal Commission of Inquiry as a 'wanton and cruel' manner." Priyamvada Gopal, *Insurgent Empire: Anticolonial Resistance and British Dissent* (Verso, 2019), 91. Also see Gad Heuman, *The Killing Time: The Morant Bay Rebellion in Jamaica* (University of Tennessee Press, 1994).

40 Despatches from Governor Eyre, no. 1, October 20, 1865, pg. 7.

41 Despatches from Governor Eyre, no. 1, October 20, 1865, pg. 1.

42 Despatches from Governor Eyre, no. 1, October 20, 1865, pg. 3.

43 Heuman, *Killing Time*, 172.

44 Gopal, *Insurgent Empire*, 112.

45 Michelle Cliff, *Abeng* (Plume, 1995), 31.

46 Some of this erasure had to do with labor leaders' reluctance to recognize domestic labor as unionizable. As Colin Palmer explains, "In spite of their numerical strength, these women were ignored entirely by [Allan George St. Claver] Coombs, [Alexander] Bustamante, and the other labor leaders. Some of them probably employed women in their households as domestic servants. . . . Domestic work was deemed to be unimportant and lacking in social prestige. The union may have thought that the relationship between employers and domestics was so intimate that it was beyond the purview and scrutiny of any organization of workers. Fearing reprisals from their employers, domestics may also have been unwilling to be unionized. It was undeniable, however, that many of these women worked under the most appalling conditions, laboring from sunup to sundown and frequently much later." Colin Palmer, *Freedom's Children: The 1938 Labor Rebellion and the Birth of Modern Jamaica* (University of North Carolina Press, 2014), 128.

47 Diana Paton, *The Cultural Politics of Obeah: Religion, Colonialism, and Modernity in the Caribbean World* (Cambridge University Press, 2015), 1. By placing the West and the Caribbean in quotations here, Paton is referencing Haitian historian and anthropologist Michel-Rolph Trouillot's famous critique of the West as an imaginative project and "default category" that "operates only in opposition to the populations that it marks." See Michel-Rolph Trouillot, *Global Transformations: Anthropology and the Modern World* (Palgrave Macmillan, 2003), 2.

48 Trouillot, *Global Transformations*, 3.

49 Here, I invoke "common sense"—as it is attached to both sensory rationalism and minor offense complaints generally—in conversation with Stuart Hall's and Alan O'Shea's usage, as well as Kara Keeling's. (All of these writers are themselves in conversation with Antonio Gramsci's meditations on common sense in his *Prison Notebooks*.) As Hall and O'Shea explain, "But what exactly is common sense? It is a form of 'everyday thinking' which offers us frameworks of meaning with which to make sense of the world. It is a form of popular, easily-available knowledge which contains no complicated ideas, requires no sophisticated argument and does not depend on deep thought or wide reading. It works intuitively, without forethought or reflection. It is pragmatic and empirical, giving the illusion of arising directly from experience, reflecting only the realities of daily life and answering the needs of the 'common people' for practical guidance and advice." I am also guided by Keeling's insights into common sense, which emphasize that dominant commonsense regimes are themselves under "strain" and shot through with "vulnerabilities." Keeling explains,

> While much of Gramsci's attention and, consequently, much of the attention of his readers (including myself) focuses on the common sense of subaltern or marginalized and oppressed groups, dominant groups operate according to common sense as well. Their conception of the world provides the official common sense of a society, one that garners the spontaneous consent of many subaltern groups. Like subaltern common sense, "official common sense" contains elements "borrowed" (or, more likely, stolen or appropriated) from other groups, particularly those exploited by the dominant group. These "appropriated" elements provide a record of concessions made in the struggle for hegemony and a strain within official common sense that renders it vulnerable to further transformations.

See Stuart Hall and Alan O'Shea, "Common-Sense Neoliberalism," *Soundings: A Journal of Politics and Culture*, 55 (2013): 8–24; and Keeling, *Witch's Flight*, 21.

50 See, for example, Cooper, *Noises in the Blood*; Carolyn Cooper, *Sound Clash: Jamaican Dancehall Culture at Large* (Palgrave Macmillan, 2004); Julian Henriques, *Sonic Bodies: Reggae Sound Systems, Performance Techniques, and Ways of Knowing* (London: Bloomsbury, 2011); Alexandra T. Vazquez, *Listening in Detail: Performances of Cuban Music* (Duke University Press, 2013); Tsitsi Jaji, *Africa in Stereo: Modernism, Music, and Pan-African Solidarity* (Oxford University Press, 2014); Michael Veal, *Dub: Soundscapes and Shattered Songs in Jamaican Reggae* (Wesleyan University Press, 2007); Édouard Glissant, "Free and Forced Poetics," *Alcheringa/Ethnopoetics: A First International Symposium* 2 (1976): 95–101.

51 See for example Edwin C. Hill Jr., *Black Soundscapes, White Stages: The Meaning of Francophone Sound in the Black Atlantic* (Johns Hopkins University Press, 2013); Alejandra Bronfman, *Isles of Noise: Sonic Media in the Caribbean* (University of North Carolina Press, 2016).

52 Aaron Kamugisha, *Beyond Coloniality: Citizenship and Freedom in the Caribbean Intellectual Tradition* (Indiana University Press, 2019).

53 Mariame Kaba, "Yes, We Mean Literally Abolish the Police," *New York Times*, June 12, 2020, https://www.nytimes.com/2020/06/12/opinion/sunday/floyd-abolish-defund-police.html.

54 "Check Needed."

55 "Check Needed."

56 "Check Needed."

57 "Check Needed."

58 Kamala Kempadoo, "Continuities and Change: Five Centuries of Prostitution in the Caribbean," in *Sun, Sex, and Gold: Tourism and Sex Work in the Caribbean*, ed. Kamala Kempadoo (Rowman & Littlefield, 1999), 10. The irony, of course, that Kempadoo and other scholars in this collection highlight—contrary to the narrative of contagion—is that sex workers are far more fastidious about sexual hygiene than their clients. Sex workers' clients are far more likely to be vectors of disease (knowingly or unknowingly), due in part to the arbitrary belief that their gender, class, sexual, or racial privilege—and sometimes their marital status—somehow protect them from contracting or spreading disease.

59 "Check Needed."

60 Hilary Beckles, "White Women and Slavery in the Caribbean," *History Workshop Journal* 36, no. 1 (1993): 71–72.

61 Yasmin Tambieh, "Threatening Sexual (Mis)Behavior: Homosexuality in the Penal Code Debates in Trinidad and Tobago, 1986," in *Sex and the Citizen: Interrogating the Caribbean, ed. Faith Smith* (University of Virginia Press, 2011), 144.

62 Kempadoo, "Continuities and Change," 11.

63 Tao Leigh Goffe, "Bigger Than the Sound: The Jamaican Chinese Infrastructures of Reggae," *Small Axe* 63 (2020): 98.

64 "Check Needed."

65 "Check Needed."

66 Obika Gray, "The Coloniality of Power and the Limits of Dissent in Jamaica," *Small Axe* 54 (2017): 99.

67 Janeille Zarina Matthews and Tracy Robinson, "Modern Vagrancy in the Anglophone Caribbean," *Caribbean Journal of Criminology* 1, no. 4 (2019): 123.
68 Matthews and Robinson, "Modern Vagrancy," 123.
69 Matthews and Robinson, "Modern Vagrancy," 126, emphasis in original.
70 Ruth Wilson Gilmore, "Public Enemies and Private Intellectuals: Apartheid USA," *Race and Class* 35, no. 1 (1993): 74.
71 Gilmore, "Public Enemies," 74.
72 Matthews and Robinson, "Modern Vagrancy," 128.
73 Cliff, *Abeng*, 36–37.
74 Cliff, *Abeng*, 37.
75 Schwartz, "Interview with Michelle Cliff," 617.
76 Here, I reference Laurent Berlant's distinction between a "situation" and an "event." Berlant writes, "The police conventionally say: 'We have a situation here.' A situation is a state of things in which *something* that will perhaps matter is unfolding amid the usual activity of life. It is a state of animated and animating suspension that forces itself on consciousness, that produces a sense of the emergence of something in the present that may become an event [. . .] The situation is therefore a genre of social time and practice in which a relation of persons and worlds is sensed to be changing but the rules for habitation and the genres of storytelling about it are unstable, in chaos." See Lauren Berlant, *Cruel Optimism* (Duke University Press, 2011), 5.
77 Riffing on Deleuze's concept of "perturbation," Berlant underscores that "situations" carry the potential to "[release] subjects from the normativity of intuition and [make] them available for alternative ordinaries." Also see Kara Keeling's lyrical and pathbreaking analysis of common sense, where Keeling writes, "There is not just one common sense, but various common senses—as many as there are groups of living beings with brains. I pay attention to black common sense and, later, to butch-femme common sense in an attempt to reveal where these conceptions of the world and the modes of sensory-motor habituation through which they are supported and expressed harbor viable alternatives to white bourgeoisie North American common sense." See Berlant, *Cruel Optimism*, 6. Also see Gilles Deleuze, *The Logic of Sense*, ed. Constantin V. Boundas, trans. Mark Lester and Charles Stivale (Columbia University Press, 1990); and Keeling, *Witch's Flight*, 21.
78 Michelle Cliff, "Colonial Girl, and What It Would Be Like," in Smith, *Sex and the Citizen*, 251.
79 Cliff, "Colonial Girl," 254.
80 Cliff, "Colonial Girl," 254.
81 Cliff, "Colonial Girl," 253–254.
82 Cliff, "Colonial Girl," 254.
83 Makeda Silvera, "Man Royales and Sodomites: Some Thoughts in the Invisibility of Afro-Caribbean Lesbians," *Feminist Studies* 18, no. 3 (1992): 522–523.
84 Cliff, *Abeng*, 3.
85 See Gerald Horne, *The Dawning of the Apocalypse: The Roots of Slavery, White Supremacy, Settler Colonialism, and Capitalism in the Long Sixteenth Century* (Monthly Review Press, 2020).
86 Michelle Cliff, *Free Enterprise: A Novel of Mary Ellen Pleasant* (City Lights, 2004), 123.
87 Cliff, *Free Enterprise*, 123.
88 Kamugisha, *Beyond Coloniality*, 3.

89 "Why Abeng," *Abeng*, February 1, 1969.
90 Cliff, *Abeng*, 29.
91 Cliff, *Abeng*, 23.
92 Edmondson, *Making Men*, 133.
93 Cliff, *Abeng*, 6.
94 Cliff, *Abeng*, 6.
95 Cliff, *Abeng*, 6.
96 Cliff, *Abeng*, 97.
97 Michelle Cliff, *If I Could Write This in Fire* (University of Minnesota Press, 2008), 14.
98 Cliff, *Abeng*, 99.
99 Cliff, *No Telephone to Heaven*, 137.
100 Cliff, *No Telephone to Heaven*, 137.
101 Cliff, *No Telephone to Heaven*, 137.
102 Cliff, *No Telephone to Heaven*, 137.
103 Cliff, *No Telephone to Heaven*, 139.
104 Cliff, *No Telephone to Heaven*, 139.
105 Cliff, *No Telephone to Heaven*, 189.
106 Cliff, *No Telephone to Heaven*, 207–208.
107 Michelle Cliff, "Caliban's Daughter: The Tempest and the Teapot," *Frontiers: A Journal of Women Studies* 12, no. 2 (1991): 45–46.

Chapter 2 Aural Privacy

1 Here, I reference "Brown" in its particularity as a color and class category in Jamaica. As Deborah Thomas explains, "brownness" can be understood as "an intermediary color and class construction that is linked historically with the population of free people of color that emerged during the slavery period. . . . 'Brown' is as much a way of life as it is a phenotype, however, as it signifies respectability or at least aspirations toward respectability. This is the segment of the national middle class most often associated with the creole multiracial nationalist project and with [. . .] values and visions of progress." Especially in the decades preceding and following independence—which saw the ascendency of a "'brown' middle-class leadership" class—brownness, for many, marked a set of moderate, respectable nationalist visions for Jamaica's future. Yet as Thomas explains, "The 'brown' middle classes, seen as having originated from the free colored offspring of plantation owners and their slave concubines, have always occupied a rather problematic structural position in relation to the majority of the population. As the class born in Jamaica, they have been seen as the most creole of Jamaicans (in the sense of being a 'new' social group, the result of the new socioeconomic conditions of plantation-based production) and [. . .] as exhibiting the greatest loyalty both to Jamaica and to Great Britain. . . . At the same time and for the same reasons, they have been viewed with suspicion due to the extent to which they have distanced themselves—materially and socially—from the insecurities faced by the majority of the population." See Deborah Thomas, *Modern Blackness: Nationalism, Globalization, and the Politics of Culture in Jamaica* (Duke University Press, 2004), 24, 51.
2 Claudia Gardner, "Sean Paul's Wife Jodi Jinx Dragged over 'Condescending' All-Inclusive Hotel Food Comment," *Dancehall Mag*, June 16, 2021, https://www

.dancehallmag.com/2021/06/16/news/sean-pauls-wife-jodi-jinx-dragged-over-condescending-all-inclusive-hotel-food-comment.html.

3 Caroline Graham, "Party-Mad Usain Bolt Is 'Neighbour from Hell': Model Wife of Rapper Sean Paul Slams Sprinter's Non-stop Noise—and Claims Jamaican Police Turn a Blind Eye Because He's a National Hero," *Daily Mail*, June 6, 2015, https://www.dailymail.co.uk/news/article-3113977/Model-wife-rapper-Sean-Paul-claims-suffered-Usain-Bolt-moved-door-two-years-ago.html.

4 I reference "stranger-neighbour" as it is proposed by Sara Ahmed as a way to describe the conundrum of living with those who are in one's (spatial, national, etc.) community but with whom one claims no commonality. Ahmed explains, "The other, then, the one whom I may not know, is always my neighbour, living by my side, living 'with' me. The other is the 'stranger-neighbour': she is distant in the sense that I cannot assume community or commonality with her, and yet she is close by, so that she will haunt me, stay with me, as a reminder of the unassimilable in my life, or that which cannot be assimilated into the 'my' of 'my life.' The pain of the other's nearness suggests that encountering the other opens the self to the world, an opening that touches the self, makes it feel: the self becomes an opening, a boundless space of torment, the tiredness of being by the other, and of being with and for that which is *not yet*." See Sara Ahmed, *Strange Encounters: Embodied Others in Post-Coloniality* (Routledge, 2000), 37, 138, emphasis in original.

5 Kei Miller, *Things I Have Withheld: Essays* (Grove Press, 2021), 29.

6 Carolyn Cooper, "Sound Clash in Uptown Ghetto," *Gleaner*, June 12, 2015, https://jamaica-gleaner.com/article/commentary/20150614/sound-clash-uptown-ghetto.

7 Cooper, "Sound Clash."

8 Jodi "Jinx" Henriques, "Letter of the Day: Jinx—I Should Never Have Dissed Bolt," *Gleaner*, June 2, 2015, https://web5.jamaica-gleaner.com/article/letters/20150603/letter-day-jinx-i-should-never-have-dissed-bolt.

9 Belinda Edmondson, "Public Spectacles: Caribbean Women and the Politics of Public Performance," *Small Axe* 7, no. 1 (2003): 4–5.

10 Jovan Johnson, "Usain Bolt Beating Classism and Racism in Jamaica," *Gleaner*, January 25, 2016, https://jamaica-gleaner.com/article/news/20160125/usain-bolt-beating-classism-and-racism-jamaica.

11 Gardner, "Sean Paul's Wife."

12 Gardner, "Sean Paul's Wife."

13 Justin Mann brilliantly analyzes the ways vigilantism appears as an expression of what he terms "security imaginaries": "Security imaginaries relate and translate imagined sources of insecurity as they exist in culture and discourse into real world manifestations of security policy and practice." For more see, Justin Mann, *Breaking the World: Blackness and Insecurity After the New World Order* (Duke University Press, 2025); and Justin Mann, "The Vigilante Spirit: Bernhard Goetz, Batman, and Racial Violence in 1980s New York," *Surveillance and Society* 15, no. 1 (2017): 56–67.

14 *Oxford English Dictionary*, s.v. "privacy (*n.*)," accessed June 19, 2025, https://www.oed.com/dictionary/privacy_n.

15 I explore the link between Western notions of sonic etiquette and privacy in the Caribbean elsewhere in my work. See Petal Samuel, "The Sound of Luxury: Antiblackness, Silence, and the Private Island Resort," *Black Scholar* 51, no. 1 (2021): 30–42.

16 For more on this, see Steve Goodman, *Sonic Warfare*. He discusses, for example, the use of loud, unceasing heavy metal music as a torture tactic used against prisoners at Guantanamo Bay and the Israeli military practice of using low flying planes to break the barrier of sound over the Gaza strip as a tactic of sonic-psychological terror used against Palestinians.

17 On January 19, 2025, during his last day in office, the U.S. president Joe Biden issued a posthumous pardon to Garvey. Garvey's sons had long worked to secure a pardon for their father, including petitioning the Obama administration for a pardon, which was denied at the time.

18 This impulse to command overwhelming police force to respond to incidents of Black noise is not uncommon. See for instance the 2015 case of Sistahs on a Reading Edge, a Black women's book club, who were taking the Napa Valley Wine Train tour and were evicted midway through the tour because other passengers complained that they were laughing too loudly. They were, to their humiliation, escorted through six train cars before they were able to exit and were met by four armed officers upon disembarking. See Riya Bhattacharjee, "11 Women Kicked Off Napa Valley Wine Train for Laughing Too Loudly Settle Racial Discrimination Suit," NBC Bay Area, April 19, 2016, https://www.nbcbayarea.com/news/local/11-Women-Kicked-Off-Napa-Valley-Wine-Train-File-11M-Racial-Discrimination-Suit-376139281.html.

19 Talise D. Moorer, "Police 'Shakedowns' Send Tremors Through Community," *New York Amsterdam News*, July 26, 2007, quoted in Khadijah White, "Belongingness and the Harlem Drummers," *Urban Geography* 36, no. 3 (2015): 340–358.

20 White, "Belongingness," 349.

21 Timothy Williams, "An Old Sound in Harlem Draws New Neighbors' Ire," *New York Times*, July 6, 2008, http://www.nytimes.com/2008/07/06/nyregion/06drummers.html.

22 "A Drumbeat of Tension in Harlem," *New York Daily News*, August 12, 2007, https://www.nydailynews.com/2007/08/12/a-drumbeat-of-tension-in-harlem/.

23 Khadijah White richly and compellingly unpacks the four-hour limit as exemplary of the ways temporal control, aural control, noise, and the governance of public space operate in league: "Four hours becomes her established boundary for the drumming before it *becomes* noise. Thus, it is not the presence of the drummers or merely the noise of the drums that the woman underpins as her primary complaint—it is the time. Temporal control is a useful device, as it is a passive indicator that distinguishes what, or whom, is important within a space. Many parks close at night to prevent homeless people from sleeping in them—thus, a temporal constraint can be employed to effectively remove a member of the public from the public space. . . . Restrictions regarding noise can also be employed in the same ways, revealing different ideas about what is allowed in a space, undermined by the 'who' gets to set and establish codified norms. Time and sound are thus mutually dependent in constructing boundaries of an aural landscape—for while time is important because it allows for the presence of a certain public within a space, noise is integral because it establishes an aural public who is being addressed. . . . [T]he establishment of temporal and aural boundaries alludes to the deviant 'other' and functions to exclude those 'others' from a space, while embracing some individuals or groups who are deemed more important." See White, "Belongingness," 352, emphasis in original.

24 Williams, "Old Sound," my emphasis.

25 White, "Belongingness," 341.
26 White, however, also very compellingly points out that this is a double-edged sword. It also "endowed middle-class Blacks with a type of *gentrifier exceptionality* and allowed them to use 'counterclaims of racial communality' to justify their move to Harlem (and potential displacement of working-class minorities) (Jackson, 2006, p. 204)." White, "Belongingness," 347, emphasis in original.
27 Patricia J. Williams, *The Alchemy of Race and Rights: Diary of a Law Professor* (Harvard University Press, 1991), 28.
28 This is the same logic that energizes the reactionary response of "All lives matter" to the racial justice call of "Black lives matter." The former relies on obscuring the uneven distribution of racial violence against Black communities and instead reenvisions "all people" as equally vulnerable to structural violence. To do so, it must deploy the fiction that Black people are committing an initial assault by attempting to establish an alternative supremacy wherein Black lives matter *more* than all others. As such, it reenvisions the privileged subjects of rights and civil liberties as vulnerable to violation in precisely the way Black communities actually are.
29 Agnes Johnson, "In Marcus Garvey Park, Gentrifiers vs. Drummers," *Workers World*, July 26, 2007, https://www.workers.org/2007/us/drummers-0802/.
30 Verena Dobnik, "Drummers Clash with New Harlem Residents," *Washington Post*, August 11, 2007, http://www.washingtonpost.com/wp-dyn/content/article/2007/08/11/AR2007081100624_pf.html, quoted in White, "Belongingness."
31 Some of the news coverage of the case explicitly framed the co-op residents' complaints not only as engines of gentrification but as heirs of the U.S. domestic colonial project. One periodical, *Workers World* (the periodical of the Marxist-Leninist Workers World Party), explicitly described the case as an example of "the internal struggle the colonizers and colonized must face" and described the co-op residents as "plotters of gentrification or recolonization" seeking to "subjugate the African identity." The article closes by linking the case to the ban placed against singing the anthem "NKosi Sikelel'I Africa" in apartheid South Africa. This article's situation of the Harlem drummers' circle case within a broad transnational program of antiblack soundscape governance is precisely the kind of analytical move I seek to make in this manuscript. See Johnson, "In Marcus Garvey Park."
32 White expands on "belongingness" as a framework that "can both facilitate and resist the gentrification of an urban area." As such, she also uses racial belongingness to think through how new white middle- and upper-class residents of a gentrifying neighborhood deploy "urban cowboy" and "frontier imagery" as part of their claim to the neighborhood. I follow White's example of attending to the variety of ways claims to belonging—which are always at once spatial, aural, and temporal—can exceed property rights. However, I reframe the inquiry by dwelling on how privileged subjects deploy rights-based claims both by appropriating the ethical momentum of racial claims to rights while—and in order to—inhibit and deter analyses of racial, class, and national privilege that enable their claims. See White, "Belongingness," 341.
33 Brandon LaBelle, *Acoustic Territories: Sound Culture and Everyday Life* (Bloomsbury Academic, 2019), 36.
34 LaBelle, *Acoustic Territories*, 36.
35 LaBelle, *Acoustic Territories*, 38.
36 Noise Free America, "Videos," archived May 13, 2020, at https://web.archive.org/web/20200929145430/https://noisefree.org/videos/.

37 M. NourbeSe Philip, *Blank: Essays and Interviews* (Book*hug, 2017), 217.

38 TT Citizens Against Noise, "Are You Satisfied Living Like This?," archived November 26, 2023, at https://web.archive.org/web/20231126023459/trinbagocan.blogspot.com/2006/09/are-you-satisfied-living-like-this.html.

39 Neil Alexander, "How to Control Noise from Bars, Restaurants," *Trinidad and Tobago Guardian*, December 21, 2010, https://www.guardian.co.tt/article-6.2.463880.ff867c3831.

40 "Noise and Inconsideration Are Our Culture," *Trinidad and Tobago Guardian*, January 15, 2013, https://www.guardian.co.tt/article-6.2.393367.d3bc443d50.

41 TT Citizens Against Noise, "Are You Satisfied?"

42 Jonathan Sterne, in the context of the nineteenth- and twentieth-century United States, shows how the conversion of acoustic space into a form of private property was integral to the marketing of new sound technologies (such as the telephone, phonograph, and radio) and the production of what he calls "techniques of listening." He explains: "Acoustic space modeled on the form of private property allows for the commodification of sound. There needs to be a form of private property before there can be a commodity form—people must be able to own something before it can be bought and sold. Hearing tubes and audile technique construct an individualized, localized sound space, allowing the experience to be sold to a single individual." See Jonathan Sterne, *The Audible Past: Cultural Origins of Sound Reproduction* (Duke University Press, 2003), 162–163.

43 Hortense Spillers, "Mama's Baby, Papa's Maybe: An American Grammar Book," *Diacritics* 17, no. 2 (1987): 75.

44 M. Jacqui Alexander, *Pedagogies of Crossing: Meditations on Feminism, Sexual Politics, Memory, and the Sacred* (Duke University Press, 2005), 34, emphasis in original.

45 City of Vaughan (@City_of_Vaughan), "City of Vaughan By-law and Compliance, Licensing and Permit Service staff revoked the permit of the Carnival Kingdom 2018 SOS Fest event after it was determined that organizers did not comply with the terms of the permit.1/2," Twitter (now X), August 5, 2018, https://x.com/city_of_vaughan/status/1026181774597074944.

46 Anders Yates, "Caribana to be Replaced by 'Scotiabank Celebration of Noise Complaints,'" *Beaverton*, August 6, 2018, https://www.thebeaverton.com/2018/08/caribana-to-be-replaced-by-scotiabank-celebration-of-noise-complaints/.

47 M. NourbeSe Philip, "Black W/Holes: A History of Brief Time," in *For the Geography of a Soul: Emerging Perspectives on Kamau Brathwaite*, ed. Timothy J. Reiss (Africa World Press, 2001), 263.

48 Philip, "Black W/Holes," 263–264.

49 Philip, *Blank*, 18.

50 Philip, *Blank*, 211.

51 Environmental Management Authority, "2012 Annual Report," https://www.ema.co.tt/ema-legal/ema-annual-reports/, p. 136.

52 Environmental Management Authority, "2012 Annual Report," ii.

53 Environmental Management Authority, "2012 Annual Report," 136.

54 Environmental Management Authority, "2012 Annual Report," 136.

55 M. Jacqui Alexander, "Not Just (Any)Body Can Be a Citizen: The Politics of Law, Sexuality and Postcoloniality in Trinidad and Tobago and the Bahamas," *Feminist Review* no. 48 (1994): 5–6.

56 Alexander, "Not Just (Any)Body, 6.

57 Edmondson, *Creole Noise*, 10.
58 Edmondson, *Creole Noise*, 10.
59 Naylan Dwarika, "EMA Noise Campaign—Phase 1," posted January 30, 2012, YouTube, 30 sec., https://www.youtube.com/watch?v=kinlP3sSYbs.
60 Faith Smith, "Introduction: Sexing the Citizen," in Smith, *Sex and the Citizen*, 12–13.
61 Naylan Dwarika, "EMA Noise Campaign—Phase 2," posted January 30, 2012, YouTube, 30 sec., https://www.youtube.com/watch?v=QRlFeD2isfg.
62 Naylan Dwarika, "EMA Noise Campaign—Phase 3," posted January 30, 2012, YouTube, 30 sec., https://www.youtube.com/watch?v=yaUFoVZfRiE.
63 "Noise and Inconsideration."
64 Environmental Management Authority, "2012 Annual Report," 46.
65 Environmental Management Authority, "2012 Annual Report," 46.
66 "United Nations Conference on Environment and Development, Rio de Janeiro, Brazil, June 3–14, 1992," accessed June 19, 2025, https://www.un.org/en/conferences/environment/rio1992.
67 "United Nations Conference."
68 Jemima Pierre, "The Racial Vernaculars of Development: A View from West Africa," *American Anthropologist* 122, no. 1 (2019): 92.
69 "United Nations Conference."
70 "EMA History," Environmental Management Authority, accessed September 10, 2022, https://www.ema.co.tt/about/ema-history/.
71 "EMA History."
72 Jemima Pierre, "Racial Vernaculars of Development," 87.
73 Rajendra Ramlogan, "Using the Law to Achieve Environmental Democracy and Sustainable Development: An Elusive Dream for Trinidad and Tobago," *Electronic Green Journal* no. 30 (2010): 11.
74 Ramlogan, "Using the Law," 5.
75 My sincere gratitude to Faith Barter who called this connection to my attention. Barter's work brilliantly elaborates how Black writers labored as "architects of legal possibility," creatively deploying legal forms in order to challenge the logics of their oppression. See Faith Barter, *Black Pro Se: Authorship and the Limits of Law in Nineteenth-Century African American Literature* (University of North Carolina Press, 2025).
76 George Lamming, *Sovereignty of the Imagination: Conversations III* (House of Nehesi Publishers, 2009), 10.

Chapter 3 Vibration

1 Steve McQueen's aunt served as an inspiration for the character Martha Trenton. McQueen recounts in several interviews that his aunt was prohibited by McQueen's grandmother from attending blues parties when she was younger, but his uncle used to "leave the back door open for her" to make it easier for her to sneak out of the house. He noted she would leave and return in time for church the next morning, as does Martha in the film. McQueen describes this—the transformation that became possible at night but then faded back to normality in the morning—as a kind of Cinderella tale. See Dennis Lim and Steve McQueen, "Steve McQueen on Making an Ecstatic Musical with Lovers Rock | NYFF58," interview, September 18, 2020, posted by Film at Lincoln Center, YouTube, 21 min., 1 sec., https://www.youtube.com/watch?v=aTPck4Tu3xo.

2 Jeremy Gordan, "The Beat at the Heart of 'Lovers Rock,'" *New York Times*, November 29, 2020, https://www.nytimes.com/2020/11/29/arts/music/lovers-rock-small-axe.html.
3 Saba Mahmood, "Feminist Theory, Embodiment, and the Docile Agent: Some Reflections on the Egyptian Islamic Revival," *Cultural Anthropology* 16, no. 2 (2001): 225.
4 K. Austin Collins, "The Dance Floor Is Always at the Center of Steve McQueen's 'Lovers Rock,'" *Rolling Stone*, November 28, 2020, https://www.rollingstone.com/tv-movies/tv-movie-reviews/lovers-rock-steve-mcqueen-small-axe-1090869/.
5 Collins, "Dance Floor."
6 Collins, "Dance Floor."
7 Michael McMillan underscores that what distinguished a "house party" from a "blues party" was the illegal sale of alcohol. This fact made these parties more vulnerable to police surveillance and incursions. See Michael McMillan, "Who Feels It Knows It: Black Bodies and the Sensory Experience of the Dance-Hall," *Senses and Society* 17, no. 2 (2022): 223–227.
8 Paul Gilroy and Steve McQueen, "Transcript: In Conversation with Steve McQueen," UCL Sarah Parker Remond Centre for the Study of Racism and Racialisation, October 26, 2020, https://www.ucl.ac.uk/racism-racialisation/transcript-conversation-steve-mcqueen.
9 Paul Gilroy, *There Ain't No Black in the Union Jack* (Routledge, 1992), 37.
10 For example, see Steve Goodman's discussion of "quantum modulation" as a corporate productivity strategy. Referring to Muzak's strategy deployments of sound, Goodman explains, "Muzak [. . .] provides a sonic microcosm of what Deleuze described as the shift from disciplinary societies to societies of control. From the surveillance of stimulus progression that constituted an early form of sonic discipline by Muzak, to the horizontality of background, atmospheric control in quantum modulation that no longer needs to correct individual action directly. Quantum modulation affects mood rather than just trying to manipulate attention. . . . Quantum modulation therefore, simulating the logic of the DJ, attempts a smooth affective control by creating a plateau of musical intensity." See Goodman, *Sonic Warfare*, 144.
11 Lim, "Steve McQueen," 0:44–1:38.
12 Gilroy remarks about the film, "And actually the sensuous part of it wasn't just the sound—because the sound of the music seems to kind of saturate the visual presentation of the film in some very rare way. And I found myself being able to smell what was being cooked in that kitchen. It came together into the body in that way. It's a very rare thing; I don't know how you managed to do that." See Gilroy and McQueen, "Transcript."
13 Stuart Hall critiques this analytical simplification for "collud[ing], however unconsciously, with the construction of West Indians as objects, always 'outside time,' outside history." He notes that representations of "the frequently unrecorded, unrecognised, unspoken history of everyday life and practice in the black communities in Britain" often "*resist[s]* simplification and disrupt[s] our reading" in part because they demand attention to the ways West Indians often vitally shaped and invested in the very representational codes that routinely placed them in a "subordinate position." See Stuart Hall, "Reconstruction Work: Images of Post-war Black Settlement," in *Selected Writings on Visual Arts and Culture:*

Detour to the Imaginary, ed. Gilane Tawadros and Bill Schwarz (Duke University Press, 2024), 239–249, emphasis in original.

14 McMillan, "Who Feels," 224.

15 Hall, "Reconstruction Work," 245.

16 Sara Ahmed, *Strange Encounters: Embodied Others in Post-coloniality* (Routledge, 2000).

17 Mahmood, "Feminist Theory, Embodiment, and the Docile Agent," 225.

18 Mireille Miller-Young, *A Taste for Brown Sugar: Black Women in Pornography* (Duke University Press, 2014), 273.

19 Nash, "Pleasurable Blackness," 261–262.

20 While *12 Years a Slave* received a bevy of awards (and represented, as Jasmine Nichole Cobb points out, "the first ever major motion picture to base its portrayal of US slavery on a slave narrative"), many scholars, artists, and cultural critics expressed reservations about the film's stark depictions of racial and sexual violence, its claims to historical fidelity and accuracy, its use of the white savior trope, and more. The Tobagonian-Canadian writer M. NourbeSe Philip called *12 Years* "a profoundly problematic film," arguing that it "remains [. . .] locked in the hold of a sort of historical verite approach—a belief that you can tell the story. This is what gives it the Slavery 101 feel—every trope of slavery must be hit. . . . We understand how horrible slavery was, and therefore, are all the better for it." Jasmine Nichole Cobb called attention to the role of "validating," legitimizing gestures on the press tour for the film—including foregrounding that the film was based on a slave narrative, noting the role of Henry Louis Gates Jr. as a historical consultant for the film, and the "presence of violence" in the film itself to signal its legitimacy as a portrayal of slavery. "Questions of precision about slavery," Cobb reminds us, "stem from a long history of blackness as fit for observation, wrought within the peculiar institution." Others praised the film for its treatment of the character Patsey (played by Lupita Nyong'o), a character that, Salamishah Tillet notes, "begins to undo the limiting and hypermasculine categories of the 'Heroic Slave,'" and whose presence has been excised from other adaptations of the slave narrative. See Paul Watkins, "We Can Never Tell the Entire Story of Slavery: In Conversation with M. NourbeSe Philip," *Toronto Review of Books*, April 13, 2014, https://torontoreviewofbooks.com/2014/04/in-conversation-with-m-nourbese-philip/; Jasmine Nichole Cobb, "Directed by Himself: Steve McQueen's *12 Years a Slave*," *American Literary History* 26, no. 2 (2014): 339–346; and Salamishah Tillet, "'I Got No Comfort in this Life': The Increasing Importance of Patsey in *12 Years a Slave*," *American Literary History* 26, no. 2 (2014): 354–361.

21 Bobby Sands's importance as an icon of anticolonial struggle, particularly in the Caribbean but also globally, should not be understated. For example, in 2001, Fidel Castro unveiled a monument to Bobby Sands in Havana, Cuba. In June Jordan's 2003 essay "Report from the Bahamas, 1982," she recounts the story of a white Irish student named Cathy, "a young woman active in campus IRA activities," who helps her to aid a Black South African student, Sokutu, who is experiencing intimate partner violence at the hands of her husband (who Jordan knows through his involvement in the campus anti-apartheid movement). Jordan writes about the connection she feels with Cathy when she sees a BOBBY SANDS FREE AT LAST sticker on her car. She meditates on this unexpected alliance, writing, "This was another connection: Bobby Sands and Martin Luther King Jr. and who would believe it? I would not have believed it; I grew up terrorized by

Irish kids who introduced me to the word 'nigga.' And here I was following an Irish woman to the room of a Black South African. We were going to that room to try to save a life together." See June Jordan, "Report from the Bahamas, 1982," *Meridians* 3, no. 2 (2003): 15.

22 "Order of the British Empire," *London Gazette*, supplement no. 1, December 31, 2010, https://www.thegazette.co.uk/London/issue/59647/supplement/8.

23 The Windrush generation has repeatedly been met with extraordinary antiblack and anti-immigrant backlash, police brutality, and attacks on their legal status. The Windrush scandal of 2018, during which the Home Office under then Prime Minister Theresa May, an anti-immigration conservative, pushed to denationalize U.K. citizens of Caribbean descent who migrated to the United Kingdom during the Windrush generation, represents only the most recent of these attacks. The 1960s to 1980s in London were marked by a sharp uptick in antiblack police brutality and extrajudicial policing and violence, race riots, and more.

24 The anthology is named after Bob Marley's and Lee "Scratch" Perry's 1973 anthem of defiance "Small Axe," in which Marley sings, "If you are a big tree / we are the small axe / sharpened to cut you down."

25 Collins, "Dance Floor."

26 YaleBritishArt, "Steve McQueen Symposium," posted February 2, 2023, YouTube, 6 hr., 31 min., 20 sec., https://www.youtube.com/watch?v=1zXgeZc5tmE.

27 "Caribs' Leap/Western Deep," Art Institute Chicago, accessed June 19, 2025, https://www.artic.edu/artworks/181091/caribs-leap-western-deep.

28 Donnie Moreland, "Steve McQueen's 'Bear' Is an Exploration of Intimacies Among Black Men," Black Youth Project, August 12, 2022, https://blackyouthproject.com/steve-mcqueens-bear-is-an-exploration-of-intimacies-among-black-men/.

29 Pumla Dineo Gqola, *Female Fear Factory: Unravelling Patriarchy's Cultures of Violence* (Cassava Republic, 2022), xxix. Also see Jessica Horn, "Re-righting the Sexual Body," *Feminist Africa* 6 (2006): 7–19.

30 Here, I reference Christina Sharpe's theorization of the "weather." Sharpe writes, "In my text, the weather is the totality of our environments; the weather is the total climate; and that climate is antiblack." See Sharpe, *In the Wake*, 104.

31 "On the Dancehall scene," Julian Henriques reminds us, "the term 'massive' is used for the crowd and their intensive, immersive, visceral experience of *sonic dominance*." See Henriques, *Sonic Bodies*, 13.

32 Steve McQueen, *Lovers Rock* (BBC Studios; BBC Films; Turbine Studios; Lamas Park; Amazon Studios; EMU Films; Six Temple Productions, 2020), https://www.amazon.com/Small-Axe-Season-1/dp/B08J4HRR4P, 07:42–08:21.

33 McQueen, *Lovers Rock*, 07:42–08:21. The use of the term "outernational" here matters; as Carolyn Cooper explains, outernational is a "Rastafari inversion of international"; the emcee is deliberately centering Rastafari linguistics and philosophy in his set. In a context where Rastafarians get mobilized as the quintessential emblems of Black unruliness and criminality (both in Jamaica and in the United Kingdom in this period), to celebrate their philosophy and language is itself a declaration of the party's intention to provide safe harbor for, and express solidarity with, oppressed Black people globally (as is central to Rastafarian spiritual and political principles). See "[SSO#7] Keynote Lecture by Carolyn Cooper," lecture, July 12–16, 2021, posted August 13, 2021, by Sound System Outernational, YouTube, 1 hr., 29 min., 52 sec., https://youtu.be/c1idTqrcbvM?si=bIkEg-Vbl61DotaY.

34 *Oxford English Dictionary*, s.v. "vibration (*n*.)," accessed September 23, 2024, https://www.oed.com/dictionary/vibration_n?tab=meaning_and_use#15516079.

35 Wayne Marshall, "Treble Culture," in *The Oxford Handbook of Mobile Music Studies*, vol. 2, ed. Sumanth Gopinath and Jason Stanyek (Oxford University Press, 2014), 67.

36 This is a racial slur used in Britain to refer to any nonwhite, dark-skinned person—typically Black or South Asian people—and to those perceived as foreigners. British white nationalists, however, are not the only ones who have claimed and deployed the term to similarly disparage outsiders: it has circulated in similar ways in Australia and by the CIA. Curiously, the Church of Scientology also uses the term to refer to nonadherents of Scientology's principles.

37 In Powell's "Rivers of Blood" speech, he declared that mass immigration and legislation condemning racial discrimination were serving to make white British citizens "strangers in their own country"—espousing familiar white nationalist views that people of color were taking white jobs, flooding social services and barring white access to hospitals and schools, degrading the quality of British neighborhoods, and lowering the "standards of discipline and competence" at work. He urged immediate action to stem the inflow of migrants and to prevent legislation guarding their right to equal treatment under the law, lest the proportion of white Britons to nonwhite Britons "reach American proportions long before the end of the century."

38 Nadia Ellis, *Territories of the Soul: Queered Belonging in the Black Diaspora* (Duke University Press, 2015), 2–4.

39 Reference to Luke 9:23: "Whoever wants to be my disciple must deny themselves and take up their cross daily and follow me" (NIV). This routine ascetic ritual of penitence—intended to "mortify the flesh" by reenacting Jesus's walk on the Via Dolorosa carrying the cross on which he would soon be crucified—is practiced by certain sects of Christianity (typically Catholics) and confraternities of penitents.

40 McQueen, *Lovers Rock*, 08:56–08:58.

41 McQueen, *Lovers Rock*, 45:45–46:15.

42 The bus scene unfolds to the sounds of reggae singer Dennis Brown's 1979 song "Money in My Pocket." The lyrics of the song follow heartbreak: though the song's narrator is financially secure (there is "money in [his] pocket"), he nevertheless suffers from loneliness ("I just can't get no love"). His lover has deceived and abandoned him. More, the narrator mournfully concludes: "The love I had in mind / Was very, very hard to find." Martha, too, is a character for whom love is physically and emotionally painful, despite her family's hard-won financial security. She is also in search of a way of loving and being loved that is hard to find.

43 Michael McMillan, "Taste-Cultures in the Black British Home," in *The Persistence of Taste: Art, Museums and Everyday Life After Bourdieu*, ed. Malcolm Quinn, Dave Beech, Michael Lehnert, Carol Tulloch, and Stephen Wilson (Routledge, 2018), 306.

44 Though homeownership was on the rise in the 1980s—a result of the 1980 Housing Act, a key policy push of Thatcher's conservative administration—this must be understood as a part of a push to privatize public housing. The act offered longtime tenants in council housing (or British public housing) the right to buy the homes they lived in at a discount. However, this ultimately reduced the availability of public housing and generally privileged those with the economic

means to buy their homes (disadvantaging single-parent households, lone renters, and young people in general). More, much council housing was in a state of severe disrepair; many buyers would, years later, sell their homes to private buyers. In effect, this conservative policy led to a mass privatization of the housing sector.

45 In a spare room, we see a cluster of items that have presumably been transplanted from the front room. Here, what McMillan describes as the thoughtful "kitsch" of the West Indian front room in postwar Britain is on full display—a busy cluster of floral-patterned wallpaper, flamingo-colored satin bedsheets, a drinks bar, and a dresser brimming with ornaments and family photos.

46 McMillan, "Taste-Cultures," 308, emphasis in original.

47 Julian Henriques explains his concept of "sonic dominance"—a rebuttal to the dominance of vision as the governing sensory modality of knowledge-production—in his study of the dancehall and of sound systems. He writes, "The sheer power of the set in a dancehall session makes for an inescapable sonic experience, described as *sonic dominance*. This identifies the crowd's *intensive* experience of the *extensive* presence of the material vibrations of sound, as well as its corporeal and sociocultural vibrations." More, Henriques stresses the importance of analyses of gender: "One important issue for further discussion is the gendering of this sonic power, together with the engineer's embodied way of knowing, by which he understands it." See Henriques, *Sonic Bodies*, 86, emphasis in original.

48 Henriques, *Sonic Bodies*, xxviii.

49 This event is often referred to as the "New Cross Fire"; however, several Black organizers and scholars have instead referred to it as the "New Cross Massacre" to insist on its treatment as a hate crime, a deliberate killing rather than an accident. Because the coverage of the event (or the lack thereof) at all in the news pivoted around the question of whether or not antiblack racism was indeed a systemic scourge in London in this period, and whether this event constituted evidence of it, I, too, choose intentionally to name this event a massacre.

50 Kehinde Andrews, "Forty Years on from the New Cross Fire, What Has Changed for Black Britons?," *Guardian*, January 17, 2021, https://www.theguardian.com/world/2021/jan/17/forty-years-on-from-the-new-cross-fire-what-has-changed-for-black-britons. It should be noted that the National Front, a far-right, white supremacist political party, had a major presence in the neighborhood where the New Cross Massacre occurred.

51 Andrews, "Forty Years."

52 Kurt Barling, "Who Rules the Roost?," BBC News, January 26, 2011, https://www.bbc.co.uk/blogs/kurtbarling/2011/01.

53 "All-Night Parties," HC Deb, February 11, 1981, vol. 998, cc958–966, https://api.parliament.uk/historic-hansard/commons/1981/feb/11/all-night-parties.

54 "All-Night Parties."

55 "New Cross Massacre 13 Young Blacks Dead 26 Injured," October 2, 1981, LMA/4463/B/02/02/046, Eric and Jessica Huntley Collection, London Metropolitan Archives, London, U.K.

56 In Jamaican writer Michelle Cliff's 1987 novel *No Telephone to Heaven*, the Jamaican protagonist Clare is disturbed and angered after witnessing a National Front march that takes place right outside the university in London where she is pursuing her graduate work. See Michelle Cliff, *No Telephone to Heaven* (E. P. Dutton, 1987).

57 Eddie Chambers, "The Jamaican 1970s and Its Influence on the Making of Black Britain," *Small Axe* 23, no. 1 (2019): 134.

58 Jafari Allen, *There's a Disco Ball Between Us: A Theory of Black Gay Life* (Duke University Press, 2022), 8.

59 Allen, *There's a Disco Ball*, 9.

60 Gilroy and McQueen, "Transcript."

61 McQueen, *Lovers Rock*, 17:52–18:05.

62 McQueen, *Lovers Rock*, 18:21–18:35.

63 Lisa Amanda Palmer, "Hopelessly in Love: Carroll Thompson's Reflections and Insights into the Patriarchal Politics within the Lovers Rock Reggae Scene," in *Black Music in Britain in the 21st Century*, ed. Monique Charles and Mary Gani (Liverpool University Press, 2023), 76.

64 Lisa Amanda Palmer, "'LADIES A YOUR TIME NOW!': Erotic Politics, Lovers Rock and Resistance in the UK," *African and Black Diaspora* 4, no. 2 (2011): 177.

65 Lovers rock bore the weight of a kind of ongoing erasure of the historical, social, and creative particularities of U.K. diasporic Blackness. In contrast with lovers rock, reggae, as Njelle Hamilton explains, "was articulated as the sound of Jamaican 'authenticity,' both in its coterminous rise with independence and in its characteristic elements and techniques of reconciling disparate and foreign influences into a 'hybrid and coherent' sound that is uniquely referential to Jamaican reality." Building on the arguments of scholars like Belinda Edmondson and Faith Smith, Hamilton underscores that "the prospect of losing Jamaican specificity to international blackness is consonant with turn-of-the-millennium anxieties about 'authenticity' ushered in by globalization," anxieties that produced attachments to "external markings of Jamaicanness that the diasporic citizen must master in order to qualify for repatriation." See Njelle W. Hamilton, *Phonographic Memories: Popular Music and the Contemporary Caribbean Novel* (Rutgers University Press, 2019), 117–118, 121–122, 196. Also see Belinda Edmondson, *Caribbean Middlebrow: Leisure Culture and the Middle Class* (Cornell University Press, 2009); and Faith Smith, "'You Know You're West Indian If . . .': Codes of Authenticity in Colin Channer's *Waiting in Vain*," *Small Axe* 10 (2001): 41–59.

66 Palmer, "'LADIES A YOUR TIME NOW!,'" 188–189.

67 Palmer, "'LADIES A YOUR TIME NOW!,'" 185.

68 *The Story of Lover's Rock*, Menelik Shabazz, dir. (BFM Media and SunRa Pictures, 2011), https://play.xumo.com/free-movies/the-story-of-lovers-rock/XMoM7J9J-EIB3T2, 1:36:42.

69 For example, the interviewees cite Louisa Mark's 1978 "Six Sixth Street" as the song that captured the anticipation of a fallout for a couple after the discovery of infidelity; Carroll Thompson's 1981 "Hopelessly in Love" as the song that captured the feeling of being "really moved" by a romantic interest; and Carroll Thompson's 1981 "I'm So Sorry" as the song that articulated an apology to a betrayed lover.

70 *The Story of Lover's Rock*, 05:42–05:49.

71 McQueen, *Lovers Rock*, 44:00–44:15.

72 McQueen, *Lovers Rock*, 46:02–46:15.

73 McQueen, *Lovers Rock*, 51:42–52:10.

74 McQueen, *Lovers Rock*, 46:57–47:25.

75 Antonia Randolph, "Platonic Couples and the Limits of Queer Theory: The Case of Black Masculinity in Hip-Hop Culture," in *Outskirts: Queer Experiences on the Fringe*, edited by D'Lane Compton and Amy L. Stone (NYU Press, 2024), 218–219.

76 Randolph, "Platonic Couples," 220.
77 See Krystal Nandini Ghisyawan, "Kith and Kin: The Making of Queer Communities," *Small Axe* 28, no. 2 (2024): 147–155. Also see Krystal Nandini Ghisyawan, *Erotic Cartographies: Decolonization and the Queer Caribbean Imagination* (Rutgers University Press, 2022).
78 The dancefloor crescendo of the film might even be said to display what Randolph names "illegible intimacy," or "relationships that confound norms within both dominant and Black culture about how Black men interact." See Randolph, "Platonic Couples," 220–221.
79 Nadia Ellis, "Black Migrants, White Queers and the Archive of Inclusion in Postwar London," *Interventions: International Journal of Postcolonial Studies* 17, no. 6 (2015): 895.
80 Ellis, "Black Migrants," 896.
81 Ellis, "Black Migrants," 895.
82 Henriques, *Sonic Bodies*, 13.
83 Henriques, *Sonic Bodies*, 16.
84 "Exhibitions and Projects: Steve McQueen," Dia Art, accessed October 18, 2024, https://www.diaart.org/exhibition/exhibitions-projects/steve-mcqueen-exhibition.
85 "Exhibitions and Projects."
86 Siddhartha Mitter, "Steve McQueen, on a Different Wavelength," *New York Times*, May 10, 2024, https://www.nytimes.com/2024/05/10/arts/design/steve-mcqueen-filmmaker-art-dia-beacon-bass.html.
87 Mitter, "Steve McQueen."
88 Here, I reference "self-regard" in Kaiama Glover's usage of the term, describing "the ambivalent nature of social being wherein it is at once crucial to love oneself, deeply and protectively, and to publicly perform modesty, selflessness and love for one's community." See Kaiama Glover, *A Regarded Self: Caribbean Womanhood and the Ethics of Disorderly Being* (Duke University Press, 2021), 6.
89 Mitter, "Steve McQueen."
90 Mitter, "Steve McQueen."
91 Mitter, "Steve McQueen."
92 "Further Details Announced on Dia Art Foundation and Laurenz Foundation's Major Commission by Steve McQueen," Dia Art, accessed October 18, 2024, https://www.diaart.org/about/press/further-details-announced-on-dia-art-foundation-and-laurenz-foundations-major-commission-by-steve-mcqueen/type/text.

Chapter 4 Ultrasound, or Subtlety

1 Miller, "In Praise of."
2 Miller, "In Praise of."
3 Royal Collection Trust, "About the Collection," accessed June 23, 2025, https://www.rct.uk/collection/about-the-collection.
4 Royal Collection Trust, "Gold," accessed June 23, 2025, https://www.rct.uk/collection/exhibitions/gold/the-queens-gallery-buckingham-palace.
5 Key West Literary Seminar, "'Jamaican Letters' | Marlon James, Nicole Dennis-Benn, and Kei Miller in Conversation," posted September 26, 2019, YouTube, 11:40–12:00, https://youtu.be/IUC2SqxKJhg?si=MyPOmIzbZjYTsIxD&t=700.

6 Royal Collection Trust, "Poetry Evening with Kei Miller," accessed June 23, 2025, https://www.rct.uk/collection/exhibitions/gold/the-queens-gallery-buckingham-palace/poetry-evening-with-kei-miller.
7 Though now debunked, the capacity of infrasound to damage the human body was a major fear fueling the coverage of the spread of so-called "Havana syndrome" among the U.S. military personnel and diplomats in Cuba in 2017. Those affected experienced symptoms such as hearing loss, nausea, and tinnitus.
8 Postcolonial Writers Make Worlds, "Kei Miller Interviewed by Ellen Boehmer," posted October 14, 2019, YouTube, 3:33–7:02, https://www.youtube.com/watch?v=tKLTMGN8RDk&t=422s.
9 *Oxford English Dictionary*, s.v. "subtlety (*n.*)," accessed June 23, 2025, https://www.oed.com/dictionary/subtlety_n?tab=meaning_and_use#20136912; *Oxford English Dictionary*, s.v. "subtle (*adj.*)," accessed June 23, 2025, https://www.oed.com/dictionary/subtle_adj?tab=meaning_and_use#20135035.
10 Visual artist Kara Walker, however, invokes the word "subtlety" in its meaning in the early modern period as a form of dinner entertainment comprised of a small course made of sugar and taking on an ornamental design. The irony of Walker's piece, of course, is that it is not at all subtle: it is 35 feet tall and 75 feet long. We might read this as a critique of the ways these forms of "subtle" dinner entertainment required spectacular antiblack violence in the British colonies.
11 Kevin Quashie, *The Sovereignty of Quiet: Beyond Resistance in Black Culture* (Rutgers University Press, 2012), 1.
12 Sara Ahmed, *Living a Feminist Life* (Duke University Press, 2017), 107.
13 WNYC, "Spoken Word: Staceyann Chin Performs 'Homophobia,'" posted January 17, 2017, YouTube, 8 min., 20 sec., https://www.youtube.com/watch?v=-LV_aqfoXVc.
14 Cathy J. Cohen, "Punks, Bulldaggers, and Welfare Queens: The Radical Potential of Queer Politics?," in *Black Queer Studies: A Critical Anthology*, ed. E. Patrick Johnson and Mae G. Henderson (Duke University Press, 2005), 21.
15 Cohen, "Punks, Bulldaggers," 25–26.
16 Jennifer C. Nash and Samantha Pinto, "A New Genealogy of 'Intelligent Rage,' or Other Ways to Think About White Women in Feminism," *Signs: Journal of Women in Culture and Society* 46, no. 4 (2021): 893.
17 Nash and Pinto, "New Genealogy," 888.
18 Nash and Pinto, "New Genealogy," 892–893.
19 In the blurbs for Staceyann Chin's 2019 poetry collection *Crossfire: A Litany for Survival*, Rosanne Cash calls Chin's work "brave" and "forthright"; Sonia Sanchez calls the book one that is "irresistible" that "hums / sings / talks / seduces us with words"; and Eve Ensler describes the book as evidence that Chin "has come into her raw, sexual, revolutionary poetic power" and calls the poems "jet fuel from the hot center of her body—from rage, from sorrow, from pure, unmitigated life-force." In the blurb for her 2010 memoir *The Other Side of Paradise*, Walter Mosley describes Chin's work as "heartbreaking and unflinching."
20 From Ensler's blurb for *Crossfire*.
21 From Mosley's blurb for *Crossfire*.
22 Amber Jamilla Musser, *Between Shadows and Noise: Sensation, Situatedness, and the Undisciplined* (Duke University Press, 2024), 5.
23 Musser, *Between Shadows and Noise*, 5.
24 Miller, "In Praise of."

25 Miller, "In Praise of."
26 Miller, "In Praise of."
27 Miller, "In Praise of."
28 Audre Lorde, "Uses of the Erotic," in *Sister Outsider*, 56.
29 Shoniqua Roach, "Black Sex in the Quiet," *Differences* 30, no. 1 (2019): 127–128.
30 Roshanak Kheshti, "Sound Studies," *Feminist Media Histories* 4, no. 2 (2018): 182.
31 Roshanak Kheshti, "Toward a Rupture in the *Sensus Communis*: On Sound Studies and the Politics of Knowledge Production," *Current Musicology* 99–100 (2017): 18.
32 Roger Reeves, "Minor Characters, Major Silence, or Against the Compulsion to Talk," *Black Scholar* 51, no. 1 (2021): 44.
33 Roach, "Black Sex in the Quiet," 127.
34 Roach, "Black Sex in the Quiet," 127.
35 Sarah Schulman, *Stagestruck: Theater, AIDS, and the Marketing of Gay America* (Duke University Press, 1998), 102.
36 Ahmed, *Living a Feminist Life*, 222.
37 Kwame Holmes, "What's the Tea: Gossip and the Production of Black Gay Social History," *Radical History Review* 122 (2015): 64.
38 Quashie, *Sovereignty of Quiet*, 6, 4.
39 Quashie, *Sovereignty of Quiet*, 4.
40 Derefe Chevannes, "Euromodernity's Undertone: On Reconceptualizing Political Speech" (PhD diss., University of Connecticut, 2019), 1.
41 Chevannes, "Euromodernity's Undertone," 4.
42 Chevannes, "Euromodernity's Undertone," 9, emphasis in original.
43 Marlene NourbeSe Philip, "Interview with an Empire," in *Assembling Alternatives: Reading Postmodern Poetries Transnationally*, ed. Romana Huk (Wesleyan University Press, 2003), 195.
44 Philip, "Interview," 195.
45 Philip, "Interview," 195.
46 Philip, "Interview," 195.
47 Philip, "Interview," 195, my emphasis.
48 Philip, "Interview," 195.
49 Samantha Pinto, *Difficult Diasporas: The Transnational Feminist Aesthetic of the Black Atlantic* (New York University Press, 2013), 189.
50 Pinto, *Difficult Diasporas*, 189.
51 Philip, "Interview," 195.
52 Pinto, *Difficult Diasporas*, 179.
53 Paul Barrett, "The Poetic Disturbances of M. NourbeSe Philip," *Walrus*, September 21, 2018, https://thewalrus.ca/the-poetic-disturbances-of-m-nourbese-philip/.
54 M. NourbeSe Philip, *Blank: Essays and Interviews* (Book*hug, 2017), 154.
55 Philip, *Blank*, 154.
56 Philip, *Blank*, 154.
57 Philip, *Blank*, 156.
58 Barrett, "Poetic Disturbances."
59 The discussion of particular Black women writers as "difficult" is a distinctly raced, gendered, and sexualized form of commentary. We might immediately think of a writer like Toni Morrison, who was routinely critiqued for "marginalizing" white audiences. In her infamous 1998 interview with Jana Wendt, Wendt queries, "You have, in your writing, certainly marginalized whites. Why are they

of no particular interest to you?" Morrison chuckles before responding, "Well, I was interested in another kind of literature that was not just confrontational: Black vs. White. I was really interested in Black readership. . . . For me, the allegory or the parallel is Black music, which is as splendid and complicated and wonderful as it is because its audience was within. Its primary audience. The fact that it has become universal, worldwide—anyone, everyone can play it, and it has evolved—is because it wasn't tampered with and editorialized within the community." See thepostarchive, "Toni Morrison—Intro and Interview," posted May 22, 2019, YouTube, 27 min., 55 sec., https://www.youtube.com/watch?v=WoTELoC8QoM.

60 M. NourbeSe Philip, *The Collected Short Stories of Marlene NourbeSe Philip* (Alexander Street Press, 2006), 22.

61 Philip, *Collected Short Stories*, 22.

62 Philip, *Collected Short Stories*, 22.

63 Philip, *Collected Short Stories*, 22.

64 Philip, *Collected Short Stories*, 29.

65 Philip, *Collected Short Stories*, 27. As Kelly Baker Josephs reminds us, representations of madness in Caribbean literature were often linked to writers' meditations on the transition from the late colonial period to de jure independence. "Not surprisingly," Josephs writes, "the representations of madness increased as, with the process of political decolonization underway, writers began experimenting with routes to social and mental decolonization. . . . Various terms of insanity became part of this search for new forms of expression as writers contemplated communal neuroses and schizophrenic existences." See Kelly Baker Josephs, *Disturbers of the Peace: Representations of Madness in Anglophone Caribbean Literature* (University of Virginia Press, 2013), 11.

66 Philip, *Collected Short Stories*, 27.

67 M. NourbeSe Philip, *Showing Grit: Showboating North of the 44th Parallel* (Poui, 1993).

68 Sarah Phillips Casteel, *Calypso Jews: Jewishness in the Caribbean Literary Imagination* (Columbia University Press, 2016), 204.

69 Casteel, *Calypso Jews*, 204, 206.

70 Carol Bailey, "Performing 'Difference': Reading Gossip in Olive Senior's Short Stories," in *Constructing Vernacular Culture in the Trans-Caribbean*, ed. Holger Henke and Karl-Heinz Magister (Lexington Books, 2008), 124.

71 Bailey, "Performing 'Difference.'"

72 Bailey, "Performing 'Difference.'"

73 Raphael Dalleo, *Caribbean Literature and the Public Sphere: From the Plantation to the Postcolonial* (University of Virginia Press, 2011), 102.

74 Philip, *Collected Short Stories*, 29.

75 Philip, *Collected Short Stories*, 27.

76 Philip, *Collected Short Stories*, 27.

77 Philip, *Collected Short Stories*, 26.

78 Philip, *Collected Short Stories*, 26.

79 Philip, *Collected Short Stories*, 26.

80 Philip, *Collected Short Stories*, 26.

81 Dalleo, *Caribbean Literature*.

82 Philip, *Collected Short Stories*, 22.

83 Philip, *Collected Short Stories*, 23.

84 Philip, *Collected Short Stories*, 27.
85 Philip, *Collected Short Stories*, 24.
86 Miranda recalls the memories of her mother's staged suicide attempt iteratively, gradually adding more detail with each iteration: "my mother lying on the floor screaming; stop frame: my mother lying on the floor screaming that she drinking poison; stop frame: my mother lying on the floor screaming that she drinking poison and killing herself."
87 Philip, *Collected Short Stories*, 29.
88 Philip, *Collected Short Stories*, 30.

Coda

1 Nicole Dennis-Benn, *Here Comes the Sun* (Oneworld, 2017), 341, emphasis added.
2 Dennis-Benn, *Here Comes the Sun*, 33.
3 Dennis-Benn, *Here Comes the Sun*, 46.
4 Dennis-Benn, *Here Comes the Sun*, 19.
5 Dennis-Benn, *Here Comes the Sun*, 342.
6 Dennis-Benn, *Here Comes the Sun*, 343.
7 Dennis-Benn, *Here Comes the Sun*, 343–344.
8 Dennis-Benn, *Here Comes the Sun*, 64.
9 Dennis-Benn, *Here Comes the Sun*, 43.
10 Dennis-Benn, *Here Comes the Sun*, 48.
11 Dennis-Benn, *Here Comes the Sun*, 49.
12 Dennis-Benn, *Here Comes the Sun*, 43.
13 Dennis-Benn, *Here Comes the Sun*, 43.
14 Nadia Ellis, "Out and Bad: Toward a Queer Performance Hermeneutic in Jamaican Dancehall," *Small Axe* 15, no. 2 (2011): 12.
15 Isis Semaj-Hall, "[Sic] with Contagion: Communicating Prohibition in Pre-Independence Trinidad," *Caribbean Quarterly* 66, no. 1 (2020): 92–94.

Bibliography

Abdur-Rahman, Aliyyah. "The Black Ecstatic." *GLQ: A Journal of Lesbian and Gay Studies* 24, no. 2–3 (2018): 343–365.

Abeng. "Why Abeng." February 1, 1969.

Adisa, Opal Palmer. "Journey into Speech—A Writer Between Two Worlds: An Interview with Michelle Cliff." *African American Review* 28, no. 2 (1994): 273–281.

Ahmed, Sara. *Living a Feminist Life*. Duke University Press, 2017.

———. *Strange Encounters: Embodied Others in Post-Coloniality*. Routledge, 2000.

Alexander, M. Jacqui. "Not Just (Any)Body Can Be a Citizen: The Politics of Law, Sexuality and Postcoloniality in Trinidad and Tobago and the Bahamas." *Feminist Review*, no. 48 (1994): 5–23.

———. *Pedagogies of Crossing: Meditations on Feminism, Sexual Politics, Memory, and the Sacred*. Duke University Press, 2005.

Alexander, Neil. "How to Control Noise from Bars, Restaurants." *Trinidad and Tobago Guardian,* December 21, 2010. https://www.guardian.co.tt/article-6.2.463880.ff867c3831.

Allen, Jafari. *There's a Disco Ball Between Us: A Theory of Black Gay Life*. Duke University Press, 2022.

Anatol, Giselle Liza. *The Things That Fly in the Night: Female Vampires in Literature of the Circum-Caribbean and African Diaspora*. Rutgers University Press, 2015.

Andrews, Kehinde. "Forty Years on from the New Cross Fire, What Has Changed for Black Britons?" *Guardian*, January 17, 2021. https://www.theguardian.com/world/2021/jan/17/forty-years-on-from-the-new-cross-fire-what-has-changed-for-black-britons.

Anim-Addo, Joan. "Gendering Creolisation: Creolizing Affect." *Feminist Review* 104 (2013): 5–23.

Anzaldúa, Gloria. *Making Face, Making Soul/Haciendo Caras: Creative and Critical Perspectives by Feminists of Color*. Aunt Lute Books, 1990.

Bailey, Carol. "Performing 'Difference': Reading Gossip in Olive Senior's Short Stories." In *Constructing Vernacular Culture in the Trans-Caribbean*, edited by Holger Henke and Karl-Heinz Magister. Lexington Books, 2008.

Barling, Kurt. "Who Rules the Roost?" BBC News, January 26, 2011. https://www.bbc.co.uk/blogs/kurtbarling/2011/01.

Barrett, Paul. "The Poetic Disturbances of M. NourbeSe Philip." *Walrus*, September 21, 2018. https://thewalrus.ca/the-poetic-disturbances-of-m-nourbese-philip/.

Barter, Faith. *Black Pro Se: Authorship and the Limits of Law in Nineteenth-Century African American Literature.* University of North Carolina Press, 2025.

Beckles, Hilary. "Caribbean Anti-Slavery: The Self-Liberation Ethos of Enslaved Blacks." *Journal of Caribbean History* 22, no. 1 (1988): 1–19.

———. "White Women and Slavery in the Caribbean." *History Workshop Journal* 36, no. 1 (1993): 66–82.

Bell, Archie. *The Spell of the Caribbean Islands.* L. C. Page, 1926.

Berlant, Lauren. *Cruel Optimism.* Duke University Press, 2011.

Bhattacharjee, Riya. "11 Women Kicked Off Napa Valley Wine Train for Laughing Too Loudly Settle Racial Discrimination Suit." NBC Bay Area, April 19, 2016. https://www.nbcbayarea.com/news/local/11-Women-Kicked-Off-Napa-Valley-Wine-Train-File-11M-Racial-Discrimination-Suit-376139281.html.

Bleby, Henry. *The Reign of Terror: A Narrative of the Facts Concerning Ex-Governor Eyre, George William Gordon, and the Jamaica Atrocities.* W. Nichols, 1868.

Bronfman, Alejandra. *Isles of Noise: Sonic Media in the Caribbean.* University of North Carolina Press, 2016.

Brooks, Daphne. *Liner Notes for the Revolution: The Intellectual Life of Black Feminist Sound.* Harvard University Press, 2021.

Casteel, Sarah Phillips. *Calypso Jews: Jewishness in the Caribbean Literary Imagination.* Columbia University Press, 2016.

Chambers, Eddie. "The Jamaican 1970s and Its Influence on the Making of Black Britain." *Small Axe* 23, no. 1 (2019): 134–149.

Chancy, Myriam J. A. *Searching for Safe Spaces: Afro-Caribbean Women Writers in Exile.* Temple University Press, 1997.

Chevannes, Derefe. "Euromodernity's Undertone: On Reconceptualizing Political Speech." PhD diss., University of Connecticut, 2019. ProQuest (31077822).

Chin, Matthew. "Tracing 'Gay Liberation' Through Postindependence Jamaica." *Public Culture* 31, no. 2 (2019): 323–341.

Cliff, Michelle. *Abeng.* Plume, 1995.

———. "Caliban's Daughter: The Tempest and the Teapot." *Frontiers: A Journal of Women Studies* 12, no. 2 (1991): 36–51.

———. "Colonial Girl, and What It Would Be Like." In Smith, *Sex and the Citizen.*

———. *Free Enterprise: A Novel of Mary Ellen Pleasant.* City Lights, 2004.

———. *If I Could Write This in Fire.* University of Minnesota Press, 2008.

———. *The Land of Look Behind: Prose and Poetry.* Firebrand Books, 1985.

———. *No Telephone to Heaven.* E. P. Dutton, 1987.

———. "Notes on Speechlessness." *Sinister Wisdom: A Journal of Words and Pictures for the Lesbian Imagination in All Women* 5 (1978): 5–9.

Cobb, Jasmine Nichole. "Directed by Himself: Steve McQueen's 12 Years a Slave." *American Literary History* 26, no. 2 (2014): 339–346.

Cohen, Cathy J. "Punks, Bulldaggers, and Welfare Queens: The Radical Potential of Queer Politics?" In *Black Queer Studies: A Critical Anthology*, edited by E. Patrick Johnson and Mae G. Henderson. Duke University Press, 2005.

Collins, K. Austin. "The Dance Floor Is Always at the Center of Steve McQueen's 'Lovers Rock.'" *Rolling Stone*, November 28, 2020. https://www.rollingstone.com/tv-movies/tv-movie-reviews/lovers-rock-steve-mcqueen-small-axe-1090869/.

Collins, Patricia Hill. *Black Feminist Thought: Knowledge, Consciousness, and the Politics of Empowerment.* 2nd ed. Routledge, 2000.

Condé, Mayse. "Order, Disorder, Freedom, and the West Indian Writer." *Yale French Studies* 97 (2000): 151–165.

Cooper, Carolyn. *Noises in the Blood: Orality, Gender, and the "Vulgar" Body of Jamaican Popular Culture.* Duke University Press, 1995.

———. "Sound Clash in Uptown Ghetto." *Gleaner,* June 12, 2015. https://jamaica-gleaner.com/article/commentary/20150614/sound-clash-uptown-ghetto.

———. *Sound Clash: Jamaican Dancehall Culture at Large.* Palgrave Macmillan, 2004.

———. "[SSO#7] Keynote Lecture by Carolyn Cooper." Posted August 13, 2021, by Sound System Outernational. YouTube, 1 hr., 29 min., 52 sec. https://youtu.be/c1idTqrcbvM?si=bIkEg-Vbl61DotaY.

Crawley, Ashon. *Blackpentecostal Breath: The Aesthetics of Possibility.* Fordham University Press, 2016.

Dadzie, Stella. "The Complicated Resistance Efforts of Enslaved Women in the West Indies." Literary Hub, October 20, 2020. https://lithub.com/the-complicated-resistance-efforts-of-enslaved-women-in-the-west-indies/.

Daily Gleaner. "A Check Needed." February 28, 1934.

Dalleo, Raphael. *Caribbean Literature and the Public Sphere: From the Plantation to the Postcolonial.* University of Virginia Press, 2011.

Dana, Richard Henry. *To Cuba and Back: A Vacation Voyage.* Ticknor and Fields, 1859.

Davies, Carole Boyce, and Elaine Savory Fido, eds. *Out of the Kumbla: Caribbean Women and Literature.* Africa World Press, 1990.

Day, Susan de Forest. *The Cruise of the Scythian in the West Indies.* F. Tennyson Neely, 1899.

Deleuze, Gilles. *The Logic of Sense.* Edited by Constantin V. Boundas. Translated by Mark Lester and Charles Stivale. Columbia University Press, 1990.

Dennis-Benn, Nicole. *Here Comes the Sun.* Oneworld, 2017.

Dwarika, Naylan. "EMA Noise Campaign—Phase 1." Posted January 30, 2012. YouTube, 30 sec. https://www.youtube.com/watch?v=kinlP3sSYbs.

———. "EMA Noise Campaign—Phase 2." Posted January 30, 2012. YouTube, 30 sec. https://www.youtube.com/watch?v=QRlFeD2isfg.

———. "EMA Noise Campaign—Phase 3." Posted January 30, 2012. YouTube, 30 sec. https://www.youtube.com/watch?v=yaUFoVZfRiE.

Edmondson, Belinda. *Caribbean Middlebrow: Leisure Culture and the Middle Class.* Cornell University Press, 2009.

———. *Creole Noise: Early Caribbean Dialect Literature and Performance.* Oxford University Press, 2022.

———. *Making Men: Gender, Literary Authority, and Women's Writing in Caribbean Narrative.* Duke University Press, 1999.

———. "Public Spectacles: Caribbean Women and the Politics of Public Performance." *Small Axe* 7, no. 1 (2003): 1–16.

Eidsheim, Nina Sun. "Marian Anderson and 'Sonic Blackness' in American Opera." *American Quarterly* 63, no. 3 (2011): 641–671.

Ellis, Nadia. "Black Migrants, White Queers and the Archive of Inclusion in Postwar London." *Interventions: International Journal of Postcolonial Studies* 17, no. 6 (2015): 893–915.

———. "Out and Bad: Toward a Queer Performance Hermeneutic in Jamaican Dancehall." *Small Axe* 15, no. 2 (2011): 7–23.

———. *Territories of the Soul: Queered Belonging in the Black Diaspora*. Duke University Press, 2015.

Foster, Harry La Tourette. *The Caribbean Cruise*. Dodd, Mead, 1935.

Franck, Harry A. *Roaming Through the West Indies*. Century, 1920.

Fuentes, Marisa. *Dispossessed Lives: Enslaved Women, Violence, and the Archive*. University of Pennsylvania Press, 2016.

Gardner, Claudia. "Sean Paul's Wife Jodi Jinx Dragged over 'Condescending' All-Inclusive Hotel Food Comment." *Dancehall Mag*, June 16, 2021. https://www.dancehallmag.com/2021/06/16/news/sean-pauls-wife-jodi-jinx-dragged-over-condescending-all-inclusive-hotel-food-comment.html.

Ghisyawan, Krystal Nandini. *Erotic Cartographies: Decolonization and the Queer Caribbean Imagination*. Rutgers University Press, 2022.

———. "Kith and Kin: The Making of Queer Communities." *Small Axe* 28, no. 2 (2024): 147–155.

Gilmore, Ruth Wilson. "Public Enemies and Private Intellectuals: Apartheid USA." *Race and Class* 35, no. 1 (1993): 69–78.

Gilroy, Paul. *There Ain't No Black in the Union Jack*. Routledge, 1992.

Gilroy, Paul, and Steve McQueen. "Transcript: In Conversation with Steve McQueen." UCL Sarah Parker Remond Centre for the Study of Racism and Racialisation, October 26, 2020. https://www.ucl.ac.uk/racism-racialisation/transcript-conversation-steve-mcqueen.

Glissant, Édouard. "Free and Forced Poetics." *Alcheringa/Ethnopoetics: A First International Symposium* 2 (1976): 95–101.

Glover, Kaiama. *A Regarded Self: Caribbean Womanhood and the Ethics of Disorderly Being*. Duke University Press, 2021.

Glover, Kaiama, Erna Brodber, and Nicole Dennis-Benn. "Critical Caribbean Feminisms: Erna Brodber and Nicole Dennis-Benn." Posted November 28, 2018, by Barnard Center for Research on Women. YouTube, 1 hr., 23 min., 20 sec. https://www.youtube.com/watch?v=DqWJ3WemXL8.

Goffe, Tao Leigh. "Bigger Than the Sound: The Jamaican Chinese Infrastructures of Reggae." *Small Axe* 63 (2020): 97–127.

Goodman, Steve. *Sonic Warfare: Sound, Affect, and the Ecology of Fear*. MIT Press, 2010.

Good Morning Britain. "Is the Song 'Rule Britannia!' Racist? | Good Morning Britain." Posted August 24, 2020. YouTube, 8 min., 31 sec. https://youtu.be/4lYwwNrUmcc?si=Ua-M2B4nRB065waw.

Gopal, Priyamvada. *Insurgent Empire: Anticolonial Resistance and British Dissent*. Verso, 2019.

Gordan, Jeremy. "The Beat at the Heart of 'Lovers Rock.'" *New York Times*, November 29, 2020. https://www.nytimes.com/2020/11/29/arts/music/lovers-rock-small-axe.html.

Gqola, Pumla Dineo. *Female Fear Factory: Unravelling Patriarchy's Cultures of Violence*. Cassava Republic, 2022.

Graham, Caroline. "Party-Mad Usain Bolt Is 'Neighbour from Hell': Model Wife of Rapper Sean Paul Slams Sprinter's Non-stop Noise—and Claims Jamaican Police Turn a Blind Eye Because He's a National Hero." *Daily Mail*, June 6, 2015. https://www.dailymail.co.uk/news/article-3113977/Model-wife-rapper-Sean-Paul-claims-suffered-Usain-Bolt-moved-door-two-years-ago.html.

Grant, Colin. "Jamaica: The Loudest Island on the Planet?" BBC News, September 27, 2012. https://www.bbc.com/news/world-latin-america-19636160.

Gray, Obika. "The Coloniality of Power and the Limits of Dissent in Jamaica." *Small Axe* 54 (2017): 98–110.

Griffin, Farah Jasmine. "When Malindy Sings: A Meditation of Black Women's Vocality." In *Uptown Conversation: The New Jazz Studies Reader*, edited by Robert O'Meally, Brent Hayes Edwards, and Farah Jasmine Griffin. Columbia University Press, 2004.

Guilbault, Jocelyne, and Timothy Rommen, eds. *Sounds of Vacation: Political Economies of Caribbean Tourism*. Duke University Press, 2019.

Hall, Stuart. "Reconstruction Work: Images of Post-War Black Settlement." In *Selected Writings on Visual Arts and Culture: Detour to the Imaginary*, edited by Gilane Tawadros and Bill Schwarz. Duke University Press, 2024.

Hall, Stuart, and Alan O'Shea. "Common-Sense Neoliberalism." *Soundings: A Journal of Politics and Culture* 55 (2013): 8–24.

Hamilton, Njelle W. *Phonographic Memories: Popular Music and the Contemporary Caribbean Novel.* Rutgers University Press, 2019.

Harewood, Susan. "Listening for Noise: Seeking Disturbing Sounds in Tourist Spaces." In *Sounds of Vacation: Political Economies of Caribbean Tourism*, edited by Jocelyne Guilbault and Timothy Rommen. Duke University Press, 2019.

Harris-Perry, Melissa. *Sister Citizen: Shame, Stereotypes, and Black Women in America*. Yale University Press, 2011.

Hartman, Saidiya. "Venus in Two Acts." *Small Axe* 12, no. 2 (2012): 1–14.

Henriques, Jodi "Jinx." "Letter of the Day: Jinx—I Should Never Have Dissed Bolt." *Gleaner*, June 2, 2015. https://web5.jamaica-gleaner.com/article/letters/20150603/letter-day-jinx-i-should-never-have-dissed-bolt.

Henriques, Julian. *Sonic Bodies: Reggae Sound Systems, Performance Techniques, and Ways of Knowing*. Continuum, 2011.

Heuman, Gad. *The Killing Time: The Morant Bay Rebellion in Jamaica*. University of Tennessee Press, 1994.

Hill, Edwin C., Jr. *Black Soundscapes, White Stages: The Meaning of Francophone Sound in the Black Atlantic*. Johns Hopkins University Press, 2013.

Holland, Sharon Patricia. *The Erotic Life of Racism*. Duke University Press, 2014.

Holmes, Kwame. "What's the Tea: Gossip and the Production of Black Gay Social History." *Radical History Review* 122 (2015): 55–69.

Horn, Jessica. "Re-righting the Sexual Body." *Feminist Africa* 6 (2006): 7–19.

Horne, Gerald. *The Dawning of the Apocalypse: The Roots of Slavery, White Supremacy, Settler Colonialism, and Capitalism in the Long Sixteenth Century*. Monthly Review Press, 2020.

Hudson, Peter James. *Bankers and Empire: How Wall Street Colonized the Caribbean*. University of Chicago Press, 2017.

Jaji, Tsitsi. *Africa in Stereo: Modernism, Music, and Pan-African Solidarity*. Oxford University Press, 2014.

Jamaica Gleaner. "Hell Begins Again." March 21, 1934.

Jamaica Observer. "Dogs' Incessant Barking Irritates Ambassador." February 13, 2007. https://www.jamaicaobserver.com/2007/02/13/dogs-incessant-barking-irritates-ambassador/.

Johnson, Agnes. "In Marcus Garvey Park, Gentrifiers vs. Drummers." Workers World, July 26, 2007. https://www.workers.org/2007/us/drummers-0802/.

Johnson, Jovan. "Usain Bolt Beating Classism and Racism in Jamaica." *Gleaner*, January 25, 2016. https://jamaica-gleaner.com/article/news/20160125/usain-bolt-beating-classism-and-racism-jamaica.

Jordan, June. "Report from the Bahamas, 1982." *Meridians* 3, no. 2 (2003): 6–16.

Josephs, Kelly Baker. *Disturbers of the Peace: Representations of Madness in Anglophone Caribbean Literature*. University of Virginia Press, 2013.

Kaba, Mariame. "Yes, We Mean Literally Abolish the Police." *New York Times*, June 12, 2020. https://www.nytimes.com/2020/06/12/opinion/sunday/floyd-abolish-defund-police.html.

Kamugisha, Aaron. *Beyond Coloniality: Citizenship and Freedom in the Caribbean Intellectual Tradition*. Indiana University Press, 2019.

Keeling, Kara. *The Witch's Flight: The Cinematic, the Black Femme, and the Image of Common Sense*. Duke University Press, 2007.

Kempadoo, Kamala, ed. *Sun, Sex, and Gold: Tourism and Sex Work in the Caribbean*. Rowman & Littlefield, 1999.

Key West Literary Seminar. "'Jamaican Letters' | Marlon James, Nicole Dennis-Benn, and Kei Miller in Conversation." Posted September 26, 2019. YouTube, 50 min., 37 sec. https://youtu.be/IUC2SqxKJhg?si=MyPOmIzbZjYTsIxD.

Kheshti, Roshanak. *Modernity's Ear: Listening to Race and Gender in World Music*. New York University Press, 2015.

———. "Sound Studies," *Feminist Media Histories* 4, no. 2 (2018): 179–184.

———. "Toward a Rupture in the *Sensus Communis*: On Sound Studies and the Politics of Knowledge Production," *Current Musicology* 99–100 (2017): 7–20.

Kincaid, Jamaica. *Lucy*. Farrar, Straus and Giroux, 2002.

———. *A Small Place*. Farrar, Straus and Giroux, 1988.

King, Rosamond. *Island Bodies: Transgressive Sexualities in the Caribbean Region*. University Press of Florida, 2014.

LaBelle, Brandon. *Acoustic Territories: Sound Culture and Everyday Life*. Bloomsbury Academic, 2019.

Lamming, George. *Sovereignty of the imagination: Conversations III*. House of Nehesi, 2009.

Langfitt, Frank. "A Row Erupts in Britain over 'Rule, Britannia!' at the Proms." NPR, September 11, 2020. https://www.npr.org/2020/09/11/912045003/a-row-erupts-in-britain-over-rule-britannia-at-the-proms.

Levy, Andrea. "This Is My England." *Guardian*, February 18, 2000. https://www.theguardian.com/books/2000/feb/19/society1.

Lim, Dennis, and Steve McQueen. "Steve McQueen on Making an Ecstatic Musical with Lovers Rock | NYFF58." Posted September 18, 2020, by Film at Lincoln Center. YouTube, 21 min., 1 sec. https://www.youtube.com/watch?v=aTPck4Tu3xo.

London Gazette. "Order of the British Empire." Supplement no. 1, December 31, 2010. https://www.thegazette.co.uk/London/issue/59647/supplement/8.

Lorde, Audre. *Sister Outsider: Essays and Speeches*. Crossing Press, 1984.

Lordi, Emily. *Black Resonance: Iconic Women Singers and African American Literature*. Rutgers University Press, 2013.

Mahmood, Saba. "Feminist Theory, Embodiment, and the Docile Agent: Some Reflections on the Egyptian Islamic Revival." *Cultural Anthropology* 16, no. 2 (2001): 202–236.

Mann, Justin. *Breaking the World: Blackness and Insecurity After the New World Order*. Duke University Press, 2025.

———. "The Vigilante Spirit: Bernhard Goetz, Batman, and Racial Violence in 1980s New York." *Surveillance and Society* 15, no. 1 (2017): 56–67.

Marshall, Wayne. "Treble Culture." In *The Oxford Handbook of Mobile Music Studies*. Vol. 2. Edited by Sumanth Gopinath and Jason Stanyek. Oxford University Press, 2014.

Matthews, Janeille Zarina, and Tracy Robinson. "Modern Vagrancy in the Anglophone Caribbean." *Caribbean Journal of Criminology* 1, no. 4 (2019): 123–154.

McMillan, Michael. "Taste Cultures in the Black British Home." In *The Persistence of Taste: Art, Museums and Everyday Life After Bourdieu*, edited by Malcolm Quinn, Dave Beech, Michael Lehnert, Carol Tulloch, and Stephen Wilson. Routledge, 2018.

———. "Who Feels It Knows It: Black Bodies and the Sensory Experience of the Dance-Hall." *Senses and Society* 17, no. 2 (2022): 223–227.

McQueen, Steve, dir. *Lovers Rock*. BBC Studios; BBC Films; Turbine Studios; Lamas Park; Amazon Studios; EMU Films; Six Temple Productions, 2020. https://www.amazon.com/Small-Axe-Season-1/dp/B08J4HRR4P.

Miller, Kei. "In Praise of the Fat Black Woman and Volume." *PN Review* 44, no. 5 (2018). https://www.pnreview.co.uk/cgi-bin/scribe?item_id=10209.

———. *There Is an Anger That Moves*. Carcanet Press, 2007.

———. *Things I Have Withheld: Essays*. Grove Press, 2021.

Miller-Young, Mireille. *A Taste for Brown Sugar: Black Women in Pornography*. Duke University Press, 2014.

Mitter, Siddhartha. "Steve McQueen, on a Different Wavelength." *New York Times*, May 10, 2024. https://www.nytimes.com/2024/05/10/arts/design/steve-mcqueen-filmmaker-art-dia-beacon-bass.html.

Mordecai, Pamela, and Betty Wilson, eds. *Her True-True Name: An Anthology of Women's Writing from the Caribbean*. Heinemann, 1989.

Moreland, Donnie. "Steve McQueen's 'Bear' Is an Exploration of Intimacies Among Black Men." Black Youth Project, August 12, 2022. https://blackyouthproject.com/steve-mcqueens-bear-is-an-exploration-of-intimacies-among-black-men/.

Morgan, Jennifer. *Laboring Women: Reproduction and Gender in New World Slavery*. University of Pennsylvania Press, 2011.

Moten, Fred. *In the Break: The Aesthetics of the Black Radical Tradition*. University of Minnesota Press, 2003.

Munro, Martin. *Different Drummers: Rhythm and Race in the Americas*. University of California Press, 2010.

———. *Listening to the Caribbean: Sounds of Slavery, Revolt, and Race*. Liverpool University Press, 2022.

Musser, Amber Jamilla. *Between Shadows and Noise: Sensation, Situatedness, and the Undisciplined*. Duke University Press, 2024.

Naipaul, V. S. *The Middle Passage: The Caribbean Revisited*. Vintage Books, 1962.

Nash, Jennifer C. "Black Feminist Self-Help: Or Notes on the Genres of Contemporary Black Feminist Political Life." *Signs: Journal of Women in Culture and Society* 49, no. 3 (2024): 557–578.

———. "Pleasurable Blackness." In *The Palgrave Handbook of Sexuality Education*, edited by Louisa Allen and Mary Lou Rasmussen. Palgrave Macmillan, 2017.

Nash, Jennifer C., and Samantha Pinto. "A New Genealogy of 'Intelligent Rage,' or Other Ways to Think About White Women in Feminism." *Signs: Journal of Women in Culture and Society* 46, no. 4 (2021): 883–910.

New York Daily News. "A Drumbeat of Tension in Harlem." August 12, 2007. https://www.nydailynews.com/2007/08/12/a-drumbeat-of-tension-in-harlem/.

Nixon, Angelique. *Resisting Paradise: Tourism, Diaspora, and Sexuality in Caribbean Culture*. University Press of Mississippi, 2015.

Obadike, Mendi Dessalines Shirley Lewis Townsend. "Low Fidelity: Stereotyped Blackness in the Field of Sound." PhD diss., Duke University, 2005. ProQuest (3179330).

O'Callaghan, Evelyn. *Woman Version: Theoretical Approaches to West Indian Fiction by Women*. St. Martin's Press, 1993.

Palmer, Colin. *Freedom's Children: The 1938 Labor Rebellion and the Birth of Modern Jamaica*. University of North Carolina Press, 2014.

Palmer, Lisa Amanda. "Hopelessly in Love: Carroll Thompson's Reflections and Insights into the Patriarchal Politics within the Lovers Rock Reggae Scene." In *Black Music in Britain in the 21st Century*, edited by Monique Charles and Mary Gani. Liverpool University Press, 2023.

———. "'LADIES A YOUR TIME NOW!': Erotic Politics, Lovers' Rock and Resistance in the UK." *African and Black Diaspora* 4, no. 2 (2011): 177–192.

Paton, Diana. *The Cultural Politics of Obeah: Religion, Colonialism, and Modernity in the Caribbean World*. Cambridge University Press, 2015.

Philip, Marlene NourbeSe. "Black W/Holes: A History of Brief Time." In *For the Geography of a Soul: Emerging Perspectives on Kamau Brathwaite*, edited by Timothy J. Reiss. Africa World Press, 2001.

———. *Blank: Essays and Interviews*. Book*hug, 2017.

———. *The Collected Short Stories of Marlene NourbeSe Philip*. Alexander Street Press, 2006.

———. "Fugues, Fragments and Fissures—A Work in Progress." *Anthurium* 3, no. 2 (2005): 1–15.

———. *A Genealogy of Resistance: And Other Essays*. Mercury Press, 1997.

———. "Interview with an Empire." In *Assembling Alternatives: Reading Postmodern Poetries Transnationally*, edited by Romana Huk. Wesleyan University Press, 2003.

———. *Showing Grit: Showboating North of the 44th Parallel*. Poui, 1993.

Pierre, Jemima. "Haiti and the 'Savage Slot.'" *Journal of Haitian Studies* 19, no. 2 (2013): 110–116.

———. "The Racial Vernaculars of Development: A View from West Africa." *American Anthropologist* 122, no. 1 (2019): 86–98.

Pinto, Samantha. *Difficult Diasporas: The Transnational Feminist Aesthetic of the Black Atlantic*. New York University Press, 2013.

Post, Tina. *Deadpan: The Aesthetics of Black Inexpression*. New York University Press, 2022.

Postcolonial Writers Make Worlds. "Kei Miller Interviewed by Ellen Boehmer." Posted October 14, 2019. YouTube, 20 min., 18 sec. https://www.youtube.com/watch?v=tKLTMGN8RDk.

Quashie, Kevin. *Black Aliveness, or A Poetics of Being*. Duke University Press, 2021.

———. *The Sovereignty of Quiet: Beyond Resistance in Black Culture*. Rutgers University Press, 2012.

Radano, Ronald. *Lying Up a Nation: Race and Black Music*. University of Chicago Press, 2003.

Radano, Ronald, and Philip V. Bohlman. *Music and the Racial Imagination*. University of Chicago Press, 2000.

Ramlogan, Rajendra. "Using the Law to Achieve Environmental Democracy and Sustainable Development: An Elusive Dream for Trinidad and Tobago." *Electronic Green Journal* no. 30 (2010): 1–13.

Randolph, Antonia. "Platonic Couples and the Limits of Queer Theory: The Case of Black Masculinity in Hip-Hop Culture." In *Outskirts: Queer Experiences on the Fringe*, edited by D'Lane Compton and Amy L. Stone. NYU Press, 2024.

Rappke, Annike. "The Pain of Senses Escaping: Eighteenth-Century Europeans and the Sensory Challenges of the Caribbean." In *Empire of the Senses: Sensory Practices of Colonialism in Early America*, edited by Daniela Hacke and Paul Musselwhite. Brill Press, 2017.

Reddock, Rhoda E. *Women, Labour, and Politics in Trinidad and Tobago: A History*. Zed Books, 1994.

Reeves, Roger. "Minor Characters, Major Silence, or Against the Compulsion to Talk." *Black Scholar* 51, no. 1 (2021): 43–50.

Roach, Shoniqua. "Black Sex in the Quiet." *Differences* 30, no. 1 (2019): 126–147.

Samuel, Petal. "Black Gravity, or a Hidden History of Empire." *Differences* 35, no. 2 (2024): 132–156.

———. "The Sound of Luxury: Antiblackness, Silence, and the Private Island Resort." *Black Scholar* 51, no. 1 (2021): 30–42.

Samuel, Petal, and Erna Brodber. "Put Your Bucket Down." *SX Salon* 19 (2015). http://smallaxe.net/sxsalon/interviews/put-your-bucket-down.

Schulman, Sarah. *Stagestruck: Theater, AIDS, and the Marketing of Gay America*. Duke University Press, 1998.

Schultz, Dagmar, dir. *Audre Lorde: The Berlin Years: 1984–1992*. Third World Newsreel, 2012.

Schwartz, Meryl F. "An Interview with Michelle Cliff." *Contemporary Literature* 34, no. 4 (1993): 595–619.

Semaj-Hall, Isis. "[Sic] with Contagion: Communicating Prohibition in Pre-Independence Trinidad." *Caribbean Quarterly* 66, no. 1 (2020): 90–107.

Shabazz, Menelik, dir. *The Story of Lover's Rock*. BFM Media and SunRa Pictures, 2011.

Sharpe, Christina. *In the Wake: On Blackness and Being*. Duke University Press, 2016.

Sharpe, Jenny. *Immaterial Archives: An African Diaspora Poetics of Loss*. Northwestern University Press, 2020.

Sheller, Mimi. *Consuming the Caribbean: From Arawaks to Zombies*. Routledge, 2003.

Silvera, Makeda. "Man Royales and Sodomites: Some Thoughts in the Invisibility of Afro-Caribbean Lesbians." *Feminist Studies* 18, no. 3 (1992): 521–532.

Slave Law of Jamaica: With Proceedings and Documents Relative Thereto. James Ridgway, 1828.

Smith, Barbara, ed. *Home Girls: A Black Feminist Anthology*. Rutgers University Press, 2000.

Smith, Faith. "Introduction: Sexing the Citizen." In *Smith, Sex and the Citizen*.

———, ed. *Sex and the Citizen: Interrogating the Caribbean*. University of Virginia Press, 2011.

———. "'You Know You're West Indian If . . .': Codes of Authenticity in Colin Channer's *Waiting in Vain*." *Small Axe* 10 (2001): 41–59.

Smith, Mark M. *How Race Is Made: Slavery, Segregation, and the Senses*. University of North Carolina Press, 2008.

Spillers, Hortense. "Mama's Baby, Papa's Maybe: An American Grammar Book." *Diacritics* 17, no. 2 (1987): 64–81.

Sterne, Jonathan. *The Audible Past: Cultural Origins of Sound Reproduction*. Duke University Press, 2003.

Stoever, Jennifer Lynn. *The Sonic Color Line: Race and the Cultural Politics of Listening*. New York University Press, 2016.
Strachan, Ian Gregory. *Paradise and Plantation: Tourism and Culture in the Anglophone Caribbean*. University of Virginia Press, 2003.
Sullivan, Mecca Jamilah. "Pedagogies of the 'Irresistible': Imaginative Elsewheres of Black Feminist Learning." *Journal of Feminist Scholarship* 20 (2022): 1–18.
Tambieh, Yasmin. "Threatening Sexual (Mis)Behavior: Homosexuality in the Penal Code Debates in Trinidad and Tobago, 1986." In *Smith, Sex and the Citizen*.
thepostarchive. "Toni Morrison—Intro and Interview." Posted May 22, 2019. YouTube, 27 min., 55 sec. https://www.youtube.com/watch?v=WoTELoC8QoM.
Thomas, Deborah. *Modern Blackness: Nationalism, Globalization, and the Politics of Culture in Jamaica*. Duke University Press, 2004.
Thompson, Krista. *An Eye for the Tropics: Tourism, Photography, and Framing the Caribbean Picturesque*. Duke University Press, 2007.
———. *Shine: The Visual Economy of Light in the African Diasporic Aesthetic Practice*. Duke University Press, 2015.
Tillet, Salamishah. "'I Got No Comfort in This Life': The Increasing Importance of Patsey in 12 Years a Slave." *American Literary History* 26, no. 2 (2014): 354–361.
Trinidad and Tobago Guardian. "Noise and Inconsideration Are Our Culture." January 15, 2013. https://www.guardian.co.tt/article-6.2.393367.d3bc443d50.
Trotman, David V. "Spectacle and the Colonial Imagination: Performances of White Power in Trinidad." *Caribbean Quarterly* 68, no. 4 (2002): 485–505.
Trouillot, Michel-Rolph. *Global Transformations: Anthropology and the Modern World*. Palgrave Macmillan, 2003.
———. *Trouillot Remixed: The Michel-Rolph Trouillot Reader*. Edited by Yarimar Bonilla, Greg Beckett, and Mayanthi L. Fernando. Duke University Press, 2021.
Vazquez, Alexandra T. *Listening in Detail: Performances of Cuban Music*. Duke University Press, 2013.
Veal, Michael. *Dub: Soundscapes and Shattered Songs in Jamaican Reggae*. Wesleyan University Press, 2007.
Walcott, Rinaldo. "'Inner Plantation': Caribbean Studies, Black Studies, and a Black Theory of Freedom." *Small Axe* 25, no. 3 (2021): 116–126.
Waterson, Jim. "Proms Row: Johnson Calls for End to 'Cringing Embarrassment' over UK History." *Guardian*, August 25, 2020. https://www.theguardian.com/music/2020/aug/25/boris-johnson-scolds-bbc-over-suggestion-proms-would-drop-rule-britannia.
Watkins, Paul. "We Can Never Tell the Entire Story of Slavery: In Conversation with M. NourbeSe Philip." *Toronto Review of Books*, April 13, 2014. https://torontoreviewofbooks.com/2014/04/in-conversation-with-m-nourbese-philip/.
White, Khadijah. "Belongingness and the Harlem Drummers." *Urban Geography* 36, no. 3 (2015): 340–358.
Williams, Patricia J. *The Alchemy of Race and Rights: Diary of a Law Professor*. Harvard University Press, 1991.
Williams, Timothy. "An Old Sound in Harlem Draws New Neighbors' Ire." *New York Times*, July 6, 2008. http://www.nytimes.com/2008/07/06/nyregion/06drummers.html.
Willis, Nathaniel Parker. *Health Trip to the Tropics*. C. Scribner, 1853.
WNYC. "Spoken Word: Staceyann Chin Performs 'Homophobia.'" Posted January 17, 2017. YouTube, 8 min., 20 sec. https://www.youtube.com/watch?v=-LV_aqfoXVc.

Wright, Keril. "No Barking . . . Please." *Jamaica Observer*, February 14, 2007. https://www.jamaicaobserver.com/2007/02/14/no-barking-please/.

YaleBritishArt. "Steve McQueen Symposium." Posted February 2, 2023. YouTube, 6 hr., 31 min., 20 sec. https://www.youtube.com/watch?v=1zXgeZc5tmE.

Yates, Anders. "Caribana to be Replaced by 'Scotiabank Celebration of Noise Complaints.'" *Beaverton*, August 6, 2018. https://www.thebeaverton.com/2018/08/caribana-to-be-replaced-by-scotiabank-celebration-of-noise-complaints/.

Yates-Richard, Meina. "'What Is Your Mother's Name?': Maternal Disavowal and the Reverberating Aesthetic of Black Women's Pain in Black Nationalist Literature." *American Literature* 88, no. 3 (2016): 477–507.

Index

About the Author

PETAL KIMBERLY SAMUEL is an assistant professor of African, African American, and Diaspora Studies at the University of North Carolina at Chapel Hill. She holds a PhD in English from Vanderbilt University. Her work on African diasporic women's writing, Caribbean feminist and queer literary aesthetics, and Black speculative imagination has appeared in the *Journal of West Indian Literature*, *The Black Scholar*, *Differences*, and *Public Books*. Her current work and scholarly interests include Caribbean anticolonial literature and aesthetics, the sensorium, and transnational Black feminist thought.

Available titles in the Critical Caribbean Studies series

Giselle Anatol, *The Things That Fly in the Night: Female Vampires in Literature of the Circum-Caribbean and African Diaspora*
Alaí Reyes-Santos, *Our Caribbean Kin: Race and Nation in the Neoliberal Antilles*
Milagros Ricourt, *The Dominican Racial Imaginary: Surveying the Landscape of Race and Nation in Hispaniola*
Katherine A. Zien, *Sovereign Acts: Performing Race, Space, and Belonging in Panama and the Canal Zone*
Frances R. Botkin, *Thieving Three-Fingered Jack: Transatlantic Tales of a Jamaican Outlaw, 1780–2015*
Melissa A. Johnson, *Becoming Creole: Nature and Race in Belize*
Carlos Garrido Castellano, *Beyond Representation in Contemporary Caribbean Art: Space, Politics, and the Public Sphere*
Njelle W. Hamilton, *Phonographic Memories: Popular Music and the Contemporary Caribbean Novel*
Lia T. Bascomb, *In Plenty and in Time of Need: Popular Culture and the Remapping of Barbadian Identity*
Aliyah Khan, *Far from Mecca: Globalizing the Muslim Caribbean*
Rafael Ocasio, *Race and Nation in Puerto Rican Folklore: Franz Boas and John Alden Mason in Porto Rico*
Ana-Maurine Lara, *Streetwalking: LGBTQ Lives and Protest in the Dominican Republic*
Anke Birkenmaier, ed., *Caribbean Migrations: The Legacies of Colonialism*
Sherina Feliciano-Santos, *A Contested Caribbean Indigeneity: Language, Social Practice, and Identity Within Puerto Rican Taíno Activism*
H. Adlai Murdoch, ed., *The Struggle of Non-Sovereign Caribbean Territories: Neoliberalism Since the French Antillean Uprisings of 2009*
Robert Fatton Jr., *The Guise of Exceptionalism: Unmasking the National Narratives of Haiti and the United States*
Rafael Ocasio, *Folk Stories from the Hills of Puerto Rico/Cuentos folklóricos de las montañas de Puerto Rico*
Yveline Alexis, *Haiti Fights Back: The Life and Legacy of Charlemagne Péralte*
Katerina Gonzalez Seligmann, *Writing the Caribbean in Magazine Time*
Jocelyn Fenton Stitt, *Dreams of Archives Unfolded: Absence and Caribbean Life Writing*
Alison Donnell, *Creolized Sexualities: Undoing Heteronormativity in the Literary Imagination of the Anglo-Caribbean*
Vincent Joos, *Urban Dwellings, Haitian Citizenships: Housing, Memory, and Daily Life in Haiti*
Krystal Nandini Ghisyawan, *Erotic Cartographies: Decolonization and the Queer Caribbean Imagination*
Yvon van der Pijl and Francio Guadeloupe, eds., *Equaliberty in the Dutch Caribbean: Ways of Being Non/Sovereign*

Patricia Joan Saunders, *Buyers Beware: Insurgency and Consumption in Caribbean Popular Culture*

Atreyee Phukan, *Contradictory Indianness: Indenture, Creolization, and Literary Imaginary*

Nikoli A. Attai, *Defiant Bodies: Making Queer Community in the Anglophone Caribbean*

Samuel Ginsburg, *The Cyborg Caribbean: Techno-Dominance in Twenty-First-Century Cuban, Dominican, and Puerto Rican Science Fiction*

Linden F. Lewis, *Forbes Burnham: The Life and Times of the Comrade Leader*

Keja L. Valens, *Culinary Colonialism, Caribbean Cookbooks, and Recipes for National Independence*

Kim Williams-Pulfer, *Get Involved! Stories of Bahamian Civil Society*

Preity R. Kumar, *An Ordinary Landscape of Violence: Women Loving Women in Guyana*

Kezia Page, *Inside Tenement Time: Suss, Spirit, and Surveillance*

Natalie Lauren Belisle, *Caribbean Inhospitality: The Poetics of Strangers at Home*

Darlène Elizabeth Dubuisson, *Reclaiming Haiti's Futures: Returned Intellectuals, Placemaking, and Radical Imagination*

Elizabeth S. Manley, *Imagining the Tropics: Women, Romance, and the Making of Modern Tourism*

Jennifer Boum Make, *Decolonial Caregiving: Reimagining Caregiving in the French Caribbean*

Petal Kimberly Samuel, *The Quiet Zone: Caribbean Expressive Cultures and the Feminist Aesthetics of Disturbance*